ENGLAND'S ROAD
TO SOCIAL SECURITY

What a pity it is to see a proper gentleman to have such a crick in his neck that he cannot look backward! yet no better is he who cannot see behind him the actions which long since were performed. History maketh a young man to be old without either wrinkles or gray hairs; privileging him with the experience of age, without either the infirmities or inconveniences thereof. Yea, it not only maketh things past, present; but enableth one to make a rational conjecture of things to come. For this world affordeth no new accidents, but in the same sense wherein we call it a new moon, which is the old one in another shape, and yet no other than what hath been formerly. Old actions return again, furbished over with some new and different circumstances.

THOMAS FULLER, *The Historie of the Holy Warre*, 1639

ENGLAND'S
ROAD
TO
SOCIAL
SECURITY

From *the Statute of Laborers* in 1349
to the *Beveridge Report* of 1942

By

Karl de Schweinitz

A Perpetua Book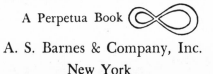

A. S. Barnes & Company, Inc.
New York

PREFACE

THOSE who are interested in the development of social security in the United States are turning today, as they have for many years, to Great Britain. Whatever happens there in this field has significance for us here. No better evidence of this could be had than the attention we have given to the recent report upon social insurance and allied services presented to Parliament by Sir William H. Beveridge. We may differ from the British in our efforts to achieve social security, but we cannot plan adequately without taking their ideas into consideration.

To understand these ideas, to appreciate, for example, the significance of the Beveridge Report, and, indeed, to understand our own past, we must look to England. There is our inheritance. For more than six hundred years, English statesmen and other English leaders have been writing in statute and in literature the record of their attempts to deal with insecurity and human need. Everything that we have addressed to this end derives from their experience or has been influenced by it.

Nothing in philosophy or principle that could be called our own began to develop with respect to the problem of poverty until well toward the end of the last century. Only after 1930 did the discussion of the subject reach the place of importance in our national forum that it had occupied in Parliament since the reign of Henry VIII; and the commencement, with the Act of 1935, of our national program of social security came a quarter of a century after the inauguration of the British system. So it is that the person who is interested in the expedients that have been tried in the past, in the shifts in theory and in public policy, and in the thought and action out of which the concept of social security has developed, will find his sources of basic information in the wealth of documents and books that have come to us from Great Britain.

I have endeavored to summarize what have seemed to me to be the most significant trends in the English development, hoping that such a recapitulation by someone on this side of the water would carry a special appropriateness for readers in the United States and, written from an experience in both public and private administration, would have the value of what might be called an operative perspective.

Since most of the years which this history spans have been concerned with the problem of assistance, social insurance being only a generation old, I had at first thought of calling the book *Six Centuries of Relief;* but the appearance of the Beveridge Report, focusing trends in thought that have beeen expressing themselves with growing strength since the coming of social insurance in 1911, makes it possible to include a discussion of Britain's plans for the future. Our story starts with the English experience and ends with a British program. It begins with six centuries of relief and, pausing after thirty years of insurance, includes both past and future in the title *England's Road to Social Security*.

In writing, I am addressing: first, administrators of social security —both insurance and assistance—and men and women preparing themselves for such work, as well as the members of county, state, and federal boards in this field; and second, college students—graduate and undergraduate—in sociology, political science, and related areas; but I believe that some knowledge of the long duel between government and poverty and the efforts of the people to achieve security is part of a general culture, and so I offer this book also to the person who would like to become acquainted with one of the most interesting aspects of English history.

Social insurance today needs no definition. The word "relief" however, is becoming so much a part of the past as even now to call for explanation. It may be described as money, goods, or services supplied by an organization, philanthropic or governmental, to an individual who has applied for economic assistance because he has not enough in earnings or other resources to obtain for himself the necessities of life. Such aid, when provided in the form of maintenance in an institution, has been spoken of as "indoor relief"; when supplied to people in their own homes, as "outdoor relief."

"Relief" is an old word. It appears in the first statute—1536— in which Parliament placed on the government of England the responsibility of seeing to it that the poor received help. The term is now passing out of use. Today, in the United States as in Great Britain, it is being replaced by the word "assistance." Differently conceived, as indicated by its change of name, it is playing its part along with social insurance in the program and organization of social security.

As a means of avoiding footnotes, I have listed the sources of quotations or specific facts in an appendix, the number in the text indicating the reference. There is no occasion for the reader to pursue these references unless he is seeking the authority for a given statement. Everything else has been included in the running text.

Permission to quote from the sources cited in the Bibliography has been sought and has been received from most of the publishers whose names appear in the list of books. The difficulties in communication because of the war have prevented me from hearing from a few of those to whom I wrote. It has not seemed wise to delay publication on their account and I am therefore, by way of acknowledgment, mentioning them along with those from whom I have had word.

In addition to drawing upon statutes, documents, and books, I have had the special help of four persons. My wife, Elizabeth de Schweinitz, has read the manuscript in all its various stages, contributing to the development of the project from her experience in private social work and in public assistance; Karl de Schweinitz, Jr., has read it with a view to its appropriateness for undergraduates; Elisabeth Schneider, associate professor of English in Temple University, Philadelphia, from a background of historical scholarship and research both in this country and in Great Britain; and Michael Ross, now Research Director of the Union of Marine and Shipbuilding Workers of America, from a broad knowledge in the economics of social security and an early association with the labor movement of his native England.

K. DE S.

Philadelphia
April 1943

CONTENTS

I

POVERTY BECOMES A CONCERN OF
GOVERNMENT

Verily he who dooms a worse doom to the friendless and the
comer from afar than to his fellows, injures himself.

LAWS OF KING CNUT,
A.D. 1017 to 1035.[2]

SIX centuries ago Edward III of England issued a proclamation
from which the administration of social security in Great Britain
and in the United States may be said to date. This proclamation, which
commences the famous Statutes of Laborers, was an attempt by the
English landowners to assure themselves of a supply of agricultural
workers. One of its paragraphs is of special significance:

Because that many valiant beggars, as long as they may live of begging, do refuse to labor, giving themselves to idleness and vice, and
sometime to theft and other abominations; none upon the said pain of
imprisonment, shall under the color of pity or alms, give anything to
such, which may labor, or presume to favor them towards their desires, so that thereby they may be compelled to labor for their necessary living.[3]

In this prohibitory regulation we have the beginning of the long
and varied series of laws and establishments through which, during
six hundred years, Anglo-Saxon government has attacked the problem of economic distress. There had been occasional legal recognition of the subject much earlier than the Statute of Laborers of 1349.
Thomas Fuller, in his *Church History of Britain*, comments upon
an enactment of a council at Greatlea in 928 during the reign of
Athelstan:

*That the King's Officers maintain one Poor-body in the King's Vil-
lages; and in case none be found therein, fetch him from other places.*

Christ saith, the poor you have always with you. The Church in general is well stocked with them, though some particular parish may want
such as are in want. If any would know the bill of fare allowed these
poor people; it was monthly a measure of meal, una perna, a gammon

of bacon, a ram worth a groat, four cheeses, and 30 pence on Easter-Wednesday to buy them clothes.[441a]

Centuries before this, there existed organized provision for the relief of destitution. In Greece, in Palestine, in Rome, there were extensive measures for the care of the poor; and in the cultural background from which we approach any discussion of poverty is the influence of Aristotle, St. Paul, Cicero, St. Francis of Assisi, and many other classical and medieval thinkers.

If, however, one is seeking a starting point for a study of the development of social security as we have it today, the Proclamation of Edward III offers itself as the logical place. With it begins the chain of related circumstances that leads to our present system. The governmental relief of classic times is separated from us by the economy of the Middle Ages; and that separation is so great that for the start of administrative attempts to deal with the problem of destitution, we appropriately look to the Statute of Laborers of 1349.

It is in the years of the shift from feudalism to a capitalistic democratic society that the consecutive history of social security commences. Under feudalism there could, at least in theory, be no uncared-for distress. The people who today would be in the greatest economic danger were, in the Middle Ages, presumably protected by their masters from the most acute suffering. They were serfs or villeins who, by virtue either of their slavery or of what F. W. Maitland calls their "unfreedom," had coverage against disaster.[473a] Insurance against unemployment, sickness, old age was theirs in the protection of their liege lords.

While the nation [writes Sir Frederic Eden in his *State of the Poor*] consisted principally of the two classes of landholders and servile cultivators, the latter had, at least in ordinary times, a fund to which they might resort for maintenance; and, although they could not acquire property, they were, in general, certain of food; because it was the obvious interest of those, who could command their services, to provide for their support. . . .

This, however, furnishes no solid argument against the blessings of liberty. A prisoner under the custody of his keeper, may perhaps be confident of receiving his bread and his water daily; yet, I believe, there are few who would not, even with the contingent possibility of starving, prefer a precarious chance of subsistence, from their own industry, to the certainty of regular meals in a gaol. . . .

Dr. Johnson's remark, on marriage and celibacy, may, perhaps, be applied with propriety to freedom and servitude: the one has many pains; the other no pleasures. (Rasselas)

However deplorable, therefore, the effects produced by the want of personal freedom, may have been, . . . and . . . however degraded the general condition of the great mass of the people, then employed principally in agriculture, might be, they were still, unless in extraordinary cases of national misery, assured of the bare necessaries of life. The villein, I apprehend, if unable to work, was maintained by his lord; as the pauper is now supported by his parish; . . . the Legislature was not called upon to enact laws, either for the punishment of vagrants, or the relief of the impotent and aged.[432a]

By the middle of the fourteenth century feudalism was nearing its end. Wages had come largely into use. They were both a symbol and a means of the emancipation of the laborer from serfdom. The number of men who worked for anyone who would pay them, and where they pleased, had steadily grown. Along with this advance toward freedom, however, went the loss of the economic security that inhered in the having of a master. Now, when misfortune came, there was no patron in whom the liberated individual had a guarantee of help. Lacking this, many persons when in need turned to mendicancy or theft. To the landowners, the new conditions were a source of great dissatisfaction. They were losing much of their control over labor. In addition, there was the menace to safety and property of men who existed on the basis of what they could take by stealth or force.

The issue arose most vividly and most acutely in connection with the vagrant and the transient and migratory worker. As they and their kind increased, they became significant enough to warrant action by King and Parliament. For years after the Statute of Laborers the problem they presented was a main consideration in legislation designed to affect the state of the poor. Today, after six centuries, it is still unsolved.

Perhaps the most significant and the most prized aspects of freedom in those times of emergence from feudalism had to do with ownership and movement. Did a man own himself? Could he sell ox or calf, could he marry son or daughter without his lord's consent? If he chose to leave his place of birth, could he be compelled to return? Could his master go and bring him back; could he be brought home by the officers of the law?

Ownership and movement were not unrelated. Often movement

was the way in which a man might own himself. Travel was an indication of independence. There was, moreover, a temptation to take to wandering in the example of the mendicant friars who went about from manor to manor and from village to village. They were evidence that a man could subsist by begging. At the same time, forest and moor offered the possibility both of escape and of sustenance. The population of England, as deduced from the economic survey initiated by William the Conqueror in 1085 and recorded in the Domesday Book, may have been as low as 1,375,000.[473b] In the latter part of the fourteenth century it is estimated to have been about 2,500,000.[430a] As compared with a present 40,000,000 the country was relatively unoccupied and there was ample room for the man who wanted to emancipate himself by flight and who knew how to live off the land. He could maintain a gypsy life not unlike that lived by the more adventurous of the pioneers in colonial North America.

A recognized and acceptable occasion for wandering was that provided by the time of harvest. Nature then as now demanded an accession of labor to gather in the ripening crops, and workers migrated during the summer from one part of the country to another. An interesting evidence of this exists in the second Statute of Laborers enacted in the twenty-fifth year of Edward III. Having found that the Proclamation of 1349 was not observed, the King submitted the problem to Parliament, which in 1351 passed a law reaffirming and making more specific the regulations of the first Statute, though, incidentally, without the section on beggars. The new law provided among other things that

the people of the Counties of Stafford, Lancaster, and Derby, and the people of Craven, and of the marches of Wales and Scotland, and other places, may come in time of August, and labor in other counties, and safely return, as they were wont to do before this time.[4]

The wars in France offered another opportunity for movement and for freedom. The men who followed their lord or the king across the Channel, having cut loose from the restrictions of the manor, often on their return to England betook themselves to a wanderer's life or established themselves in town.

Then as now the city was an attraction. In 1377 the population of London was, it is estimated, 35,000; of York, nearly 11,000; of Bristol, 9,500.[487a] Though to modern eyes such figures may seem small, these and many other towns were able to maintain a not in-

4

considerable measure of independence, and in the fourteenth century were securing franchises and privileges, both corporate and individual, that made them places of comparative freedom for the man who would leave the feudal estate.

The movement from country to city was accelerated by the introduction of woolen manufacture. William the Conqueror had brought several Flemish weavers with him at the time of the Conquest, but it was not until Edward III that this industry began to be a factor in English economic life. Edward III encouraged the immigration of weavers from Holland and in less than forty years after 1331, when the first of these came, woolen manufacture in England had become extensive enough to permit the export of cloth. "By drawing the superfluous hands from the country into towns and cities," says Sir Frederick Eden, "it contributed more than any other cause to meliorate the condition of the laboring classes." [432b]

While by the middle of the fourteenth century all these elements of change were operating to emancipate men from their lords, it required a national catastrophe to give to the problem the final vividness necessary to precipitate legislative action. From 1315 to 1321 there was famine in England, particularly in the first two and the last of these years—famine serious enough to reduce the number of laborers. There followed a steep rise in wages. Then in 1347, the Black Death swept westward from Constantinople. It reached England in 1348; and by 1349 upwards of one-third of the population had died.[430a] Two lesser epidemics came within a generation, each bringing a heavy mortality. The result was a reduction in the supply of labor, great enough to cause the latter part of the fourteenth century to be a time of prosperity and strategic advantage for the surviving workers. The laborer could ask what wages he wanted, work when he liked, and observe holiday when he pleased. He was solicited by competing employers and began to enjoy a freedom he had not known before.

By the middle of the 1300's agriculture had been so seriously affected that the landed proprietors set about to secure remedial legislation. They looked back to the golden days of feudalism when men were attached to the land and gave proper service to their lords; and they sought to establish and conserve what they could of the passing system. This was the purpose of the Statute of Laborers of 1349. Its opening paragraph states the problem, and the second paragraph contains the proposed remedy:

Because a great part of the people, and especially of workmen and servants, late died of the pestilence, many seeing the necessity of masters, and great scarcity of servants, will not serve unless they may receive excessive wages, and some rather willing to beg in idleness, than by labor to get their living; we, considering the grievous incommodities, which of the lack especially of ploughmen and such laborers may hereafter come, have upon deliberation and treaty with the prelates and the nobles, and learned men assisting us, of their mutual counsel ordained:

That every man and woman of our realm of England, of what condition he be, free or bond, able in body, and within the age of threescore years, not living in merchandize, nor exercising any craft, nor having of his own whereof he may live, nor proper land, about whose tillage he may himself occupy, and not serving any other, if he in convenient service, his estate considered, be required to serve, he shall be bounden to serve him which so shall him require; and take only the wages, livery, meed, or salary, which were accustomed to be given in the places where he oweth to serve, the twentieth year of our reign of England, or five or six other common years next before. . . . And if any such man or woman, being so required to serve, will not the same do, . . . he shall anon be taken . . . and committed to the next gaol, there to remain under strait keeping, till he find surety to serve in the form aforesaid.[3]

A subsequent paragraph contains the prohibition about alms to beggars quoted at the beginning of this chapter.

What might be called the companion or confirmatory Statute of Laborers enacted by Parliament in 1351 forbade any servant except dwellers in certain privileged areas to "go out of the town, where he dwelleth in the winter, to serve the summer, if he may serve in the same town, taking as before is said."[4]

The King and his lords saw begging, movement and vagrancy, and the labor shortage as essentially the same problem, to be dealt with in one law. They proposed to solve this problem by fixing a maximum wage, by compelling the unattached man to work for whoever wanted him, by forbidding the laborer to travel, and by stopping alms to the man who if he could beg would presumably refuse to work. The beggar, in the concern of the Statute of Laborers, was not a problem in destitution but a seepage from the supply of labor.

The economic and social changes that occasioned this Statute were, however, far more powerful than the law which was designed to stop them. The progress from feudalism toward a capitalistic-democratic society continued, and not always peaceably. The first statute, in the year 1377, to be enacted in the reign of Richard II, complains that villeins and land tenants "do daily withdraw their services and customs due to their said lords" and "affirm them to be quite and utterly discharged of all manner of servage, due as well of their body as of their said tenures," and "which more is, gather themselves together in great routs, and agree by such confederacy, that every one shall aid other to resist their lords with strong hand." [5]

Here was material for revolt, and four years later came Wat Tyler's attempt to force by rebellion further concessions in the direction of freedom for the serfs. He failed, but the changes of which he was evidence continued. In 1388 Parliament enacted a statute— 12th Richard II—which restated the problem and attempted to improve upon the measures imposed by the first and second Statutes of Laborers. The new law makes complaint as follows:

That servants and laborers will not, nor by a long season would, serve and labor without outrageous and excessive hire, and much more than hath been given to such servants and laborers in any time past, so that for scarcity of the said servants and laborers, the husbands and land-tenants may not pay their rents, nor [scarcely] live upon their lands, to the great damage and loss as well of the Lords as all the Commons. [7]

The Statute moves further toward coercion by attempting in much more specific language than before to restrict the laborer to his place of residence:

No servant nor laborer, be he man or woman, shall depart at the end of his term out of the hundred, rape, or wapentake where he is dwelling, to serve or dwell elsewhere, or by color to go from thence in pilgrimage, unless he bring a letter patent containing the cause of his going, and the time of his return. . . . If . . . without such letter, . . . he shall be . . . put in the stocks, and kept till he hath found surety to return to his service, or to serve or labor in the town from whence he came, till he have such letter to depart for a reasonable cause. [6]

The penalty which the 12th Richard II inflicted upon the servant or laborer traveling without letter patent, it also employed against the beggar:

Of every person that goeth begging, *and is able to serve or labor*, [italics mine] it shall be done of him as of him that departeth out of the hundred and other places aforesaid without letter testimonial. [8]

While this law introduces the long series of attempts to control begging through punishment, it also recognizes for the first time the possible existence of need requiring relief. The Statutes of Laborers treated the beggar, the transient, and the bargainer for high wages as problems relating to the supply of labor. The 12th Richard II, 1388, grants the plight of the unemployable, and by implication approves begging as an appropriate way by which they may obtain support:

That the beggars *impotent to serve*, [italics mine] shall abide in the cities and towns where they be dwelling at the time of the proclamation of this statute; and if the people of cities or other towns will not or may not suffice to find them, that then the said beggars shall draw them to other towns within the hundreds, rape, or wapentake, or to the towns where they were born, within forty days after the proclamation made, and there shall continually abide during their lives.[8]

More than one hundred years passed before there was any further indication that there might be a difference of condition or status among those who begged. Even then the reference was again indirect. In 1495, under Henry VII, when the penalty for vagrancy was redefined as "three days and three nights" in the stocks, "diminution of punishment of vagabonds and beggars aforesaid," was established "for women great with child, and men and women in extreme sickness." [12]

Nine years later, in 1504, "persons being impotent and above the age of sixty years," were added to those who were to receive special consideration.[13]

These permissible exemptions from harsh punishment, together with the law of 1388 that impotent beggars should "abide in the cities and towns where they be dwelling," comprise the only legal recognition for nearly two centuries after the Statute of Laborers that people might be in need and be unable to support themselves except by alms. The main aim of the laws relating to the poor was repressive, with penalties being directed against vagrants and wandering beggars.

This is not surprising, for the fifteenth century was a period of comparative prosperity for the average English laborer if one considers wages in relation to his standard of life and cost of living. His numbers had been decimated by famine and by the Black Death in the preceding century, but his earnings had risen. He lived in a hovel, he had few utensils and fewer articles of furniture; he was the frequent victim of disease. His food was simple and without great variety, but he had enough for his needs. Even those who in the change from the feudal system had taken to the forests and the roads could, nevertheless, pick up here and there the meager little that their living involved. Under such circumstances necessity, as related to the standards of the time, did not call forth measures of relief.

But as the fifteenth century began to close, the factors separating people from the land multiplied and poverty began to increase. The wars on the Continent had been followed by the Wars of the Roses, ending at Bosworth in 1485. The wool industry had continued to develop, making the raising of sheep a source of large profit. Tilled lands were being converted to pasturage, with a consequent destruction of homesteads and the scattering of cottagers.

A vivid statement of the situation is to be found in one of the statutes in the fourth year of Henry VII, 1488-89:

The King our sovereign Lord, having a singular pleasure above all things to avoid such enormities and mischiefs as be hurtful and prejudicial to the commonweal of this his land and his subjects of the same, remembreth that among all other things great inconveniences daily doth increase by desolation and pulling down and wilful waste of houses and towns within this his realm, and laying to pasture lands which customarily have been used in tilth, whereby idleness, ground and beginning of all mischiefs, daily do increase; for where in some towns two hundred persons were occupied and lived by their lawful labors, now be there occupied two or three herdsmen, and the residue fall in idleness, the husbandry which is one of the greatest commodities of this realm is greatly decayed, churches destroyed, the service of God withdrawn, the bodies there buried not prayed for, the patron and curates wronged, the defense of this land against our enemies outward feebled and impaired; to the great displeasure of God, to the subversion of the policy and good rule of this land, and remedy be not hastily therefore purveyed.[11]

What such conditions must have meant to the people affected, we can perhaps appreciate by comparison with the similar plight of many mining communities in the United States during our portion of the twentieth century. Introduce modern terminology and the statute of four hundred and fifty years ago would describe any one of our ghost towns.

The remedy proposed as a solution of this problem was to compel owners to maintain their houses and properties. This did not, however, stop the trend toward pasturage, particularly for the raising of sheep. Writing in 1516, Sir Thomas More describes in *Utopia* the sufferings of the dispossessed farmers, reminding one of the tragedies of the migrants from the Dust Bowl in southwestern United States during the 1930's:

The husbandmen be thrust out of their own, or else either by covin or fraud, or by violent oppression they be put besides it, or by wrongs and injuries they be so wearied, that they be compelled to sell all: by one means therefore or by other, either by hook or crook they must needs depart away, poor, silly [simple], wretched souls, men, women, husbands, wives, fatherless children, widows, woeful mothers, with their young babes, and their whole household small in substance and much in number, as husbandry requireth many hands. Away they trudge, I say, out of their known and accustomed houses, finding no place to rest in. All their household stuff, which is very little worth, though it might well abide the sale, yet being suddenly thrust out, they be constrained to sell it for a thing of naught. And when they have wandered abroad till that be spent, what can they then else do but steal, and then justly pardy be hanged, or else go about a begging. And yet then also they be cast in prison as vagabonds, because they go about and work not: whom no man will set at work, though they never so willingly profer themselves thereto.[480a]

Elsewhere in the same book he pleads the need of the workingman for economic security, compared with whose lot

the state and condition of the laboring beasts may seem much better and wealthier. . . . But these silly, poor wretches be presently tormented with barren and unfruitful labor. And the remembrance of their poor indigent and beggarly old age killeth them up. For their daily wage is so little, that it will not suffice for the same day, much less it yieldeth any overplus, that may daily be laid up for the relief of old age.

Is not this an unjust and an unkind public weal, which giveth great fees and rewards to gentlemen, as they call them, and to goldsmiths, and to such other, which be either idle persons or else only flatterers, and devisers of vain pleasures; and of the contrary part maketh no gentle provision for poor plowmen, colliers, laborers, carters, ironsmiths, and carpenters: without whom no common wealth can continue? [480b]

The situation grew no better. The 25th Henry VIII, Chapter 13, 1534, reveals a continued tendency toward large estates and blames upon this the steeply rising prices which marked the beginning of years of hard times for the laboring people of England.

This law of Henry VIII was called "an act concerning farms and sheep." It proposed to limit the number of sheep in any one holding to two thousand and set forth the following situation as a reason for this restriction:

Divers and sundry of the King's subjects . . . have not only pulled down churches and towns and enhanced the old rates of the rents . . . but also have raised and enhanced the prices of all manner of corn, cattle, wool, pigs, geese, hens, chickens, eggs and such other almost double above the prices which hath been accustomed. . . . One of the greatest occasions that moveth and provoketh these greedy and covetous people so to accumulate and keep in their hands such great portions and parts of the grounds and lands of this realm . . . is only the great profit that cometh of sheep . . . by the which a good sheep for victual that was accustomed to be sold for two shillings four pence or three shillings at the most, is now sold for six shillings or five shillings or four shillings at the least, and a stone of clothing wool that in some shire of this realm was accustomed to be sold for eighteen pence or twenty pence is now sold for four shillings or three shillings four pence at the least.[15]

How much the movement toward the enclosure of land was responsible for the rise in prices that characterized the sixteenth century, it is difficult to know. There were other factors in the higher cost of living, as for example the increase in the production of silver and the reduction by Henry VIII and by Edward VI of the content of silver in the coinage. There were also periods of failure in the crops, such as there had been in previous centuries. What can, however, be seen as a direct result of enclosure was the dislocation of people from their former employments and the increase in the numbers of unattached persons without regular means of support.

In addition to feeling the effects of the expropriation of farmers, England was beginning to experience the economic complications arising from industrial developments. Manufacture had spread until a depression could throw all the members of a family and, indeed, the people of a whole neighborhood out of work. When, in 1528, Henry VIII declared war against the Emperor Charles V, the weavers of England suffered because of the loss of sales to the Flemish markets.

The world was no longer self-contained. A war on the Continent could mean the stoppage of the English business in export, and that in turn might mean unemployment for the workers. Times had changed. The complications of a different order of life were beginning to operate. When under feudalism crops failed and the serfs died in their huts or in the barren fields, this was famine. It was a depriving nature that was destroying man. But in the sixteenth century the problem expressed itself differently. Witness these excerpts from the municipal accounts of Newcastle-upon-Tyne, published by M. A. Richardson in *Reprints of Rare Tracts.*

1597, September. Paid for the charges of burying 9 poor folks who died for want in the streets, for their graves making 3s.

1597, October. Paid for the charge of burying 16 poor folks who died for want in the streets 6s. 8d.[486a]

Granted the failure of the crops in that year, here, nevertheless, was something different from famine. It was not merely nature against man. It was man caught in the society of his own contriving. The process which Edward III helped to put into operation when he stimulated woolen manufacture by encouraging the immigration of weavers from Holland had had implications of which he could not have been aware. This was indeed a new world: a world that, as we shall see, was changing on the Continent quite as much as in England. It was a world in which the articulated movement of life could be dislocated and in which that dislocation was already taking place.

Under feudalism, then, life for the laborer might be said to have been stable. His economy was undisturbed except for the direct impact of famine or the forays of war. With the breaking of the old system came the separation of men from the land and the beginning of movement. Thereby men escaped their bondage at the price of their security. The development of towns, of manufacture, of commerce brought new interrelationships, the balance and functioning of which were susceptible of acute disturbance. It was the substitution of the clock for the sundial. No casual clouds could affect the operation of the clock; but let something happen to the mechanism of the new timepiece, and the consequent disaster could outdo the occasional interruptions that nature had formerly brought to the measurement of the hours.

A major cause of individual economic need is dislocation—in the period just reviewed, the dislocation of the farmer and the laborer from his expropriated tenancies or holdings, the dislocation of men from life-long employment with the substitution of casual labor; the dislocation that craft and trade were beginning to be subject to through the development of commerce and manufacture. From this period forward, casual employment, underemployment, intermittent employment, seasonal employment, cyclical employment would be the portion of the worker. At the same time, an industrial civilization would be baffled by the problem of how to provide him with an equivalent of the provision against sickness, old age, and the other personal exigencies which, however inadequate, had been the corollary of his serfdom. These were the circumstances under which, perforce poverty became a concern of government. Out of the efforts to solve this problem came a long and varied series of measures and establishments; the latest of which is our present system of social security.

II

CHARITY BEFORE 1536

I give no alms to satisfy the hunger of my brother, but to fulfill and accomplish the will and command of my God; I draw not my purse for his sake that demands it, but his that enjoined it; I relieve no man upon the rhetoric of his miseries, nor to content mine own commiserating disposition; for this is still but moral charity, and an act that oweth more passion than reason. He that relieves another upon the bare suggestion and bowels of pity, doth not this so much for his sake, as for his own; for by compassion we make others' misery our own, and so by relieving them, we relieve ourselves also.

SIR THOMAS BROWNE,
Religio Medici, 1643 [411a]

U P to the sixteenth century the approach of government to the problem of poverty had been only punitive and repressive. This was partly because the existence of the destitution that accompanied the social changes of the times was but gradually and slowly appreciated. It was also because most people felt that ample facilities existed for meeting economic distress.

There was, first of all, the widespread, unorganized relief that the poor obtained for themselves through begging. This was a recognized and accepted method of help. The asking and the giving of charity was, as we all know, a part of medieval life; the beggar was one of the characteristic figures of the age. He had received a dramatic place and endorsement from St. Francis and many another religious leader. The mendicant friar, the pilgrim to or from the Holy Land, the scholar at the university—all had social approval when they sought alms. They gave to begging a kind of status, making it a much more possible method than it would be now of providing for the relief of need. So accepted indeed was mendicancy, according to current ethical standards, that the forbidding of it by law represented a revolutionary change, and when proposed at Ypres (see Chapter IV) brought forth considerable opposition. As we have seen, the first English statute which took into consideration the need of the impotent recognized begging as their means of support (12th Richard II).

In addition to mendicancy, there were three avenues of organized help that might be available to the person in distress. One of these was the ancient and long-established institution of the guilds. Whether they were social, craft, or merchant guilds, all emphasized a coöperative self-help and brotherhood. While the greater part of their efforts was manifestly in the direction of mutual benefit among their own members, who by their status in trade or craft were somewhat removed from the immediate threat of poverty, aid was provided when need occurred. In addition, many of the guilds maintained "works of charity" for the poor of their towns. This involved any of a variety of activities; as, for example, the feeding of the needy on feast days, the distribution of a certain amount of corn and barley yearly, the provision of free lodgings for destitute travelers, and other kinds of intermittent and incidental help.

More important probably than the guilds as a means of relief were the facilities established through private foundations of various kinds. Bequests and large gifts by individual benefactors were as much a part of the life of the fourteenth and fifteenth centuries and the years following as they are of the modern world. At the time of the Reformation there were in England not less than 460 charitable foundations.[403a] Money was not only willed for the establishment of almshouses, hospitals, and similar institutions, but also was designated for disbursement in connection with funeral ceremonies and on anniversaries in perpetuation of the memory of the testator. These and like philanthropies were common enough to cause Thomas Fuller to include in his *Worthies of England* a special category of notables, benefactors to the public, dividing them as with his other categories into those before and those after the Reformation. These benefactors established colleges, built bridges and other public works, in addition to erecting charitable institutions. Three quotations from the *Worthies* may serve to illustrate their philanthropy, as it affected the poor:

(1) Ambrose, son to John Nicholas, . . . thriving so well in his trade that anno 1576 he became Lord Mayor of London. He founded twelve alms-houses in Mungwel-street in that city, endowing them with competent maintenance.

(2) Sir Roger Achley . . . beheld the whole city of London as one family, and himself the mayor 1511—for the time being—the master

thereof. He observed that poor people who never have more than they need, will sometimes need more than they have. This Joseph collected from the present plenty, that a future famine would follow, as in this kind a lank constantly attendeth a bank. Wherefore he prepared Leaden-Hall, therefore called the Common Garner, and stored up much corn therein, for which he received the praise of the rich and the blessing of the poor.

(3) Thomas Curson born in Allhallows Lumbard street, Armorer, dwelt without Bishop-gate. It happened that a stage player borrowed a rusty musket, which had lain long leger in his shop; now though his part was comical he therewith acted an unexpected tragedy, killing one of the standers by, the gun casually going off on the stage, which he suspected not to be charged.

Oh the difference of divers men in the tenderness of their consciences! Some are scarce touched with a wound, whilst others are wounded with a touch therein. This poor armorer was highly afflicted therewith, though done against his will, yea without his knowledge, in his absence, by another, out of mere chance. Hereupon he resolved to give all his estate to pious uses; no sooner had he gotten a round sum, but presently he posted with it in his apron to the Court of Aldermen, and was in pain till by their direction he had settled it for the relief of the poor in his own and other parishes, and disposed of some hundreds of pounds accordingly, as I am credibly informed by the then church wardens of the said parish. Thus as he conceived himself casually—though at a great distance—to have occasioned the death of one, he was the immediate and direct cause of giving a comfortable living to many, he died anno 16. . . .[443a]

Much of this sort of giving was indiscriminate and missed its best purpose. Moreover, the administration of many of the institutions was such as to favor the administrators rather than the designated beneficiaries. The situation had become serious enough by the beginning of the fifteenth century to call for the enactment of a statute providing for the investigation of hospitals and for the reform of their management. The preamble to this Statute of 1414 indicates in its complaint the scope of these enterprises:

. . . to sustain impotent men and women, lazars, men out of their wits and poor women with child, and to nourish, relieve and refresh other poor people.[10]

That misapplications of funds had reached a scale great enough to warrant the attention of Parliament is evidence of the existence of an extensive spread of institutions of benevolence, a resource that must at one time have offered considerable help to those in need, but that by the sixteenth century had been greatly reduced in its efficiency.

Far exceeding the relief thus afforded in casual or organized ways, much of it religiously inspired, was the aid that was provided by the church in its various departments. The two chief sources of Christian thought—the Hebraic and the Greek—each included the relief of distress in its conception of the good life, seeing it as important for the giver, for the individual in need, and for the community. Derived from these origins, the combined effect of the teaching of St. Paul, St. Augustine, St. Bernard, St. Francis, and St. Thomas Aquinas, however much they may have differed individually in what they emphasized, was to give to poverty a kind of dignity and to make the granting of alms a meritorious deed. The condition of being poor could not help gaining a certain social acceptance when the doing away with one's material possessions was advocated as a step in the discipline of salvation and when those in need were designated as the desirable recipients of this spiritual act. The church, incorporating both concepts—poverty as a way of grace, almsgiving as a meritorious deed—became a symbol of relief.

Tithing was an early feature of ecclesiastical finance. In England the church funds thus secured were divided: one-third for the maintenance of the church, one-third for the poor, and one-third for the priests. In 1014 a law of King Ethelred provided that

Respecting tithe: The king and his witan have chosen and decreed, as is just, that one third part of the tithe which belongs to the Church go to the reparation of the church; and a second part to the servants of God, the third to God's poor, and to needy ones in thraldom.[1]

That under feudalism the church should have been an established source of relief is not a denial of the economic security that serfdom involved for the serf. It is only an indication that no social system 'is complete. Our capitalistic society is not without its collectivistic aspects, and Russian communism has its capitalistic elements. So, too, in feudal England security could be inherent in slavery and villeinage, although the church might be needed to fill overlooked vacuities or even to be the means by which the master occasionally aided his servants.

As the Middle Ages advanced the principle of applying one-third of the income of the parish church to the relief of the poor was neglected. The omission was serious enough and general enough to call for remedial legislation. In 1391 a statute provided that "a convenient sum of money . . . be paid and distributed yearly of the fruits and profits" of certain churches to their poor parishioners.[9] Despite this law, it is doubtful whether the parish offered relatively as much provision against destitution at the opening of the sixteenth century as it had four hundred years earlier.

More important than the parish as a source of assistance to the poor were the monasteries. Thomas Fuller, in his *Church History of Britain*, speaks of the entertainment they afforded:

Their hospitality was beyond compare. . . . Especially in Christmas time, they kept most bountiful houses. Whosoever brought the face of a man, brought with him a patent for his free welcome, till he pleased to depart. This was the method: Where he break his fast, there he dined; where he dined, there he supped; where he supped, there he break his fast next morning: and so in a circle. Always provided, that he provided lodging for himself at night, abbeys having great halls and refectories, but few chambers and dormitories, save for such of their own society.

Some will object, that this their hospitality was but charity mistaken, promiscuously entertaining some who did not need, and more who did not deserve it. Yea, these abbeys did but maintain the poor which they made. For some vagrants, accounting the abbey-alms their own inheritance, served an apprenticeship, and afterwards wrought journey-work, to no other trade than begging. . . .

All this is confessed; yet, by their hospitality, many an honest and hungry soul had his bowels refreshed, who otherwise would have been starved; and better it is, two drones should be fed, than one bee famished. We see the heavens themselves, in dispensing their rain, often water many stinking bogs and noisome lakes,—which moisture is not needed by them,—yea, they the worse for it,—only because much good ground lies inseparably intermingled with them; so that either the bad with the good must be watered, or the good with the bad must be parched away.[441b]

By the second quarter of the sixteenth century the monastery, like the parish, had ceased to be as important in this respect as it had been in earlier times. It was primarily an ecclesiastical not an eleemosynary institution, and was not even in site necessarily located with a view to what was only incidental to its main purpose.

Nevertheless, it must be remembered that the church—by mandate, in principle, and often in fact—was outstanding as a means for the relief of economic distress. It occupied the field, both in its operation and in the place assigned to it in people's minds. It was a reason why for years government could take a wholly punitive and repressive attitude toward the problem of poverty.

In 1536 and 1539 Henry VIII expropriated the monasteries and turned their properties over to his followers. This action, like the Black Death in the fourteenth century, gave dramatic point to an already bad situation. A social resource, inadequate at its best, was now substantially diminished. What was more, one of the great symbols of charity had been removed, and there was consequently double occasion for public action.

The church, along with the hospitals and other religiously inspired philanthropies, represented the positive approach to human distress. With this resource available to the person in need, government could be negative in attitude and action. It was only when, in the presence of the overwhelming effects of great social change, the church and private charity could manifestly not relieve the vastly increased distress that public provision supported by funds secured through taxation was introduced. Even then, this was done only after government had tried through the church to use and develop the voluntary method—and had failed.

III

THE BEGINNING OF PUBLIC RELIEF

The necessity of a permanent establishment for supporting the poor is, I conceive, admitted to a certain degree, in every country, in which there are public schools for the education of their children; dispensatories from which medicines are gratuitously supplied; hospitals for the reception and cure of the sick; or almshouses for lodging and maintaining the aged and necessitous. In England, however, the claims of the indigent, whether infirm, industrious, or idle, to a national provision, whatever the law may say upon the subject, are recognized, by the practice consequent upon that law, in their fullest extent; and whilst the streams of individual charity flow as copiously as in other countries, through the channels of private benevolences and through many great public, but local institutions, the poor man, whether his wants are of a permanent or temporary nature, is assured, that if he should not be supplied from these sources, he can still have recourse to the never failing reservoir of parochial contribution.

Sir Frederic Morton Eden,
The State of the Poor, 1797[432c]

Government in England first took positive responsibility for the relief of economic distress in the reign of Henry VIII. The initial statute looking in this direction was enacted in 1531. The occasion for the new law is indicated in its preamble:

In all places throughout this realm of England, vagabonds and beggars have of long time increased, and daily do increase in great and excessive numbers, by the occasion of idleness, mother and root of all vices, whereby hath insurged and sprung, and daily insurgeth and springeth, continual thefts, murders, and other heinous offences and great enormities, to the high displeasure of God, the unquietation and damage of the king's people, and to the marvelous disturbance of the common weal of this realm. . . . Many and sundry good laws, strict statutes and ordinances have been before this time devised and made as well by the King our Sovereign Lord as also by divers his most noble progenitors Kings of England for the most necessary and due reformation of the premises, yet not withstanding, the said number of vagabonds and beg-

gars be not seen in any part to be diminished, but rather daily augmented and increased into great routs and companies.

The problem, as stated, is that of beggary and vagabondage; but
before dealing with the situation presented by the progeny of "idleness, mother and root of all vices," Parliament now makes provision
for those who are genuinely in need. The Act decrees that the
mayors, justices of the peace, and other local officials:

(1) Shall make diligent search and inquiry of all aged poor and impotent persons which live or of necessity be compelled to live by alms
of the charity of the people.

(2) Shall have power [to assign impotent persons limits within which
they may beg] and to give in commandment to every such aged and
impotent beggar that none of them shall beg without the limit to them
so appointed.

(3) Shall also register and write the names of every such impotent
beggar in a bill or roll indented.

(4) Shall make and deliver to every such impotent person by them
enabled to beg, a letter containing the name of such impotent person,
and witnessing that he is authorized to beg, and the limit within which
he is appointed to beg.[14]

Compared with present systems of aid for those in need, this may
seem like no provision at all. Actually it represented the beginning
of definite assumption by government of responsibility for the care
of persons in economic distress. In arranging to certify eligibility for
begging and in defining areas in which the individual might beg,
England had gone a considerable distance toward the administration of relief.

Having set up a machinery for legalizing begging, the Statute now
falls with the greater severity upon the able-bodied unemployed.
Fines are imposed upon anyone who shall

give any harboring, money, or lodging to any beggars being strong and
able in their bodies to work [and the public officials] by their discretions shall cause every such idle person so to him brought to be had to
the next market-town, or other place . . . most convenient, . . . and
there to be tied to the end of a cart naked and be beaten with whips
throughout the same market-town or other place till his body be bloody
by reason of such whipping; and after such punishment and whipping
. . . [he] shall be enjoined upon his oath to return forthwith without
delay in the next and straight way to the place where he was born, or

where he last dwelled before the same punishment by the space of three years, and there put himself to labour like as a true man oweth to do.[14]

But could the problem of the impotent be met by authorized begging, and could a man "put himself to labor like as a true man oweth to do"? Five years of experience showed that something more was needed, and in 1536 came a statute which rounded out the program started in 1531, establishing the first comprehensive system in England of relief under governmental auspices. The principal elements of the plan, as expressed in this Statute of 1536, were as follows:

(1) All and every person or persons being whipped or sent unto their countries in form aforesaid, at the end of every ten miles shall repair unto the constable of any parish, being directly in his way towards the county and place whereunto he is so appointed, and upon sight of his letters given unto him at the time of his whipping . . . every of the said constables and others the King's subjects shall and may furnish him with competent meat, drink, and lodging for one night only or for one meal, and so he shall continue his daily journey of ten miles until such time as he shall come unto the hundred and place whereunto he is assigned to go.

(2) Any of the aforesaid rufflers, sturdy vagabonds, and valiant beggars . . . upon due examinations and proof of the continuance of his said loitering, wandering and idleness, or vagabondage, shall eftsoon not only [be] whipped again . . . but also shall have the upper part of the gristle of his right ear clean cut off. . . . [If] having the upper part of the right ear cut off, as is aforesaid . . . and . . . found guilty . . . of continual loitering and idleness, then every such sturdy vagabond and valiant beggar . . . shall have judgment to suffer pains and execution of death as a felon and as enemies of the Commonwealth.

(3) [The justices and other officers] shall have authority . . . to take . . . children under the age of fourteen years and above the age of five years, in begging or idleness, and to appoint them to masters of husbandry or other crafts or labors to be taught, by the which they may get their living when they shall come of age.

(4) Mayors, governors and head officers of every city, . . . and the church wardens or two others of every parish . . . shall in good and charitable wise take such discreet and convenient order, by gathering and procuring of such charitable and voluntary alms of the good Christian people . . . with boxes every Sunday, holy day, and other festival day or otherwise . . . as the poor, impotent, lame, feeble, sick and diseased people, being not able to work, may be provided, holpen, and relieved so that in no wise they nor none of them be suffered to go openly in begging; and that such as be lusty or having their limbs strong enough

to labor, may be daily kept in continual labor, whereby every one of them may get their own sustenance and living with their own hands.

(5) Every preacher, parson, vicar, curate of this realm, as well in all and every their sermons, collations, biddings of the beads as in time of all confessions and at the making of the wills or testaments of any persons at all times of the year, shall exhort, move, stir, and provoke people to be liberal and bountifully to extend their good and charitable alms and contributions.

(6) The overplus of all and all manner of collections of the rich and wealthy parishes . . . shall be ordered and distributed for and towards the sustentation of the charges of other poor parishes.

(7) [No one is] to be constrained to any such certain contribution but as their free wills and charities shall extend.

(8) [The collectors shall] render and yield account of all sums of money as by them shall be gathered and how and in what manner it was employed.

(9) The collectors of the said alms which shall at any time forbear their own business and labor, and shall travail or take any pains in and about the execution of any part of this present act, shall have and take for his and their so doing such competent wages of the money of the said common collections as by the discretions of the mayor, aldermen, governor, bailiff, or justice of the peace and others of the parish shall be thought good and reasonable.[16]

These items in the Law of 1536 contain the characteristic elements of the Poor Law as they were to continue during four centuries. To the principles of search and registration of need as established in the Act of 1531, there is now added a definition of what the nature of the provision for that need should be. For the system of licensed begging there is substituted an administration of funds supplied through contributions. Government takes the responsibility of stimulating and securing these contributions.

For the first time also, the contingency that a person may be capable of work and yet may not be able to obtain work is recognized. The state assumes the two-fold duty of seeing that the impotent "be provided, holpen, and relieved" and that those with "limbs strong enough to labor" be "kept in continual labor whereby every one of them may get their own sustenance and living with their own hands." While there is no prescription as to how employment is to be supplied, the principle of public responsibility is established. So, too, is the function of local government in arranging for the movement of the non-resident from one jurisdiction to another. The transient supplies his own transportation—he walks—but the local officials in ten-mile stages are to feed and lodge him until he reaches his place of settlement.

Here and throughout the Act the unit of administration is indicated. Later it is to be more clearly defined; but for the present, city, borough, town, and parish are designated. In the parish the church-wardens are specified. This was natural and appropriate. The church-wardens were a board of lay governors charged with responsibility for the business affairs of the local church. Just as in the United States, at the beginning of the great unemployment of 1930, existing private agencies in many communities were first used to disburse emergency funds, so in the sixteenth century the government turned first to the established church organization for the administration of relief.

That this relief might go beyond the parish in its operations is forecast in the provision for the transfer of the overplus from the richer to the poorer parishes. The Law of 1536 calls for the recording of funds secured and expended and for the making of an accounting. There is also an arrangement for compensating the collectors for their work. The first paid public welfare official may be said to date from 1536. Subsequent legislation omitted this item, and many years passed before an employed personnel was again used to administer relief.

A decade later, in 1547—the first year of Edward VI—one of those characteristic reversals in the legislation and administration of public assistance took place. The third chapter in the Statutes of that year repeals the Acts of 1531 and 1536 and introduces the sternest kind of repression. Idlers and wanderers who "if no man otherwise will take them do not offer themselves to work for meat and drink" or "leave their work out of convenient time or run away" shall have a V "marked with a hot iron in the breast" and be enslaved for two years. If during that time the slave runs away, he shall be branded on the forehead or cheek with the letter S and be enslaved forever. Upon a repetition of his offense he shall suffer death as a felon.[17]

This Statute defeated itself by its own severity and was repealed three years later. The Law of 1531 licensing begging was revived with minor amendments, among them the provision of transportation on horseback or by cart for the return of aged and impotent persons to their places of residence.[19]

After two more years, in 1552, the law begins again the development that started in 1536. Emphasis is once more placed upon the securing of funds for the relief of destitution. This time the pressure upon the parishioners to make contributions of money is increased. Collectors of "charitable alms" are appointed, and a procedure to help them in obtaining funds is formulated:

If any person or persons being able to further this charitable work do obstinately and frowardly refuse to give towards the help of the poor or do wilfully discourage other from so charitable a deed, the parson, vicar or curate and churchwardens of the parish where he dwelleth shall gently exhort him or them towards the relief of the poor, and if he or they will not be so persuaded, then upon the certificate of the parson, vicar or curate of the parish to the Bishop of the Diocese, the same bishop shall send for him or them to induce and persuade him or them by charitable ways and means, and so according to his discretion to take order for the reformation thereof.[20]

Eleven years later, in 1563, the law moves from the social pressure of previous legislation to the use of the police power as a means of securing contributions. Voluntary giving and giving upon the persuasion of the bishop having apparently failed, the law now inserts a "must."

If, despite the gentle exhortation of the parson and the churchwardens and the subsequent efforts of the bishop, the obstinate person continues to be froward and wilful about contributing, the bishop shall have authority to bind him in the sum of ten pounds to appear before the justices of the peace at the next general session. The justices or other officials shall then "charitably and gently persuade and move the said obstinate person to extend his or their charity towards the relief of the poor of the parish where he or she inhabiteth and dwelleth and if he or she shall obstinately and wilfully stand in the same, and will not be persuaded therein by the said justices, mayor, bailiffs or other head officers," then it shall be lawful for them to "sesse, tax and limit upon every such obstinate person so refusing, according to their good discretions what sum the said obstinate person shall pay weekly towards the relief of the poor," with prison the penalty for refusal to pay the assessment.[21]

From this sort of compulsion to taxation was a short step, and a little less than a decade later that step was taken. In 1572 the Statute of 1563, together with its predecessors, was repealed and a reformulation of the Poor Law—the 14th Elizabeth, Chapter 5—was enacted.

Its forty-three sections included the principles previously established, together with an important new provision.

The justices of the peace and other local officials

shall by their good discretions tax and assess all and every the inhabitants dwelling in all and every city, borough, town, village, hamlet and place . . . to such weekly charge as they and every of them shall weekly contribute towards the relief of the said poor people and the names of all such inhabitants taxed shall also enter into the said register book together with their taxation.[23]

This marks the beginning in England of the legislation of taxes for relief. The same Statute introduces the overseer of the poor, charging him with the duty of putting rogues and vagabonds to work.

Four years later the 18th Elizabeth defines the purpose of this work:

Also to the intent youth may be accustomed and brought up in labor and work, and then not like to grow to be idle rogues, and to the intent also that such as be already grown up in idleness and so rogues at this present, may not have any just excuse in saying that they cannot get any service or work, and then without any favor or toleration worthy to be executed, and that other poor and needy persons being willing to work may be set on work.[24]

For this purpose "a competent store and stock of wool, hemp, flax, iron or other stuff" shall be provided. The mayors, justices, and other appropriate officials shall appoint "collectors and governors of the poor" who shall "of the same stock and store, deliver to such poor and needy person a competent portion to be wrought into yarn or other matter . . . for which they shall make payment to them which work the same according to the desert of the work." The collectors and governors shall sell the product.

If hereafter any such person able to do any such work shall refuse to work or shall go abroad begging or live idly, or taking such work shall spoil or embezzle the same, [then] in convenient apparel meet for such a body to wear [he] shall be received into such House of Correction there to be straightly kept, as well in diet as in work, and also punished from time to time.[24]

In this first specification of a program of work, nearly four centuries ago, appears the same mixture of purpose that has characterized the use of work in relief ever since. The Elizabethan lawmaker proposes work as training for the youth, as prevention of roguery, as a test of good intent, and as a means of providing employment for the needy. In the background is the House of Correction with its threat of punishment. How ancient is the confusion about work, and how deep-rooted is our conflict of feeling concerning it!

With the Acts of 1572 and 1576 the Poor Law is substantially complete. In 1597 the program was rewritten and clarified administratively. The hard times of 1596–97, when people died of starvation in the streets, doubtless helped to bring this about; and the first five Acts of the thirty-ninth year of Elizabeth were designed to improve and alleviate current conditions. The first two of these Statutes were directed to the problem of "the decaying of towns and of the maintenance of husbandry and tillage." [25 & 26] The fourth reënacted, with slight changes, previous regulations for the punishment of vagabonds and beggars; [28] and the fifth provided for erecting hospitals or abiding and working houses for the poor.[29] The third restated the system for the relief of the poor.[27]

In its first paragraph this third chapter of the 39th Elizabeth covers what in earlier laws was spread over several sections. The churchwardens and four substantial householders of every parish are to be appointed by the justices of the peace as overseers of the poor, charged with the responsibility of setting to work the children of parents not able to maintain them and also persons who "use no ordinary and daily trade of life to get their living by." To this end and in order to obtain "competent sums of money for and towards the necessary relief of the lame, impotent, old, blind and such other among them being poor and not able to work," they are authorized to tax every inhabitant of the parish and every occupier of lands. The justices, subject to limits set in the law, are empowered to fix the rate of assessment. It is lawful for the churchwardens and overseers to erect "convenient houses of habitation" on wastes and commons for the impotent poor, "and also to place inmates or more families than one in one cottage or house." The almshouse is thus confirmed as a part of the relief program. Section 7 of this Act introduces a new principle. It establishes the mutual liability of parents and children for each other's support.

That the parents or children of every poor, old, blind, lame and impotent person, or other poor person not able to work, being of sufficient ability, shall at their own charges relieve and maintain every such poor person in that manner and according to that rate as by the justices . . . at their general quarter session shall be assessed.[27]

With this Statute the Poor Law takes the shape that is to characterize it for three hundred years. The Act of 1601, the 43rd Elizabeth, Chapter 2, usually spoken of as the culminating Statute in the development of the Poor Law, is anticlimactic. It merely repeats the Act of 1597-98, having scarcely anything in it that is new except the extension of liability for support to grandparents.[30] What has helped to make it a landmark in the history of the relief of economic distress is the fact that it is the last rewriting of the total law. Not until 1662 is anything of substantial importance added, and that is specifically concerned with settlement. The year 1601 stands, then, as the year in which the development that started in 1531—indeed one might say in 1349—comes to a period. The Poor Law has reached the form in which it is to influence thought and operation for the next three centuries and more. The 43rd Elizabeth is the parent of governmental relief in England and in the United States, the parent in relation to which our present system of social security expresses both development and revolt.

The bare recital of a succession of statutes provides no picture of the immediate agitation that was responsible for or that accompanied each new piece of legislation. Most of the enactments were preceded by local experiments and pressures. In London and in the towns where England was making its first beginnings of manufacture, there was insistent demand for action. So great a departure as the transfer of the basic provision for relief in England from the clerical and voluntary to the temporal and compulsory, with an administrative set-up which though local in operation was country-wide in scope, could have come about only in response to a generally recognized need and an almost universal complaint. Throughout the three-quarters of a century during which the Poor Law of 1601 was taking form, appeal after appeal for remedy went forth from printing press, from pulpit, and from citizens' delegations. The writings of Sir Thomas More and of Henry Brinklow played an effective part, as did the sermons of Thomas Lever, preaching before Edward VI; of Hugh Latimer, Bishop of Worcester; and of Nicholas Ridley, Bishop of London, who was the moving spirit of a committee that agitated and planned for relief.

All this activity was progressively precipitated upon Parliament. Each new legislative step was preceded and accompanied by pressure, discussion, and debate. What happened in law was, in a sense, a confirmation of what had already happened in practice. The statutes formulated, defined, and established existing experience and theory.

That laws were passed did not, however, mean that they were enforced. There is scarcely an act relating to relief which does not begin with a reference to the unsuccess or non-observance of previous legislation. Administration was local, beyond anything we know today, and largely independent of the national authority. The statutes often did little more in effect than indicate intention, and the officials in the parishes usually did what they pleased.

Nevertheless, the pattern is set in these laws of Parliament. The statutes from Henry VIII to Elizabeth established a principle and a tradition of relief locally financed and locally administered for local residents, with the overseer of the poor as the responsible relief official, and a system of public assistance that included direct grants of aid to the unemployable and a policy of work for the able-bodied. After two centuries of attempts to control poverty by repressive measures, government slowly and reluctantly came to accept a positive obligation for the help of people who could not provide for themselves. The experience of the years between 1349 and 1601 had convinced the rulers of England of the presence of a destitution among the poor that punishment could not abolish and that could be relieved only by the application of public resources to individual need.

IV

DEVELOPMENTS ON THE CONTINENT

We perceive well that this common office to provide for poor men
is harder than men think, considering that it can not be duly executed without great diligence, study and wisdom. And therefore
because great commodity cometh of it, it requireth also great men
and such as mind more the commonwealth than their own profit.
Now this is not spoken that any man should be afraid to take upon
him this business but rather that they should be forewarned that
before they take upon them so great a weight they take advice with
good deliberation whether they be meet for it or not.

Forma subventionis pauperum,
Ypres, 1531 [439a]

DURING the years that England was moving toward the organization of a system of governmental relief, Europe was passing
through a similar experience; and between the Continent and the
island there was a considerable exchange of ideas about the problem
of poverty.

One of the men who participated in this exchange was Juan Luis
Vives, a native of Spain who was educated in Paris and who made
Flanders his adopted country. He developed a plan of organized
relief which he addressed to the Consuls and Senate of Bruges, his
adopted city. He wrote it at the request of his friend Ludvig van
Praet, mayor of Bruges from 1525 to 1537.

Vives was one of the great thinkers of his day. He was at one time
associated with Erasmus and edited for him St. Augustine's City of
God. The two became estranged and Vives went to England. Here
he held a lectureship in rhetoric at Oxford. He was an intimate
friend of Sir Thomas More.

Vives was known to Queen Katharine (of Aragon) and suffered
a short period of imprisonment for supporting her in her difficulties
with Henry VIII. He had, moreover, memorialized Henry in the
interest of making higher education more widely available. There
is thus every reason to believe that he was in a position to get attention in England for his ideas. His salutation to the Consuls and

Senate of Bruges is dated January 6, 1526, and therefore falls half-way between the *Utopia* of Thomas More in 1516 and the first comprehensive Poor Law enacted by Parliament in 1536.

Vives called his plan *De Subventione Pauperum*. The following excerpts are taken from a translation by Margaret M. Sherwood, published by the New York School of Social Work under the title, *Concerning the Relief of the Poor*.[497]

I propose the following plan. Some of the poor live in those institutions commonly called hospitals . . . others beg publicly; still others bear their hardships as best they can, each one in his own home. I call "hospitals" those places where the sick are fed and cared for, where a certain number of paupers is supported, where boys and girls are reared, where abandoned infants are nourished, where the insane are confined, and where the blind dwell. . . .

Let the Senators, by twos, with a secretary, visit each of these homes, and inspect it, and write a full account of its condition, of the number of its inmates and their names, likewise from what cause each one has come there. Let all these things be reported to the Councillors and the Senate in assembly.

Let those who suffer poverty at home be registered, both they and their children, by two Senators for each parish; their needs ascertained, in what manner they have lived hitherto, and by what ill chance they have fallen into poverty. It will be easy to learn from the neighbors what sort of men they are, how they live and what their habits are. Evidence about one poor person should not be taken from another, for he would not be free from jealousy. . . .

Should the native poor be asked whether they have learned a trade? Yes; and those who have not, if they are of suitable age, should be taught the one to which they say they are most strongly inclined, provided it is feasible. If it is not feasible, let them be taught some similar trade. . . .

Even those who have dissipated their fortunes in riotous living—by gambling, harlots, extravagance, and gluttony—must be relieved, for no one must die of hunger. But to them more irksome tasks should be assigned and smaller rations, that they may be an example to others, and may repent of their former life and may not relapse easily into the same vices, being restrained both by lack of food and by the severity of their tasks. They must not die of hunger, but they must feel its pangs. . . .

Let a certain number of those who cannot find any work by themselves be assigned to each artisan. If anyone has progressed far enough in his trade let him open a workshop. Both to these and to those to whom the magistrates have assigned apprentices let contracts be given for making the numerous things which the state uses for public purposes: such as

31

pictures, statues, tapestries, sewers, ditches, buildings, and the things which the hospitals need. . . .

Nor would I allow the blind either to sit idle or to wander around in idleness. There are a great many things at which they may employ themselves. Some are suited to letters; let them study, for in some of them we see an aptitude for learning by no means to be despised. Others are suited to the art of music; let them sing, pluck the lute, blow the flute. Let others turn wheels and work the treadmills; tread the wine-presses; blow the bellows in the smithies. We know the blind can make little boxes and chests, fruit baskets, and cages. Let the blind women spin and wind yarn. . . .

Let two censors be appointed every year out of the Senate, eminent men and of tried integrity, to inquire into the life and morals of the poor —boys, youths, and old men. Of the boys, what they are doing, what progress they are making, what sort of lives they lead, what talents they possess, what promise they show, and if any do wrong, who is to blame. . . . Those who frequent gaming places, and wine and beer taverns, should be censured. If no sort of reproof has any effect, they must be punished. . . .

I would suggest also that the same censors inquire about the youth and the sons of the wealthy. It would be most profitable to the state if they should compel them to render an account to the magistrates, as if to fathers, of the manner in which their time is spent, what pursuits and what employments they follow. . . .

This sounds very fine, someone will say, but where are we to get funds for all these things? . . .

His answer is, that under his plan there should be a surplus rather than a deficit; but that should more money be needed, he would assess the income of the hospitals, he would provide for a careful administration of bequests, would set up collection boxes in the churches, and ask the city to apply to relief some of the money spent for banquets, public games, and other festivities.

However, if the state does not want to do this, let it at all events loan what it may later on recover at a season more propitious for almsgiving.[502a]

It is interesting to observe how many of Vives' ideas appeared in current or subsequent relief administration in England. He advocated registering the poor. This was provided for by Henry VIII in the Act of 1531. He went further than the English law in prescribing methods of investigation. He relied upon private contributions to finance his program, as did the English law of 1536. Vives shared the convictions of subsequent writers that considerable savings in expenditures for relief could be effected through the creation of employment for the poor. He was modern in his suggestion that public improvements be used as a source of jobs. In his definition of tasks we have a forecast of the activities of the Work Projects Administration and the Public Works Administration in the United States. His belief in the potentialities of the blind anticipated the best present thought upon this subject. His theory that relief and work should be administered in such a way as to punish the individual deemed to be in need of reform was not unlike the program of deterrence which later was applied disastrously in England. His concept of censorship over the morals and behavior of the poor was appropriate to an age which accepted sumptuary legislation and in which the poor were just beginning to emerge from a status only slightly superior to slavery. Taken as a whole, Vives' plan impresses one as having been the most comprehensive and carefully formulated program of its day, more than a century in advance of the first attempts by writers in England to set down on paper their ideas of how the problem of relief might be solved.

About a year before Vives published his *De Subventione Pauperum* for the benefit of the citizens of Bruges, the governors of the neighboring city of Ypres had inaugurated a system of relief which exerted an enormous influence throughout Europe and which was brought to the attention of Queen Anne Boleyn, and probably by her to King Henry himself. This plan, put into effect on December 3, 1525, received both applause and adverse criticism. It was reviewed by the Sorbonne which gave it a qualified approval. The Emperor Charles V sent for a copy of the plan and within a month, October 6, 1531, issued his second decree forbidding begging throughout the Empire, the first having been proclaimed a year before.

It was in response to the request of the Emperor and many other similar requests that the City Council of Ypres arranged for the publication of the *Forma Subventionis Pauperum,* describing the scheme. A translation of it was published in England in 1535 by William Marshall, who dedicated the work to the Queen, Anne Boleyn. It has been reprinted by F. R. Salter in *Some Early Tracts on Poor Relief*. The following paragraphs taken from this diffuse and meandering, but delightful, statement contain the chief elements of the plan:

We have decreed . . . to choose by our common assents four of the chief of our city, men of good name and fame and such as are known to be trusty and of good life to whom by our authority we have committed the diligent execution of all such things as belong to the administration and oversight of poor folks in every behalf.

First of all they shall be like common parents to the poor of our city and bear towards them such fatherly favor as they should do to their adopted children—for so they are in very deed—providing for them meat, drink, and clothing and other necessaries as need shall require with measure and indifference [impartiality] so that every one have sufficient to maintain nature; not one in all the city be seen to go a-begging. . . .

To this also must these prefects look in especial that young men—every one accordingly as his nature is—either be set to school . . . or if their wit will not serve them thereunto then appoint and set them to handicrafts where they may learn one occupation or other by the which they may be able to get their living all the days of their lives after. . . .

These strong and lusty beggars also which have no lust to work for their livings they shall compell to handiworks. . . . Finally it shall belong to their office to admonish the rash and unruly folks with good reason and counsel, and such as will not be obedient to correct them measurably with the rod of justice—so as meet is—lest without correction they wax and grow worse. . . .

And that they may the better content many men's minds it shall be convenient that twice in every week they meet and sit together in a house . . . where they shall gently and without any sour or grim countenance receive all that make complaints. . . .

We thought it needful that these prefects choose unto them to help this matter of every parish such four as long have used to look to poor men and to distribute alms and such as both are meet for the room and also have a great zeal and desire to help poor folks. When these were chosen their office was appointed to them by the prefects to visit the poor houses, shops, and cottages of the poor and needy ones and to mark surely where, what and how much help every one needed. Yea and over this by certain tokens and conjectures to get the knowledge of their condition, their health, their homely and secret griefs, their manners and—as near as can be—their merits and to write these in a book or tables ordained for the same purpose. And at a day assigned to present the sum of the thing to the chief prefects of the poor.

The funds needed for relief were secured through a house-to-house collection of alms, boxes in the churches, exhortations by the clergy, and the use of bequests.

Then this decree was promulgated by the crier:

That the common poor folks of this our city from henceforth leave open begging and also keep their children from the same. And that they be patiently contented to be provided for at home without their labor and to have meat, drink and clothes as need shall require by meet and honest officers ordained for the same purpose by our common agreement. If they will not thus, then let them not think but to be punished after their deservings. . . .

Accounts shall be made once or twice openly before rulers and head officers at times certain, of all the money as well gathered as bestowed upon the poor. . . .

We give . . . to every strange, poor man so much as his necessity requireth and our substance will suffer us that is to say, viands to them that pass by. For such as be wearied we provide meat and drink and beds and other necessaries in common hospitals. And such as be sick and by the reason of sickness have not strength sufficient to perform their journey we entreat [treat] favorably, comforting and refreshing them two, three, or four days or sometimes longer till they were strong and be able to perform their begun voyages.

Those strangers which only for the intent to take alms come with a great flock of children to inhabit our city we do not receive except some necessary cause or some great pitious mischance—such as happen by war, by shipwreck, by burning or by some other such peril—do provoke us to receive them into the number of our poor folks. And of these we take no greater number than our common purse is able to maintain. . . .

We have decreed by an open commandment that none of our citizens presume to let any house to a stranger without our knowledge and consent for else by the daily increase of poor folks greater charge might grow unto us than we were able to bear. . . .

Now for all this no man is letted to do [hindered from doing] good deeds but every man if he will may give alms privately to whom he listeth. . . . Let them not send only the broken meats but let them rather send a mess or two of meat even purposely appointed for them that so the citizen's children may learn to visit and love the poor men's little cottages and the good man of the house and the good wife may remember that the burden of their neighbor's calamities must be relieved not only with alms but also with their presence in visiting, comforting, helping and in executing the deeds of pity. . . . For no other cause did nature mingle poor and rich together but that poor men should receive benefits of rich men.[439b]

The extent to which begging and indiscriminate giving had both religious and social sanction up into the sixteenth century is to be seen in the amount of controversy which the system of relief in Ypres aroused. The local clergy supported the inauguration of the plan but later the mendicant orders opposed it and called upon the Sorbonne for an opinion.

The faculty of the Sorbonne decided that the Ypres plan was hard but wholesome, and in agreement with the Scriptures, the teaching of the Apostles, and the laws of the church. It qualified this ruling with the proviso that the laws against begging should not lead to a greater impoverishment of the poor, who should be allowed to beg when other assistance was not provided for them. The rich who gave to the common relief fund should not feel that thereby all their charitable obligations had been fulfilled. Moreover, the mendicant orders should not be forbidden to gather alms.[499a]

Both the plan of Vives and the system of Ypres involved change from the social acceptance that begging had received in the past. They represented more an organization of private charity than a program of public relief, the sources of support being voluntary and philanthropic. Note particularly also the emphasis at Ypres upon the recognition by the good man and the good wife that their neighbor's calamities must be relieved not only with alms but also "with their presence in visiting, comforting, helping and in executing the deeds of pity." This preceded St. Vincent de Paul by one hundred years, and by three centuries and a half the friendly visitors of the charity organization movement.

Protestant Germany had been a few years ahead of Ypres in its plans for relief. In 1520 Martin Luther in an *Appeal to the Christian Nobility* of the German nation urged the abolition of begging and the establishment of provision for assistance to those in need.

Three years later at the request of the citizens of Leisnig, Saxony, Luther devised a plan for maintaining and conducting the religious, educational, and relief activities of the community. This plan calls for the establishment of a "Common Chest":

There shall be ordered for God's house and kept in place for all time, two casks or council chests in which bread, cheese, eggs, meat and other food and provisions shall be placed; and there shall also be a box or two wherein money may be put for the upkeep of the common chest.[470a]

In addition to voluntary contributions from various sources, there was a requirement that each inheritor, citizen, and peasant must contribute some money each year to the Chest. Servants and young manual laborers who did not own houses but had parish rights were to contribute a silver groat a year, their employers collecting this money.

From the Common Chest the salary of the clergyman and other officials of the church and of the schoolmaster were to be paid and the costs of relief were to be met. The fund was to be expended by ten supervisors or overseers, chosen in an open meeting of the parish. The provisions for the administration of relief were substantially the same as those put into effect a little later at Ypres, and advocated by Vives. Luther's scheme received considerable attention in Germany, and a number of other German cities followed the example of Leisnig.

A further indication of Luther's interest in relief is to be seen in a curious little book which he edited and published, first in 1528 and again in 1529. This was a book of vagabonds—*Liber Vagatorum* —issued some fifteen years earlier by an anonymous author. The original and Luther's edition went through a number of printings and had a wide circulation. It set the vogue for other books on this subject on the Continent and in England.

The *Liber Vagatorum* is divided into twenty chapters, "for there are XX ways, et ultra, whereby men are cheated and fooled." By implication, Luther in his preface makes a connection between the Reformation and the growing movement against beggars:

The right understanding and true meaning of the book, is after all, this, viz. that princes, lords, counsellors of state, and everybody should be prudent, and cautious in dealing with beggars, and learn that, whereas people will not give and help honest paupers and needy neighbors, as ordained by God, they give, by the persuasion of the devil, and contrary to God's judgment, ten times as much to vagabonds and desperate rogues —in like manner as we have hitherto done to monasteries, cloisters, churches, chapels, and mendicant friars, forsaking all the time the truly poor.

For this reason every town and village should know their own paupers, as written down in the Register, and assist them. But as to outlandish and strange beggars they ought not to be born with, unless they have proper letters and certificates; for all the great rogeries mentioned in this book are done by these. If each town would only keep an eye upon their paupers, such knaveries would soon be at an end. I have myself of late years been cheated and befooled by such tramps and liars more than I wish to confess. Therefore, whosoever hear these words let him be warned, and do good to his neighbor in all Christian charity, according to the teaching of the commandment. So help us God! Amen.[471a]

In Zurich, Switzerland, Zwingli developed a plan for relief somewhat like Luther's Common Chest, outlined in *Articles Touching Alms Giving* issued in January 1525. In France in 1536, Francis I ordered each parish to register its poor and provide for the impotent from contributed funds. Before this, Paris, Lyons, and Rouen had established systems of organized relief. Salter says that there does not seem to be any evidence that either the Ypres or the Vives plans influenced the citizens of Rouen. Apparently the developments in France were indigenous.

However much or little there was of communication between the towns and countries of Europe, attempts to organize relief on the Continent were quite general. There, as in England, the sixteenth century saw the growth of a movement to attack the long-entrenched practice of begging and an effort to systematize provision for relief. The administration was civil rather than clerical, the municipality or town being the over-all unit, with direct operations being usually delegated to the parish. The concept of overseers of the poor in function if not in title seems to have been universal. In Europe, as in England, the first financing was based on voluntary contributions, with Vives raising the question of the possibility of public funds and Martin Luther definitely including the concept of compulsory payment.

Thus, to quote Ashley in his *Introduction to English Economic History and Theory*:

The English legislation, beginning in 1536 and leading to "the poor law of Elizabeth," was but the English phase of a general European movement of reform. It was not called for by anything peculiar to England either in its economic development up to the middle of the sixteenth century, or in its ecclesiastical history. We need not suppose that the English legislation was a mere imitation of what was being done elsewhere; the same causes were everywhere at work, leading to the same general results. But it is clear that England, instead of preceding other nations, rather lagged behind, and that its action was probably stimulated by continental examples. English statesmen, at every step of their action in this matter, moved in an atmosphere of European discussion, of which they must have been aware.[403b]

V

THE LAW OF SETTLEMENT

It is certain, that the obligation on each parish to maintain its own poor, and, in consequence of that, a distinct interest, are the roots from which every evil relating to the poor hath sprung; and which must ever grow up, till they are eradicated. Every parish is in a state of expensive war with all the rest of the nation; regards the poor of all other places as aliens; and cares not what becomes of them if it can but banish them from its own society. No good therefore is ever to be expected, till parochial interest and settlements are destroyed; till the poor are taken out of the hands of the overseers, and put under the management of persons wiser, and more disinterested; and till they be set to work on a national, or at least a provincial fund, to arise from benefactions and the labor of the poor, as far as they will go; and what more is wanting to be leveled by an equal tax.

> WILLIAM HAY, *Remarks on the Laws*
> *Relating to the Poor with Proposals for*
> *Their Better Relief and Employment,* 1751.[457a]

AFTER 1601 when, with 43rd Elizabeth, Chapter 2, the Poor Law finally settled into shape, there was no important modification in the statutes upon this subject for more than fifty years. Then in 1662 came an amendment that has influenced the administration of relief down to the present time. It represented the most extreme and cruel form of localism that England had known previously or has known since. It was modified a little more than a century and a quarter later, but it still stands in history as the ultimate on the negative side of the Elizabethan system of assistance by neighbors to neighbors.

This law was the Law of Settlement. It formed part of a statute enacted in the fourteenth year of Charles II:

Whereas by reason of some defects in the law poor people are not restrained from going from one parish to another and therefore do endeavor to settle themselves in those parishes where there is the best stock, the largest commons or wastes to build cottages and the most woods for them to burn and destroy; and when they have consumed it then to another parish and at last become rogues and vagabonds to the great discouragement of parishes to provide stocks where it is liable to be devoured by strangers.

Be it therefore enacted by the authority aforesaid that it shall and may be lawful upon complaint made by the churchwardens or overseers of the poor of any parish to any justice of the peace within 40 days after any such person or persons coming to settle as aforesaid in any tenement under the yearly value of ten pounds for any two justices of the peace . . . to remove and convey such person or persons to such parish where he or they were last legally settled.[32]

The effect of this Statute was to empower the justices to return to his former residence any person, coming to occupy a property renting for less than ten pounds a year, who in the opinion of the overseers might at some future time become in need. It was not a matter of such a person's asking relief—merely the judgment of the overseers that he might on some later occasion be obliged to apply for assistance. For forty days a family or an individual moving into a parish at less than the rental indicated could not feel secure.

This Statute was a throwback to the days of serfdom and to the theory that the worker belonged where he was born. It represented both a culmination of the post-feudal effort to imprison the laborer in his parish and the most extreme development of a parochialism which recognized no human need that could possibly be charged to its neighbor.

A century before, in 1548, labor had been forbidden to combine in the interest of fixing wages and hours.[18] In 1563 the spirit of the first Statute of Laborers had been reaffirmed in the 5th Elizabeth, Chapter 4, requiring the unemployed poor man to work for whoever should require him, empowering the justices of the peace to fix wages with penalties for the employer paying in excess of the standard set, and requiring the worker to show a testimonial from his last employer before he could be at liberty to go elsewhere.[22] Now, in 1662, government went still further in repression, so that not only was travel prohibited to the poor man but the local authorities were empowered to send him back to the place from which he had come.

While this procedure was new to labor, it was an old expedient of the Poor Law. The Statutes of 1531 and 1536, and subsequent acts, had set up arrangements for returning able-bodied vagrants to their places of original residence and for providing transportation for the impotent and aged beggars. What the Act of 1662 did was to combine in one law the principle of forbidding movement to labor and the principle of conveying the poor.

The law was a logical consequence of the system of relief established under the 43rd Elizabeth. Since each parish was responsible for the maintenance of its own poor, each parish wanted to be sure that it was not supporting people who belonged elsewhere. The new Statute was the means whereby the local communities expected to protect themselves from each other. There is no evidence that people were, as implied in the preamble, going to one jurisdiction, using up its stock, and then going on to another.

"Amongst all the lamentations of the degeneracy, the vices, and the crimes of the poor with which the literature of the times abounded," writes George Coode, assistant secretary of the Poor Law Commissioners of 1834 and one of the great authorities upon the subject of settlement, "a laborious search has discovered no other reference to this class of disorders." [310a]

The Statute was an act of parochial caution. As the overseers looked across the boundaries of their parish to the parish next door they became uneasy. Might not their neighbors take advantage of them by persuading families, undesirable and costly in point of relief, to move across the line? They would therefore insure themselves against any such contingency by arranging to send back within forty days the person who they feared might become a charge upon them.

With this, the foundation of the Law of Settlement, there started the whole vicious succession of enactments and procedures about residence that have characterized local relief administration down to the present day, plaguing both officialdom and the poor. No sooner had the Act of 1662 been passed than abuses began to develop. Adam Smith thought the subject important enough to devote a section of his *Wealth of Nations* to a discussion of it.

Some frauds, it is said, were committed in consequence of this statute; parish officers sometimes bribing their own poor to go clandestinely to another parish, and by keeping themselves concealed for forty days to gain a settlement there, to the discharge of that to which they properly belonged. It was enacted, therefore, by the 1st of James II (1686) [33] that the forty days of undisturbed residence of any person necessary to gain a settlement, should be accounted only from the time of his delivering notice in writing, of the place of his abode and the number of his family, to one of the church wardens or overseers of the parish where he came to dwell.

But parish officers, it seems, were not always more honest with regard to their own, than they had been with regard to other parishes, and sometimes connived at such instructions, receiving the notice, and taking no proper steps in consequence of it. As every person in a parish, therefore, was supposed to have an interest to prevent as much as possible their being burdened by such intruders, it was further enacted by the 3rd of William III, (1691) [34] that the forty days residence should be accounted only from the publication of such notice in writing on Sunday in the church immediately after divine service.[498a]

The result of this amendment was to put the parish so on its guard that a person renting under ten pounds scarcely ever succeeded in gaining settlement in a new neighborhood. Other ways of acquiring residence through apprenticeship, employment, and taxation were devised, all of which only made the administration of relief the more complicated and none of which contributed very much to the mobility of the man in search of work.

"In order to restore in some measure that free circulation of labor," continues Adam Smith, "which those different statutes had almost entirely taken away, the invention of certificates was fallen upon." The certificate was a guarantee from the man's original place of settlement that if he should become a charge upon the parish to which he went, his former parish would pay the cost of his maintenance and of his removal to his former home. This, however, left the original parish with a contingent liability which it was loath to assume, and the result as far as the overseers were concerned was, as Adam Smith expressed it, "that certificates ought always to be required by the parish where any poor man comes to reside, and that they ought very seldom to be granted by that which he proposed to leave." [498b] In short, the effect of the Law of Settlement was to keep people where they were and to restrict greatly the opportunities for employment available to the man who was out of a job.

"It has made of the parish of the settlement a prison," to quote George Coode again, "and every other parish a hostile fortress." [310b]

While it is probable that in actual enforcement the Statute of 1662 with its amendments affected directly a comparatively small proportion of the six-sevenths of the population to whom it applied, its general influence was enormous. It was an ever present threat.

"There is scarce a poor man in England of forty years of age, I will venture to say," wrote Adam Smith, "who has not in some part of his life felt himself most cruelly oppressed by this ill contrived law of settlement." [498c]

Richard Burn, the author of the first history of the English Poor Law, describes in his book, published in 1764, how the overseers conducted their office under this law:

> To keep an extraordinary look-out, to prevent persons coming to inhabit without certificates, and to fly to the justices to remove them; and if a man brings a certificate, then to caution all the inhabitants not to let him a farm of ten pounds a year, and to take care to keep him out of all parish offices; to warn them, if they will hire servants, to hire them half yearly, or by the month, by the week, or by the day, rather than by any way that shall give them a settlement; or if they do hire them for a year, then to endeavor to pick a quarrel with them before the year's end, and to get rid of them. [413a]

An illustration of how settlement according to the Statute of 1662 could be used to the disadvantage of the most industrious workman was included by Sir Frederic Eden in his *State of the Poor*.

> A few years ago, in consequence of the increased population of a village in the West-riding of Yorkshire, a shoemaker, who resided in a distant part of the country, was induced to remove thither, with his family and stock, which consisted only of the implements of his trade, and an industrious pair of hands. An old inhabitant of the parish, of the same vocation, who had long enjoyed all the business which it afforded as exclusively as one of King James's patentees could have done, was alarmed at the intruder. With true monopolizing spirit, he represented to the parish officers, that the village could only maintain one of his trade; the probability of the newcomer's becoming chargeable was strongly urged; and his removal was, at length, determined on. The rector, however, who was a man of property, judiciously interfered; and by threatening to let a small tenement of ten pounds a year to the poor man, (whose only "security for the discharge of the parish" was his industry) silenced the clamor which had been raised against him. The short sequel of the story is, that the new comer firmly established himself, and notwithstanding a great competition in his trade, (for there are now not two only, but five shoemakers in the parish) earns a comfortable maintenance for himself and a large family. [432d]

It was not until 1795, after more than a century and a quarter of protest, that the Act of 1662 was finally amended so that the newcomer to a parish occupying a property of less than ten pounds a year could not be removed until he had actually applied for relief, but "every unmarried woman with child shall be deemed and taken to be a person actually chargeable" and therefore subject to removal if she paid a rent of less than ten pounds a year.[41] While, despite this exception, the law meant improvement for the independent laborer, it still worked great hardship upon the applicant for relief.

One of the best descriptions of the cruelty and futility of the settlement laws is to be found in an analysis of the Report of the Select Committee of the House of Commons appointed in 1837 to inquire into the administration of the Poor Law Amendment Act of 1834. The anonymous editor of the analysis gives rein to his faculty for ironical statement:

The statute of 1662 (13th & 14th Car. II.), the foundation of the Law of Settlements, which existed, with some modification, till the passing of the Poor Law Amendment Act, enounces the theory upon which the entire laboring population of England were, for more than a century and a half, doomed to be "hereditary bondsmen," "chained to the soil," "dispossessed of the power of acquiring property, or enjoying it openly and honestly."

The preamble to that statute says, "whereas by reason of some defects in the law, poor people are not restrained from going from one parish to another, and therefore do endeavor to settle themselves in those parishes where there is the best stock." Unquestionably. This is the effect of the great natural law of labor seeking exchange with capital; the labor went to the parishes "where there is the best stock"; where the funds for the maintenance of labor were most abundant.

In that period of profound legislation, when parliaments decreed that the superabundant produce of our own country should not be exchanged with the superabundant produce of another country, for fear the trade of our own country with countries which had nothing to exchange should be destroyed,—in that period in which it was thought the height of wisdom to declare that commerce should not be free, it was also declared that labor should not go to capital, lest the laborers should become "Rogues and Vagabonds," "to the great discouragement of parishes to provide stocks, when it is liable to be devoured by strangers."

The parishes therefore kept their stocks (capital) for those who were born and died within the lines of demarcation; and if the rogues and vagabonds ventured within the sacred precincts, they treated them with a taste of another species of stocks, which they could neither eat nor drink, —the

"Dungeon scarce three inches wide;
With roof so low, that under it
They never stand, but lie or sit;
And yet so foul, that whoso is in
Is to the middle leg in prison."

Hudibras, Part I, Canto 2.

To this ingenious machine for preventing the devouring of stocks by strangers were the laborers of England doomed, if they dared to venture out of their own parish, even when in their own parish they, the natives, had eaten up all the parish could give them. Other humane devices to prevent the desire for wandering, and to reconcile them to starvation at home, were derived from the good old times of branding and whipping. By degrees, however, these exertions to prevent the laborers wandering were in great part superseded by the merciful consideration of the old poor law functionaries, who employed a great portion of their time, and a larger portion of the public money, in carrying the laborers about from one end of the kingdom to the other, parcelling them out with the nicest adjustment amongst the fourteen thousand little divisions called parishes, and determining that whatever circumstances existed in any one of these fourteen thousand divisions to make the presence of the laborers desirable or otherwise, they should go, and they should stay where they had been born or apprenticed or last lived for a year.

The laborers were such tender plants that they could not be acclimated except in their native soil, or where they had taken a little root: and so a perpetual transplantation was going forward, which set the whole country alive with the movements of vagrant carts, and filled the coaches and the inns with burly overseers and fat constables, traveling from all points between the Thames and the Tweed, from Berkshire to Leicestershire, and from Sussex to Cornwall, with laborers and laborers wives, and astonished children. All this was managed to the great satisfaction of the vestry and the overseers, and the lawyers; under whose auspices it was generally arranged that the laborers, and the wives, and the children, or some of them, with many of their friends and fellow-laborers, should make a journey to the county sessions as witnesses, and after the most solemn inquiry, travel back again to the place whence they came and from whence they had been "illegally" removed.

We knew an instance in Berkshire of a man in good employ who had been allowed 2s a week upon a suspended order, being at last taken, with his wife and eight children, some hundred and fifty miles in the public stage to their place of settlement,—being brought back again at the expense of the parish to which they had been removed, with the intention that they should there obtain a settlement by renting a tenement—so renting the said tenement for a year, and then applying for relief—being again removed, to the infinite delight of overseers, constables, vestry-clerks, and stage coachmen, upon the plea that the tenement so rented was not worth 10 pounds a year, and that it was a collusive renting—and being finally brought back and settled upon the parish from which they had been first moved, after a solemn trial of two days, during which an array of surveyors was produced by the appellants and respondents, to prove the annual value of a cottage consisting of four rooms and a pig-stye. This process occupied about a year and a half, during which period the man's labor was entirely unsettled, and he and his wife and eight children were well-nigh starved.

This law of settlement was the great source of amusement amongst the parish functionaries throughout England for the last forty years. It was played at the direct cost to the country of several millions annually, and with an indirect cost in the loss of many more millions of profitable labor.[306a]

Since this report was published there have been many amendments of the Law of Settlement. The period necessary to acquire residence has been variously extended and shortened; and a multitude of rulings have been attempted to define the status of the child born where his parents have no residence, of the wife whose settlement before marriage was in a place other than the residence of her husband, of the child of the unmarried mother who had left her home before giving birth to her baby. No solution has ever been found to cover all the contingencies that birth, marriage, death, illegitimacy, and employment can bring to complicate the operation of the law that a man belongs where he was born—with variations. Never has it been possible to achieve any permanent arrangement by agreement between local jurisdictions. In this respect, they are, as William Hay pointed out in 1731, like warring principalities.

The problem of settlement has only been solved as it has been eliminated by an enlargement of the area of taxation and financial responsibility for relief. When, as we shall see later, the unit of relief administration in England was extended in a succession of steps from the parish to the county, and later for particular categories of need to the whole country, then at last the issue of settlement ceased within the expanded jurisdictions to plague the recipients and administrators of relief. The problem diminished as the size of the area settlement made it possible for a man to move about wherever he desired without losing residence.

Nevertheless, despite the progress which has thus been made, there are many communities and there are categories of assistance in respect of which the person compelled to seek relief continues to be at the mercy of local intolerance and nearsighted parsimony. In the United States, as of September 1939, the length of time needed to acquire settlement varied according to the state from six months to five years. In addition, in most states each county, and in some states each township, represented a special jurisdiction where if the individual applying for general assistance was not a resident he would not receive relief.[161] Thousands of dollars are still spent in removing people from one place to another; and, while the hardships are not what they were after the passage of the Act of 1662, the laws of settlement in Great Britain and in the United States remain with us as a token that the tradition of the feudal system has not yet passed and that the parochialism confirmed by the 43rd Elizabeth continues to hinder a fair and wise administration of assistance to those in need.

VI

THE EMPLOYMENT OF THE
UNEMPLOYED

Concerning the relief and employment of the poor: This is a calm
subject and thwarts no common or private interest amongst us, except that of the common enemy of mankind, the Devil.

SIR JOSIAH CHILD,
A New Discourse of Trade, 1670.[424a]

A T about the same time that Parliament was enacting the negative
and punitive Law of Settlement, there started a movement that
in its attitude toward poverty was positive and optimistic. This was
the proposal to relieve the destitute and at the same time stimulate
national prosperity by employing the unemployed in manufacture.

The plan was in keeping with Britain's growing urge toward in-
dustrialism. It came during the second half of the seventeenth century when England was struggling with the Dutch for supremacy
in commerce. The English writers of the period are full of ad-
miration for their rivals. Dutch thrift, Dutch industry, and Dutch
skill in turning raw materials into finished articles of trade are constantly cited. The absence of beggars and the admirable organization and operation of almshouses are held up as examples of how
poverty may be solved. The Dutch are described as having made
their populousness a source of prosperity to the nation. England
should do the same.

The proponents of this idea wanted first of all to stop exporting
raw materials, wool in particular, and instead to turn them into
finished goods for the market by the use of British workmen. They
saw England raising more wool and mining more iron and correspondingly developing more employment. They had plans also for
the stimulation of manufacture as related to fisheries and shipping.

Throughout the latter part of the seventeenth century scores of
books and pamphlets were written upon this subject. Their authors
believed that the personnel for the expansion of industry and commerce could be supplied from among the poor. The problem of re-

lief would be solved because everybody would be working or would be in training for future employment. Centers of manufacture in the form of workhouses were to be established in the parishes or in combinations of parishes throughout the country.

The optimism of these writers is illustrated by a typical title page:

England's Weal & Prosperity Proposed: or, Reasons for Erecting Publick Workhouses in Every County, for the Speedy Promoting of Industry and the Woollen Manufactury, Shoewing How the Wealth of the Nation May Be Encreased, Many Hundred Thousand Pounds per Annum. And Also That Many Thousand Persons May Be So Reformed, to Their Own and the Whol Kingdoms Present and Future Wealth and Glory, That There May No More be a Beggar Bred up in the Nation. Humbly offered to the Consideration of the Great Wisdom of the Nation, and presented to the Honourable House of Commons by R. [Richard Haines.] 1681.[450a]

The theory underlying this and many other similar proposals was that at the workhouses materials, supervision, and training would be provided. Here the poor could learn to support themselves. The wealth of the nation would increase; and, even if the program should fall short of all that was promised for it, the poor—particularly the children of the poor—would have acquired skill and habits of industry so that the country would profit through the increase in the number of efficient workers.

These ideas were not the creation of dilettantes in business and government. They were advanced by the most responsible men in England. Sir Matthew Hale, the Lord Chief Justice, was one of them. His *Discourse Touching Provision for the Poor* was published in 1683, after his death, but was written considerably earlier. While I shall not reproduce quite so much of it as did Dr. Burn in his *History of the Poor Laws,* 1764, I shall quote from it for the same reason that he did—"because almost all the subsequent schemes that have been offered, look up to this as their great pattern and as nothing that the author hath delivered is tedious to the reader." [413b]

Sir Matthew bases his premise upon the observation that in other nations

the more populous the state or country is, the richer and the more wealthy it is. But with us in England, for want of a due regulation of things, the more populous we are, the poorer we are; so *that* wherein the strength and wealth of a kingdom consists, renders us the weaker and the poorer.

Sir Matthew's proposal is contained in the first two of what he calls his remedies. The remaining items are merely elaborations of these initial propositions.

1. That the justices of the peace, at the quarter sessions, do set out and distribute the parishes in their several counties into several divisions; in each of which there may be a workhouse.

2. That the said justices do assess three, four, or five yearly payments, . . . for the raising a stock, to set the poor on work, and to build or procure a convenient workhouse for employing the poor (if need be) in it, and for lodging materials, and for instructing children in the trade or work.

Starting with what to a modern reader seems like none too impressive a beginning, the Chief Justice proceeds to build an economy, the anticipated growth of which reminds one, in part at least, of the dreamed increase of the 100 drachmae that the fifth brother of the barber in the Arabian Nights invested in merchandise.

By this means, the wealth of the nation will be increased, manufactures advanced, and every body put into a capacity of eating his own bread. . . .

The woolen manufactures of cloth, the staple commodity of this kingdom, would be more; and . . . would be by this means diffused over the whole kingdom; and those places, which have little of woolen manufacture . . . would soon fall into it. So likewise, knitting of stockings, caps, waistcoats, and the like. Also our linen manufactures, as linen cloth, laces of all sorts, nets, sails, and the like, would become native, and supply the want of the kingdom, and prevent the necessity of importation of linen cloth from Holland and France, of laces from Flanders. . . . And it is very considerable, the numbers of poor that would be by this means employed. . . . And if any shall say, we want the materials, . . . the answer is at hand: If once the manufacture were begun . . . all men would quickly sow hemp and flax. . . . Two acres of hemp and flax in every parish would employ multitudes. . . .

We may reasonably suppose, that in one seven years, by the blessing of God, the very offspring that will be able and fit to work, of poor families, will be more than double to what they are now; which will continually increase in a kind of geometrical progression, whereby there will be enough for double the employment that is now for them.[451a]

The program of the Lord Chief Justice of England was advocated also by the chairman of the East India Company, Sir Josiah Child. He urged the employment of girls and boys on the theory that whether it turns to present profit or not is not much material, the great business of the nation being first but to keep the poor from begging and starving, and enuring such as are able to labor and discipline, that they may hereafter be useful members to the kingdom.[424b]

This advocacy of child labor played an important part in nearly all the plans to achieve greater prosperity and to eliminate poverty. Illustrative of these was the proposal of Andrew Yarranton, a successful business man who reported upon his observations on the Continent in a little book, *England's Improvement by Sea and Land*, which he published in 1677.

In all these parts [he wrote, referring to a visit to Germany] there is no beggar, nor no occasion to beg; and in all towns there are schools for little girls, from six years old and upwards, to teach them to spin, and so to bring their tender fingers by degrees to spin very fine, which being young are thereby easily fitted for that use. Whereas people overgrown in age cannot so well feel the thread. Their wheels go all by the foot, made to go with much ease, whereby the action or motion is very easy and delightful. And in all towns there are schools according to the bigness, or multitude of the poor children.

I will here show you the way, method, rule, and order how they are governed. First, there is a large room, and in the middle thereof a little box like a pulpit. Secondly, there are benches built around the room as they are in our playhouses; upon the benches sit about two hundred children spinning, and in the box in the middle of the room sits the grand mistress with a long white wand in her hand. If she observes any of them idle, she reaches them a tap; but if that will not do, she rings a bell which by a little cord is fixed to a box, and out comes a woman; she then points to the offender, and she is taken away into another room and chastised. And all this is done without one word speaking. And I believe this way of ordering the young women in Germany is one great cause that the German women have so little of the twit twat. And I am sure it would be well were it so in England. . . .

Is it not a pity and shame that the young children and maids here in England should be idle within doors, begging abroad, tearing hedges, or robbing orchards, and worse, when these, and these alone, are the people that may, and must if ever, set up this trade of making fine linen here? And after a young maid hath been three years in the spinning school, that is taken in at six and then continues until nine years, she will get eight pence the day. And in these parts I speak of, a man that has most children lives best; whereas here he that has most is poorest. There the children enrich the father, but here beggar him.[508a]

These theories centering around the employment of the unemployed were not limited to discussion; they were attempted in practice. Thomas Firmin, merchant, manufacturer, philanthropist, and one of the leaders in the Unitarian movement in England, initiated and carried through an enterprise for providing work for the poor. In 1678 he published a letter entitled *Proposals for the Imploying of the Poor, Especially in and about London*, describing an enterprise in spinning he had started two years before and which continued until his death in 1697. He erected a building where people could

go and receive flax; and, when they had spun it, to carry it to the same place, and receive their money for it; . . . some of them being able to earn three-pence, and some four-pence a day, working only at such times as they could spare from their other necessary occasions; who being to work in their own houses, and when they could with most convenience attend it, many of them became so much pleased with it, that so much money given them for doing nothing would not have done them half so much good as that which they got by their own labor in this employment. . . .

Mr. Firmin also advocated the setting up of "a school in the nature of a work-house, to teach poor children to work":

I myself have at this time some children working to me, not above seven or eight years old, who are able to earn two-pence a day, and some, that are but a little older, two shillings a week; and I doubt not to bring any child about that age to do the like: and still as they grow up and become proficients, even in this poor trade of spinning, they will be able to get more and spin better than older people. . . .

Thomas Firmin went far beyond his contemporaries and his successors of later years by advocating adequacy in relief. He insisted that relief through work should be in addition to relief through pensions.

I acquainted the parish of St. Botolphs, Aldersgate, that if they had any poor people who wanted employment, and would work, I would supply them therewith, upon these conditions, viz., that they should not take away their pensions from any I employed, nor give pensions to any but such as would, being able, follow this or some other employment towards their own maintenance; by means of which, and the pension received from the parish, they might be provided for without begging: for I have long observed, that a very great number of those persons that are found begging in the streets, are such as do receive some pension from the parish in which they live, but that being too small to maintain them without work, they make up the rest by begging. . . .[437a]

Despite the enthusiasm of the promoter of the experiment in Aldersgate, the plan, by his own statement as contained in a second account published in 1681—*Some Proposals for the Imployment of the Poor*—was neither profitable nor self-sustaining. It certainly in no wise approached the dreams of those who saw the workhouse as a means of prosperity for England.

This I am sure is the worst that can be said of it, that it hath not yet been brought to bear its own charges. . . . However, this doth greatly satisfy me, that every penny that hath been lost by it, either by myself, or those friends who have helped to bear it, has been many times gained to the Poor and to the Public. . . .[438a]

Thomas Firmin's experiment was his own philanthropic undertaking. Somewhat the same kind of project was conducted under public auspices at Bristol, following a special act of Parliament creating a "corporation to continue forever within the said city of Bristol." [35] The Act established the corporation as of May 12, 1696, but it was two years later that the plan actually got under way. John Cary, its leading proponent, describes the enterprise as it stood two years after its inception. The corporation was responsible for both the relief and the employment of the poor.

Perhaps the best way of indicating the spirit in which the undertaking was carried on is to begin with Cary's description of how they administered relief:

To such as were sick, we gave warrants to our physician to visit them; such as wanted the assistance of our surgeons, were directed to them, and all were relieved till they were able to work; by which means the Poor, having been well attended, were set at work again, who by neglect might, with their families, have been chargeable to the corporation. For some we provided clothes, for others work; where we found people careful, but wanted a stock to employ themselves and their children, we either lent or gave it; where they wanted houses, we either paid the rent, or became security for it; where we found them oppressed, we stood by them; where differences arose, we endeavored to compose them; . . . and care was taken that none went away unheard.

Two workhouses were used to provide employment, one for girls and the other "for receiving in the remainder of the poor, (viz.) ancient people, boys, and young children."

[At the first workhouse] we received in 100 girls, and set them to work at spinning of worsted yarn; all which we first caused to be stripped by the mistress, washed, and newly clothed from head to foot; which, together with wholesome diet at set hours, and good beds to lie on, so encouraged the children that they willingly betook themselves to their work.

We likewise provided for them apparel for Sundays; they went to Church every Lord's day, were taught their catechisms at home, and had prayers twice every day: we appointed them set hours for working, eating, and playing; and gave them leave to walk on the hills, with their tutoresses, when their work was over, and the weather fair; by which means we won them into civility, and a love to their labor. But we had a great deal of trouble with their parents, and those who formerly kept them who, having lost the sweetness of their pay, did all they could to set both their children and others against us; but this was soon over. . . .

The committee then extended its activities in offering employment to include boys and "our ancient people."

Then we called in all the children that were on our Poor's books, and put them under nurses; those who can speak and go, are carried down into the school to learn their A, B, C, etc. As they grow up, we shall put them into the working-rooms.

Two years after the start of the enterprise, Cary is enthusiastic about it.

The success hath answered our expectations; we are freed from beggars, our old people are comfortably provided for; our boys and girls are educated to sobriety, and are brought up to delight in labor; our young children are well looked after, and not spoiled by the neglect of ill nurses; and the face of our city is so changed already that we have great reason to hope these young plants will produce a virtuous and laborious generation, with whom immorality and profaneness may find little encouragement; nor does our hope appear to be groundless, for among three hundred persons now under our charge within doors, there is neither cursing nor swearing, nor profane language to be heard. . . .[415a]

John Cary's description of the workhouses at Bristol and his comments are typical of the confusion of purpose and attitude that has always characterized the concept of the employment of the poor. He wants the enterprise to be economic, but he justifies it partly on moral grounds. He advocates it as an effort toward making the poor self-supporting, but he hopes for charitable contributions.

It is not surprising to find a report of failure from an observer who writes about the undertaking a generation later, October 2, 1731:

> From their first erection in the year 1696, to the year 1714, they continued to put the Poor to work . . . but not only without any benefit from their labor, but to the great loss of the corporation. For as soon as they came to do anything tolerably well, that they might have been assisting to the younger and less practised, they went off to sea, or were apprenticed in the city; by which means the public were so far benefited, though the corporation bore the loss of the charge of teaching them, and all of the tools with which they were to work, and of the materials for it. For they made nothing perfect or merchantable from their work, but only spoiled the materials. So that instead of lessening the charge of maintaining the Poor, they increased it; insomuch that, in the beginning of the year 1714, they had not only spent every year's income, but had sunk all their benefactions, and borrowed several thousand pounds of the city.[402a]

Though the upshot of the enterprise was failure, it created a wide favorable opinion at the time of its inception; and the example of Bristol in establishing a city workhouse was followed by a number of other communities. The idea of employing the poor at a profit continued to be brought forward at intervals through many years, but the general, enthusiastic discussion of the subject may be said to have been brought to a period by a pamphlet published anonymously in 1704 by Daniel Defoe. This pamphlet, *Giving Alms No Charity, and Employing the Poor a Grievance to the Nation*, was issued to combat a bill in Parliament permitting the overseers of the poor to embark upon any "trade or mystery" in the interest of employing their unemployed. The bill failed of passage, to which result Defoe's marshaling of the economic arguments against the plan may have contributed.

> Suppose now a work-house for employment of poor children, sets them to spinning of worsted. For every skein of worsted those poor children spin, there must be a skein the less spun by some poor family or person that spun it before. Suppose the manufacture of making bays to be erected in Bishopsgate-Street—unless the makers of these bays can at the same time find out a trade or consumption for more bays than were made before, for every piece of bays so made in London there must be a piece the less made at Colchester. . . .

> 'Tis only the transposing the manufacture from Colchester to London, and taking the bread out of the mouths of the poor of Essex to put it into the mouths of the poor of Middlesex.

If these worthy gentlemen, who show themselves so commendably forward to relieve and employ the poor, will find out some new trade, some new market, where the goods they shall make shall be sold, where none of the same goods were sold before; if they will send them to any place where they shall not interfere with the rest of that manufacture, or with some other made in England, then indeed they will do something worthy of themselves, and may employ the poor to the same glorious advantage as Queen Elizabeth did, to whom this nation, as a trading country, owes its peculiar greatness.

If these gentlemen could establish a trade to Muscovy for English serges, obtain an order from the Czar, that all his subjects should wear stockings who wore none before, every poor child's labor in spinning and knitting those stockings, and all the wool in them would be clear gain to the nation, and the general stock would be improved by it, because all the growth of our country, and all the labor of a person who was idle before, is so much clear gain to the general stock.

If they will employ the poor in some manufacture which was not made in England before, or not bought with some manufacture made here before, then they offer at something extraordinary.

But to set poor people at work, on the same thing which other poor people were employed on before, and at the same time not increase the consumption, is giving to one what you take away from another; enriching one poor man to starve another, putting a vagabond into an honest man's employment, and putting his diligence on the tenters to find out some other work to maintain his family.[431a]

Arguments such as these presented by Defoe, along with the test of actual experience, more than counterbalanced the enthusiasm of the men who had dreamed of England's prosperity arising from the employment of her poor. Occasional experiments were tried later in the eighteenth century, but the program never realized the hopes of its advocates.

The projects did not succeed for the reason that no similar projects have ever succeeded. Their promoters embarked upon competitive manufacture not because of a forecast demand for goods by consumers but because of the existence of unemployed people. It was the need of those who required relief that gave rise to the proposals and enterprises. But the skills involved in manufacture do not necessarily coincide with unemployment and need. Even granted a demand for the goods that might have been produced, the selection of employees on the basis of their being out of work, rather than by virtue of their adaptability for the trade or craft in question, meant failure before ever the undertakings began. We see the Bristol workhouse using even the impotent aged on the ground that every little that such workers could do would count; but if a man cannot earn his keep and a little more, there can be no profit in a business.

Even child labor, under these philanthropic auspices, could not be made to pay. Later, England—at terrible cost to the health and well-being of its people—founded much of its manufacture upon the work of children. Setting aside the assumption that the philanthropists were not willing to utilize the methods that the industrialists later adopted, there was this additional reason why business could succeed where they failed: The manufacturer could select his employees in the light of their aptitudes, whereas the master of the workhouse was obliged to use whatever children came to him by reason of need.

The impossibility of making aptitude the basis of employment and the necessity of operating irrespective of the demand for the product—the greatest need coming in bad times when the market for goods was lowest—defeated the hopes of those who believed that England could rise to prosperity through the productivity of her unemployed, as similar hopes have been defeated ever since.

VII

THE WORKHOUSE

With some who have written on this subject of the poor, the diminution of expense to the maintainers, rather than the production of benefit to the maintained, seems intrinsically if not professedly the grand desideratum.

> John Scott, *Observations on the Present State of the Parochial and Vagrant Poor*, 1773.[492a]

In practice, the office of an overseer of the poor seems to be understood to be this . . . to maintain their poor as cheap as possibly they can at all events; not to lay out two pence in prospect of any future good, but only to serve the present necessity.

> Richard Burn, *The History of the Poor Laws*, 1764.[413c]

THE unsuccessful movement to employ the unemployed in manufacture that had dominated the thought of the last half of the seventeenth and the beginning of the eighteenth centuries yielded in 1722 to another program representing a different philosophy. In that year a law was passed authorizing the overseers and the churchwardens to establish workhouses, to contract with private individuals for the employment and maintenance of the poor in these houses, and to refuse relief to any person not willing to enter the house.

The use of the institution, of course, was not new. The hospital, the almshouse, the house of correction had long been familiar; and in the effort to employ the poor, residential schools had been developed for children, as at Bristol, with provision in the house also for the aged.

It was not the institution, then, that represented an innovation, but the manner of its use. The plan that, beginning in 1722, was put widely into effect expressed a change in attitude toward the poor. Firmin and Cary and their fellows had been optimistic. They had believed that given opportunity the unemployed could be a source of strength to the nation. Their successors were cynical, pessimistic, and punitive.

Contrast the point of view of Thomas Firmin with that of Daniel Defoe, John Locke, or Bernard Mandeville.

Firmin: Had you seen, as I have done many a time, with what joy and satisfaction, many poor people have brought home their work, and received their money for it, you would think no charity in the world like unto it. Do not imagine that all the poor people in England, are like unto those vagrants you find up and down in the streets: No, there are many thousands whose necessities are very great, and yet they do what they can by their honest labor to help themselves; and many times they would do more than they do, but for want of employment.[437c]

Defoe: Tis the men that won't work, not the men that can get no work, which makes the numbers of our poor.[431b]

Locke: The growth of the poor must therefore have some other cause [i.e., than "scarcity of provisions" or "want of employment"] and it can be nothing else but the relaxation of discipline and corruption of manners.[468a]

Mandeville: It is impossible that a Society can long subsist, and suffer many of its members to live in idleness, and enjoy all the ease and pleasure they can invent, without having at the same time great multitudes of people that to make good this defect will condescend to be quite the reverse, and by use and patience inure their bodies to work for others and themselves besides.

The plenty and cheapness of provisions depends in a great measure on the price and value that is set upon this labor, and consequently the welfare of all societies, even before they are tainted with foreign luxury, requires that it should be performed by such of their members as in the first place are sturdy and robust and never used to ease or idleness, and in the second soon contented as to the necessaries of life; such as are glad to take up with the coarsest manufacture in every thing they wear, and in their diet have no other aim than to feed their bodies when their stomachs prompt them to eat, and with little regard to taste or relish, refuse no wholesome nourishment that can be swallowed when men are hungry, or ask anything for their thirst but to quench it. . . .

If such a people there must be, as no great nation can be happy without vast numbers of them, would not a wise legislature cultivate the breed of them with all imaginable care, and provide against their scarcity as he would prevent the scarcity of provision itself? No man would be poor and fatigue himself for a livelihood if he would help it: the absolute necessity all stand in for victuals and drink, and in cold climates for clothes and lodging, makes them submit to anything that can be bore with. If nobody did want nobody would work; but the greatest hardships are looked upon as solid pleasures, when they keep a man from starving.

Going to school in comparison to working is idleness, and the longer boys continue in this easy sort of life, the more unfit they'll be when grown up for down right labor, both as to strength and inclination. Men who are to remain and end their days in a laborious, tiresome and painful station of life, the sooner they are put upon it at first, the more patiently they'll submit to it for ever after.[474a]

The theory of Mandeville that the very nature of society demands a poor condemned to drudgery and the belief of Defoe and Locke that poverty is due to defect in character provide the basis for a different administration of relief from that implied in the schemes of Sir Matthew Hale, Thomas Firmin, and John Cary. This administration took its cue from the Law of 1722—the 9th George I, Chapter 7—which for two generations set the tone of public assistance in England.

For the greater ease of parishes in the relief of the poor . . . it shall be lawful for the churchwardens and overseers of the poor . . . to purchase or hire any house or houses in the same parish, township or place, and to contract with any person or persons for the lodging, keeping, maintaining, and employing any or all such poor in their respective parishes, townships or places, as shall desire to receive relief or collection from the same parish . . . and in case any poor person or persons . . . shall refuse to be lodged, kept, or maintained in such house or houses, such poor person or persons so refusing shall be put out of the book or books where the names of the persons who ought to receive collection in the said parish, town, township, or place, are to be registered, and shall not be entitled to ask or receive collection or relief from the churchwardens and overseers of the poor of the same parish, town or township.[37]

This Act brought an almost instant response. Within ten years of its passage there were in London and in the country outside London more than one hundred workhouses, nearly all of which had been established after the enactment of the Law.

It may be interesting in this connection to turn to a little book entitled *An Account of Several Workhouses for Employing and Maintaining the Poor*. This book was issued anonymously, first in 1725 and later, in a second and enlarged edition, in 1732. It contains, to quote Sir Frederic Eden, "much curious information respecting sixty workhouses in the country and about fifty in the metropolis."

The descriptions of these institutions were sent to the editor of the book by correspondents in the parishes of London and various other parts of England. Many of these accounts include statements about the commencement of the workhouse, the number of inmates, ranging from half a dozen adults and children to well over three hundred persons, the rules under which the institution was operated, and the dietary.

The most comprehensive account is that of the Workhouse of St. Andrew's, Holborn, Shoe-Lane, and in view of the fact that from now on there will be much discussion of workhouses I shall quote at length from this description, beginning with the statistical report of the inmates and the work assigned to them:

There are now 62 in the family, besides the master and matron, every one of which have such business assigned to them by the master, as they are most capable of, whose present allotments are as follows, viz:

7 old men and women (of which two are upwards of fourscore, and one an idiot) pick oakum

4 women and boys spin noyl, a yarn afterwards described

9 knit noyl yarn into caps for seamen

2 make the woolen clothes

2 make linen clothes

2 cooks constantly attend the kitchen

4 get up the linen and wash for the house

2 make beds, clean, and wash the house

2 mend clothes, linen and woolen

3 nurse those that are in the infirmary

1 school-mistress

21 children at school, in rotation as they can be spared from their work, besides which, three parish children are allowed to dine there three times, or oftener in the week

1 child nursed

2 lunatics

62 in all.

By this allotment the reader will take notice, that above ½ the family are wholly employed in nursing, and other necessary attendance on the house, that not above ⅓ are employed in what may be said to increase the revenue of the house, and that even those employments are no more than what is useful for their health.

They that pick oakum, are continually refreshed with the balsamic odour of it.

The following is a week's menu for the 62 persons:

	Breakfast	Dinner	Supper
Saturday	Milk pottage or water-gruel	Suet puddings baked & beer	Bread and cheese or bread and butter with beer
Sunday	Bread & beer	Beef broth, & beer	Beef broth & beer
Monday	Milk pottage or water-gruel	Rice milk and beer in summer, pease pottage of Sunday's broth in winter	Bread & cheese or bread and butter
Tuesday	Ditto	Broth beef and beer	Beef broth and beer
Wednesday	Ditto	Rice-milk and beer	as Monday
Thursday	Ditto	Broth beef bread and beer, as Sunday	as Tuesday
Friday	Ditto	Frumetty & beer at 3 o'clock	Bread & cheese or bread & butter with beer

The actual quantities of food consumed by the 62 persons, of whom 21 were children, is reported for the week of September 19 to 25, 1730:

33 1/2 peck loaves of bread	12 pounds of butter
22 pounds of flour	9 pounds of salt
11 quarts of oatmeal	6½ pounds of rice
60 quarts of milk	12 pounds of sugar
116 pounds of meat	89 gallons of beer [402b]

To complete the picture of the workhouse in Shoe-Lane, the correspondent quotes the nineteen *Orders to be Observed by Every Person Belonging to the Workhouse of St. Andrew's Holborn, Shoe-Lane*. These orders prescribe the discipline, the hours of rising and retiring, of work and of meals, the housekeeping, and the requirements in attendance at prayers and at church. The penalties included the stocks, the dungeon, denial of meals, refusal of permission to leave the house, and the following attempt "to make the punishment fit the crime."

That every person endeavor to preserve a good unity, and look upon themselves as one family; and to prevent any dispute which may create differences amongst themselves, by forging and telling lies, such persons so offending, (on good proof) shall be set on a stool, in the most public place in the diningroom, whilst at dinner, and a paper fixed on his or her breast, with these words wrote, infamous liar, and likewise to lose that meal.[402c]

The Law of 1722, it should be remembered, gave the overseers the right to refuse relief unless the person or the family applying for assistance was willing to enter the workhouse. It meant that father, mother, and children must leave their own home and live in the institution. The people thus maintained had not broken the law; they were merely destitute. But in order to receive relief, they were obliged to submit to the penal and disciplinary regimen indicated by the "orders to be observed." Harsh though the treatment was, it was only one aspect of the servitude in which the working class was kept until well into the nineteenth century.

The correspondent from St. Andrew's is optimistic about the success of the enterprise, the sponsors of which "have the pleasure of seeing it so prosperous under their management, as to hope in time to make a considerable reduction of the poor's tax." [402d]

The reports from other workhouses were equally enthusiastic. They cite the economies that had come about because people, quite understandably, would undergo almost any hardship rather than enter the institution. The following excerpts from the accounts of three workhouses may serve to illustrate the point:

Chelmsford, Essex.

I may aver that the parish has saved, by having a workhouse, between 1000 or 1100 pounds. For the people of the parish have been sorely afflicted with the smallpox, and fevers, and agues; and because they would not come into the house, they have made shift with a shilling, when four before would not content them.

Rumford, Essex.

The advantage of the workhouse to the parish does not arise from what the poor people can do towards their subsistence, but from the apprehensions the poor have of it. These prompt them to exert, and do their utmost to keep themselves off the parish, and render them exceedingly adverse to submit to come into the house, till extreme necessity compels them. Pride, though it does ill become poor folks, won't suffer some to wear the badge; others cannot brook confinement; and a third sort deem the workhouse to be a mere state of slavery, and so numbers are kept out.

Maidstone, Kent.

The advantage of a workhouse does not only consist in this, that the poor are maintained at less than half the expense which their weekly pay amounted to, but that very great numbers of lazy people, rather than submit to the confinement and labor of the workhouse, are content to throw off the mask, and maintain themselves by their own industry. And this was so remarkable here at Maidstone, that when our workhouse was finished, and public notice given, that all who came to demand their weekly pay, should immediately be sent thither, little more than half the poor upon the list came to the overseers to receive their allowance.[402e]

The advocates of the workhouse argued savings in three ways: First, that institutional care was less expensive than maintenance by relief in the family's own home, a conclusion that subsequent experience did not bear out; second, that rather than enter the workhouse people did without relief, "for," to quote again from the account of Maidstone, "we have many here who would choose to starve, rather than be maintained in plenty and cleanliness in the Bridewell, or House of Correction, as they call it"; third, that when given the choice of the workhouse or a much smaller allowance than previously received, the family would choose a decreased outdoor relief as against life in the institution.

Sir Frederic Eden in his *State of the Poor* studies the cost in taxes in sixteen of the parishes which reported initial savings, including St. Andrew's, Holborn; Bristol; and Maidstone. He shows in each case the rate before the workhouse was started, the reduction at the time the workhouse opened, the net expenses for the poor in 1776, and the assessments in 1783, 1784, and 1785. In all except one parish, costs had mounted far above the rise in the cost of living which began in the third quarter of the eighteenth century. In St. Andrew's, for example, the taxes had doubled, and in Maidstone they had trebled.

It will appear [Sir Frederic comments] that the charge of maintaining their poor has advanced very rapidly, notwithstanding the aid of workhouses, and perhaps as rapidly as in those parishes which have continued to relieve the poor by occasional pensions at their own habitations.

[He concludes that] from comparing the present state of those parishes which erected workhouses, in consequence of this act, with their condition seventy years ago, it would seem that the expectations entertained by the nation, that great and permanent benefits would be the result of these establishments, have not been realized.[432h]

The system condemned itself by reason of what it did to those who suffered under it. One of its most effective critics was that remarkable person, Jonas Hanway—merchant, traveler, dandy, philanthropist, crusader against the drinking of tea, the first man to carry an umbrella in England, and the wager of the first great campaign against infant mortality in Great Britain. Because of his activity, Parliament passed in 1761 an act providing for the registration of infants in the workhouses in and about London,[38] and then in 1767 a statute compelling their removal from the workhouse and their placement in the neighboring country until they should reach six years of age.[39]

Hanway spent years in visiting workhouses, in studying the care they offered children and their infant death rate, and in urging the facts he secured upon the public and upon Parliament. Along with other inquiries he examined the registers of fourteen of the largest parishes for 1750 to 1755 inclusive. Of 2,339 children born or received by these workhouses during the six years, 1,074 were discharged to their mothers after a stay seldom exceeding a few days or weeks. Of the remainder, only 168 were living in 1755. In one workhouse with fifty-three children none had been discharged and not one remained alive. He studied the registers of a number of workhouses as of 1764 and 1765, finding death rates as high as 82 per cent of children under a year. In a number of instances he reproduces pages from the register with the names of the children. A case in point is St. George's, Middlesex, for the year 1765. Here, of nineteen babies of from two months to three years nine months, only three survived.[455a]

These facts, with like figures, were published by Jonas Hanway in 1766 under the title *An Earnest Appeal for Mercy to the Children of the Poor*. What he said about the fate of the children who died at St. George's could be applied to the situation in many of the other workhouses which he visited:

It is true that man hath but a short time to live, and is cut down like a flower; but these poor infants were mowed like grass, for they had not so many days of life in the workhouse as the ordinary limitation of the years of man. . . .

These children were put into the hands of indigent, filthy, or decrepit women, three or four to one woman, and sometimes sleeping with them. The allowance of these women being scanty, they are tempted to take part of the bread and milk intended for the poor infants. The child cries for food, and the nurse beats it because it cries. Thus with blows, starving and putrid air, with the additions of lice, itch, and filthiness, he soon receives his quietus.[455b]

Hanway's indictment of the workhouse was confirmed in 1767 by a committee of the House of Commons appointed "to inquire into the state of the parish poor infants under the age of fourteen years within the bills of mortality." That committee found "that taking the children born in workhouses, or parish houses, or received of and under twelve months old, in the year 1763, and following the same into 1764 and 1765, only seven in a hundred appear to have survived this short period."[302]

The whole situation is epitomized by John Scott, in *Observations on the Present State of the Parochial and Vagrant Poor*, 1773.

One thing is too publicly known to admit of denial, that those workhouses are scenes of filthiness and confusion; that old and young, sick and healthy, are promiscuously crowded into ill-contrived apartments, not of sufficient capacity to contain with convenience half the number of miserable beings condemned to such deplorable inhabitation, and that speedy death is almost ever to the aged and infirm, and often to the youthful and robust, the consequence of a removal from more salubrious air to such mansions of putridity.[492b]

Bad as was the management that developed under the effort to solve the problem of relief and taxation by the use of the workhouse, it was rendered even worse by the provision in the Law of 1722, which permitted the parishes to contract with individuals for the care of the poor. Bids would be asked from men who would undertake to provide for those in need. There were various methods of doing this. There might be a per capita contract in which the operator of the workhouse would maintain the inmates at so much a head, or a man might undertake to manage the workhouse for a given lump sum; and there were others who actually contracted, in return for a flat amount, to provide in or out of the institution for all of the poor of the parish.

The result was inevitable. The contractor wanted to make money, and the parish wanted to spend as little as possible. If a per capita basis was agreed upon, it would be the lowest possible sum. Either from the work of the inmates or by skimping their food and other necessities, or both, the contractor would get the best profit he could. Where lump payments were the practice, he might, by making the house as terrible as he knew how, discourage people from entering it; or he might offer them a small allowance on condition that they would stay out of the institution.

Richard Burn epitomizes the system in his characterization of the office of overseer: "To bargain with some sturdy person to take them over by the lump, who yet is not intended to take them, but to hang over them in terrorem if they shall complain to the justices for want of maintenance." [413c]

Joseph Townsend, another commentator upon the Poor Law, writes to the same effect. "The terror of being sent to a workhouse acts like an abolition of the poor's tax on all who dread the loss of liberty." [501a]

Scores of other civic leaders spoke and wrote against the current methods of relief. One of these protestants was Thomas Gilbert, a local magistrate and a member of the House of Commons. After twenty years of efforts to reform the Poor Law, he succeeded at last in moving a bill through Parliament. This Statute, passed in 1782 and known because of its sponsor as the Gilbert Act, repealed in its first clause the part of the Law which permitted contracting for the care of the poor. Having thus struck at one of the greatest evils ever perpetrated against the destitute, it proceeded to set up a machinery for combining parishes into unions, permitting them among other things to erect and operate in common a poorhouse but with this provision:

That no person shall be sent to such poor house or houses, except such as are become indigent by old age, sickness, or infirmities, and are unable to acquire a maintenance by their labor; . . . and except for such orphan children . . . as shall be sent thither by order of the guardians . . . [an official created to replace the overseer of the poor] and . . . such children as shall necessarily go with their mothers thither for maintenance.

The person, "able and willing to work," thus excluded from the poorhouse was to be given "employment suited to his or her strength and capacity"; and the guardian of the poor was required "to maintain or cause such person or persons to be properly maintained, lodged, and provided for until such employment shall be procured." [40]

Gilbert's purpose in the passing of this Law was to solve the problem of relief by enlarging the area of administration so as to permit a classification of those in need and the establishment of appropriate types of care. According to his description of his "Plan for the Better Relief and Employment of the Poor," the aged, infirm, and impotent are to be brought into poorhouses; the "idle and dissolute are to be kept at hard labor in houses of correction; and the poor infants in their tender years, are to be placed out with proper persons. Those who are completely able and willing to labor are to be hired out where work can be procured for them." [445a]

In effect, his Act reversed the Statute of 1722, which authorized the overseers to strike from the relief rolls any person refusing their offer of the workhouse. In eliminating the able-bodied from the workhouse and in providing assistance for the unemployed until employment could be found for them, it opened the way for a new emphasis upon economic aid to people in their own homes. While comparatively few parishes took advantage of the new Law—in 1834 there were only sixty-seven Gilbert unions, combining 924 parishes, less than one-fifteenth of the number in England and Wales [481a]— this Statute of 1782 marked the first break from the system of public assistance that centered about the workhouse. The nation now began to turn toward a program of outdoor relief that was to be the method of operation for the next half century, and the subject of discussion for many more years thereafter.

VIII

THE ALLOWANCE IN SUPPORT OF
WAGES

The poor afflicted are
So that they perish fast.
If now no order taken be
Then ruin comes at last.

ANONYMOUS,
Greevous Grones for the Poore, 1621.[401a]

ALTHOUGH the protests against the evils of the workhouse played
a large part in relegating the institution to a less important place
in the efforts to deal with the problem of poverty, the decisive precipitant of change is to be found in the whole complex of economic
and social developments during the latter part of the eighteenth
century. It was a time of great suffering among the poor, greater
among agricultural laborers than anything that had been experienced
in two hundred years. Chief among the causes of this distress was
the acceleration of the movement toward enclosure.

Despite the accumulation of large estates that had marked the years
in the sixteenth century when the Poor Law began to take form,
the common land was still characteristic of country living in the
1700's. The laborer, in addition to whatever space there was around
his cottage, had the use of a sizable acreage which belonged to the
village. He would have a strip of this commons for cultivation and
could also turn his cows, sheep, and geese upon the communal grazing places. The wastelands offered him a source of fuel and an opportunity to add to his table by fishing and by the hunting of small
game. What today we would call subsistence farming was almost
universal. By virtue of the availability of the land, wages were less
important than now. Pay might be low and employment intermittent, but there was always the commons.

Then, in the second half of the eighteenth century, the agricultural proprietors began increasingly to perceive possibilities of profit
in the enlargement of their holdings. Act after act was introduced

in Parliament providing for the division of the commons and the wastelands and the turning of them from communal use to individual ownership. J. L. and Barbara Hammond quote estimates from several sources indicating that, in the forty years after 1760, there were not less than ten times as many Parliamentary authorizations of enclosure as in the forty years before, with more than three million acres affected.[453a]

In this division of the land, the laborer and the small farmer had little chance of obtaining individual shares comparable to what they had had in common use. Usually unable to read or write, inexperienced in the ways of the law, the peasant fell prey to every circumstance that could be turned against him. The man who had lived on the commons for so many years that he thought that his place was his own, now discovered that he was a squatter. The small farmer found himself with so tiny a plot of ground that he could not maintain his family upon it. The laborer with no room for grazing was obliged to give up his cow. As the common land disappeared he lost his source of fuel, while new laws against poaching deprived him of what he had previously been able to get in the way of small game. In the very years in which the Revolution was restoring the fields of France to its peasantry, England was developing a landed aristocracy and creating a landless poor.

Oliver Goldsmith wrote his "Deserted Village" under the influence of the first impact of this movement. His poem was published in 1770. Its familiar lines have special meaning for the student of social security:

> Sweet smiling village, loveliest of the lawn
> Thy sports are fled, and all thy charms withdrawn; . . .
> One only master grasps the whole domain,
> And half a tillage stints thy smiling plain. . . .
> A time there was, ere England's griefs began,
> When every rood of ground maintained its man. . . .
> But times are altered; trade's unfeeling train
> Usurp the land and dispossess the swain. . . .
> Where then, ah! where shall poverty reside,
> To 'scape the pressure of contiguous pride?
> If to some common's fenceless limits strayed
> He drives his flock to pick the scanty blade,
> Those fenceless fields the sons of wealth divide,
> And e'en the bare-worn common is denied.

While the accelerated movement toward enclosure was depriving the laborer of the subsistence farming that had reinforced his wages, the beginning of the development of power machinery brought another dislocating influence. Much of the spinning and the weaving involved in the woolen industry had been carried on in the home, the family having been the unit of production. This work was not only done in towns, it was scattered through the country where handicraft and agriculture supplemented each other.

The power machine made the industrial establishment rather than the family the basis of manufacture, and took this work away from the country, shifting it either to sites where water was available or, with the increasing use of steam, to the towns and cities. Moreover, with the use of power, cotton began to compete with wool, and the hand weaver was still further put to it to maintain himself against the machine.

On every count the rural and village worker was being deprived of a source of employment and income. Either he must move to the town or he must rely exclusively upon what he could earn as a laborer; and there was not enough work on the farms to keep him employed.

During the years at the turn of the century, from 1793 to 1815, the war with France brought a steep increase in the cost of living. Wages fell far behind prices. The demand for agricultural products rose, but that did not help the laborer. It only emphasized the importance of large scale production and made enclosure seem the more desirable to the large landholders. Also in this last decade of the eighteenth century there occurred a succession of poor harvests. In many places there was rioting and the seizure of food. Even where the people endured distress without turning to violence, their suffering was evident enough to cause general concern. The agricultural proprietors and the large farmers could only enjoy their prosperity if measures were taken to solve the problem of the poverty-stricken laborer.

The solution would seem to have been an increase in wages, and a number of such proposals were advanced. There was ample precedent in English history for governmental action in this direction. Since the first Statute of Laborers there had been legislation fixing wages, usually in the interest of a maximum, not a minimum wage. The laws to which most civic leaders of the time referred were the 5th Elizabeth, Chapter 4, 1563, empowering the justices of the peace "to limit, rate, and appoint" wages,[22] and the 1st James I, Chapter 6, 1604.[31]

The earlier Statute, despite a preamble expressing a concern about the wages of the poor in relation to the cost of living, was a piece of repressive legislation, framed in the spirit of the first Statute of Laborers, designed to restrict labor at every point. It included a provision enforcing a maximum wage. The second law, that of James I, was a more liberal statute. It represented an attempt at minimum wage legislation. "If any clothier or other shall . . . not pay so much or so great wages to their weavers, spinsters, workmen or workwomen . . . [as ordered, he] shall forfeit and lose for every such offense to the party grieved ten shillings."

Under this Act of James I, it would have been possible for the justices of the peace at the end of the eighteenth century to establish a minimum wage, and it was for this purpose that a meeting of the sheriff and the magistrates of Berkshire was called at the Pelican Inn in Speenhamland on May 6, 1795. It was there proposed that the wages of day laborers be adjusted to meet the high price of corn and other provisions, but according to the correspondent whom Sir Frederic Eden quotes in his contemporaneous account of the meeting:

There existed a difference of opinion, respecting the mode of making such increase. . . . The following plans were submitted. . . . 1st, that the magistrates should fix the lowest price to be given for labor, as they were empowered to do by the 5th Elizabeth Chapter 4; and 2ndly, that they should act with uniformity in the relief of the impotent and infirm poor, by a table of universal practice, corresponding with the supposed necessities of each family. The first plan was rejected by a considerable majority; but the second plan was adopted.[432†]

"The table of universal practice" was a basis for supplementing the income of the laborer. Instead of raising wages to a point where they would meet the cost of living, the justices of Berks proposed to use relief to make up the difference between a man's earnings and the minimum upon which they felt his family could exist. The scale which they drew up provided that when the gallon loaf sold for 1 shilling, enough relief would be added to the laborer's wages to bring his income to 3 shillings; if he had a wife, to 4 shillings 6 pence; if a wife and one child, to 6 shillings, and so on according to the size of the household.

This plan of supplementing wages became known as the Speenhamland Act because Speenhamland was the place where the meeting was held at which the scale was adopted. The system established at the Pelican Inn quickly spread throughout England. It was a method that had previously been used in individual parishes, but the action of the magistrates of the county of Berks formalized the practice. The publication of a scale made imitation easy, and for a generation this program of supplementing wages dominated the administration of relief.

The movement was facilitated and expedited by the enactment in Parliament—Royal Assent, December 24, 1795—of an enabling amendment to the Poor Law, permitting any of his Majesty's justices to order relief "to any industrious poor person or persons; and he, she, or they shall be entitled to ask and to receive such relief at his, her, or their homes." [42]

Shortly after the passage of this legislation, Parliament also had an opportunity to consider the same question as that which was voted down by the magistrates of Berkshire. Samuel Whitebread, a member of the House of Commons, introduced a bill providing for the fixing of minimum wages. The House, however, went the same way as the justices at Speenhamland. It negatived the bill on second reading, February 12, 1796, after a speech in opposition by the Prime Minister, William Pitt, who, according to the report of the proceedings, maintained that

by the regulations proposed, either the man with a small family would have too much wages or the man with a large family who had done most service to his country would have too little. So that were the minimum fixed upon the standard of a large family, it might operate as an encouragement to idleness on one part of the community; and if it were fixed on the standard of a small family, those would not enjoy the benefit of it, for whose relief it was intended. What measure then could be found to supply the deficit? Let us, said he, make relief, in cases where there are a number of children, a matter of right, and an honor instead of a ground for opprobrium and contempt.

This will make a large family a blessing, and not a curse; and thus will draw a proper line of distinction between those who are able to provide for themselves by their labor, and those who after having enriched their country with a number of children, have a claim upon its assistance for support.[201]

While the Prime Minister hedged his proposition with the suggestion that "they engraft upon it resolutions to discourage relief where it was not wanted" and that assistance be supplied in the form of work wherever possible, he was giving support to the introduction of outdoor relief on a wider range than had ever before been experienced in England.

The allowance in support of wages was the chief of four methods through which the able-bodied were aided outside the workhouse. Most closely related to it in practice was the system of roundsmen. Two quotations may serve to describe the operation of this system, which varied in the details of its application among the different parishes. The first quotation is from a correspondent of Sir Frederic Eden in Leicestershire, writing in August 1795, when the plan was new:

In the winter and at other times, when a man is out of work he applies to the overseer, who sends him from house to house, to get employ: the housekeeper who employs him, is obliged to give him victuals, and 6d a day; and the parish adds 4d (total 10d. a day) for the support of his family; persons working in this manner are called roundsmen, from their going around the village or township for employ.[432g]

The second quotation is dated nearly forty years after the first and is taken from the *Report from His Majesty's Commissioners for Inquiring into the Administration and Practical Operation of the Poor Laws* (See Chapter XII):

According to this plan, the parish in general makes some agreement with a farmer to sell to him the labor of one or more paupers at a certain price, and pays to the pauper, out of the parish funds, the difference between that price and the allowance which the scale, according to the price of bread and the number of his family awards to him. . . . In other cases the parish contracts with some individual to have some work performed for him by the paupers at a given price, the parish paying the paupers.

In many places the roundsman system is effected by means of an auction. Mr. Richardson states that in Sulgrave, Northamptonshire, the old and infirm are sold at the monthly meeting to the best bidder, at prices varying according to the time of the year from 1s. 6d a week to 3s.; that at Yardley, Hastings, all the unemployed men are put up to sale weekly, and that the clergyman of the parish told him that he had seen ten men the last week knocked down to one of the farmers for 5s. and that there were at that time about 70 men let out in this manner out of a body of 170.[305a]

Both the allowance and the roundsmen involved the supplementation of wages by relief. The allowance was the application of this principle to the man already employed; the roundsmen to the unemployed man who asked the parish for help. Either the parish gave him relief and then tried to reimburse itself by letting him out to a farmer for whatever payment it could secure, or it sent him on the rounds to obtain what wages he could, making up to him the difference between what he received and the scale as approved by the magistrates.

A third method was that which placed the responsibility for the employment of the unemployed upon the employer. This was called the labor rate. Here the parish set the pay and parceled the unemployed among the employers who were obliged to provide employment or pay the difference in increased taxes. One illustration of many in the *Report from the Commissioners for Inquiring into the Poor Laws* will serve to show how this system operated:

The overseer, on the plea that he could no longer collect the money for the poor rates without resorting to coercive measures, and that the unemployed poor must be apportioned among the occupiers of land in proportion to their respective quantities, had required him (a Mr. Nash) to take two more men. Mr. Nash was consequently obliged to displace two excellent laborers.[305b]

The fourth method of assistance to the able-bodied outside the workhouse was used comparatively little. This was the employment of the unemployed on public projects by the parish itself. Such work of this sort as was undertaken was chiefly in making roads, in digging at gravel pits, and like activities. *The Report from the Commissioners* estimated that in the year ending March 25, 1832, "scarcely more than one twentieth" of relief expenditures "was paid for work, including work on the roads and in the workhouses."[305c]

The parish was too small a unit to permit of much possibility of public work; the art of public administration had not reached a point at which effective superintendence could be given to project and workers; and the thought of the times, with its emphasis upon private enterprise, did not readily contemplate government in the role of employer.

It was not upon work, either public or private, nor for that matter upon relief, that the program for meeting distress at the end of the eighteenth century was founded. It was upon a mixture of both, with the parish assuming responsibility for the laborer in or out of work if his income fell below a certain level. Once an individual was adjudged to need assistance, he became in a sense both the duty and the property of local government, which might grant him relief and let it go at that, or might farm him out to the local proprietors, making the process more palatable to the reluctant employer by providing, according to the scale, whatever he could not or would not pay in wages. And, of course, the reverse also applied: that an employer who paid under the scale could send his hitherto independent employee to the overseer for a relief grant to meet the deficiency in wages.

The system comprehended in these measures was so vicious in its results and met with such cumulative, and ultimately almost universal, contemporary condemnation that throughout the succeeding century it was cited as the classic of ill-advised planning and administration of public assistance. The effect of the program was to lower the standard of wages and of living for the laborer, to destroy the initiative and hope with which he approached his work, and, if anything, to increase the number of those who were either forced or resigned to an acceptance of outdoor relief.

Three statements in the *Report from the Commissioners* will perhaps serve to illustrate the reasons for the failure of the program:

From a laborer, discussing the roundsmen:
That is the very worst thing that has ever happened for the laborers of this country; that is the way our wages are kept down. A farmer wants to get some work done; he proposes starving wages to the laborer. If the laborer refuses to take them, the farmer says, "Very well, I do not want you," and sends to the overseer and gets a man, whom he pays what he likes.[305d]

From an agriculturist, speaking of the allowance:
If a system of allowance is adopted in a parish, the consequences are, the whole of the laborers are made paupers; for if one occupier employs laborers that have an allowance, other occupiers will send the laborers to the parish officers, otherwise he pays part of the other occupiers' labor [i.e., through taxes].[305e]

From comments by the authors of the Report upon the effect of the system on employers of labor:
What motive has the man who is to receive 10 shillings every Saturday, not because 10 shillings is the value of his week's labor, but because his family consists of five persons, who knows that his income will be increased by nothing but by an increase of his family, and diminished by nothing but by a diminution of his family, that it has no reference to his skill, his honesty, or his diligence.[305f]

The Hammonds in their *Village Laborer* quote various testimony from the 1820's showing that where the allowance system was in effect wages were lower than where it was not in use.[453b] At the end of the third decade of the nineteenth century, the standard of the allowance itself had fallen until, according to the Hammonds, it was, at least in some places, only two-thirds of what it had been in 1795.[453c]

By 1832, on all counts—from the point of view of the taxpayers whose rates had risen steeply with the increased numbers of persons receiving relief, of the employer whose labor was less interested and less efficient, of the laborer who found his wages decreased and his incentives undermined, and of the person on relief who had less than the bare minimum of a generation before—the program of combining relief and wages had failed.

The burden of this failure was, as we shall see in Chapter XII, placed upon the relief system, and in particular upon relief to the able-bodied. This, in the light of present perspective, was an unjustified though, considering the then-existing state of knowledge of administration, an inevitable conclusion. It was not the principle of direct relief which was at fault. Granted adequate administrative skill, the supplementation of wages would, to a considerable extent, have been possible, for much of this supplementation was of part-time and of intermittent work. This is a procedure which is followed today without disastrous results, in special circumstances even extending to full-time employment.

What was destructive in the program which came to attention in 1795 was its professed intent. It was proclaimed as a project in the supplementation of wages, all the more dramatically established because it was chosen as an alternative to a minimum wage. It was done without even the protection afforded later by the bottoms fixed through collective bargaining. Labor organization was, indeed, actually forbidden within four years of the refusal by Parliament in 1796 to enact minimum-wage legislation.

Furthermore, the parish, in undertaking to farm out the labor of those on relief, took over a responsibility which was the individual's alone, and thus further emphasized its underwriting of the wage system. What expedited the ensuing disaster was the environment in which the program was applied. The area of relief was for the most part small and rural. The agricultural parish in relation to any one employer had an influence that the parishes in the larger industrial centers did not have. It could, and through this method did, affect both the standard of wages and the standard of living; and "ruin came at last."

So strong was the reaction against the system that in 1834 England reëstablished the workhouse as the central device in the administration of relief, delaying for another three-quarters of a century the development of a constructive program of assistance.

IX

ADMINISTRATION PRIOR TO 1834

One may observe in what instances the elder officer trained to this kind of business is apt to despise the younger for having more feeling than himself; and the younger the elder, for being provident and wary beyond measure. Both may be equally in fault. Acquaintance with misery is a very essential part; but it surely requires a peculiar moderation and tenderness, as well as discernment to constitute a good director of the parochial poor.

Jonas Hanway, <i>Letters to the
Guardians of the Infant Poor,</i> 1767.[456a]

THE failure of the various experiments in relief attempted during the more than two centuries that followed the Law of 1601 was due quite as much to poor administration as to mistaken policy. The attempt to employ the unemployed in manufacture, the use of the workhouse as the center of the assistance program, the allowance in support of wages—these were all so seriously handicapped by the current status of the art of government that, even if in every other respect they had been well founded, they would probably have met with little success. In organization, in method, and in personnel, the administration of relief in the seventeenth and eighteenth centuries had not developed to a point at which it could promise any degree of effectiveness.

The unit of operation was too small. In 1834, when the population of England was fourteen million, there were fifteen thousand parishes. This was an average of less than one thousand persons to a parish. In 1601 the average was much smaller. Throughout the period we have been discussing, most jurisdictions counted their people by the score or the hundred rather than by the thousand. It was a time of scattered, primitively rural living, when the village was more representative than the town, and the town than the city.

In the administration of the Poor Law, localism was carried to its greatest extreme. Relief of neighbors was administered by neighbors from taxes paid by neighbors, always remembering, however, the gulf separating the classes from one another. The parishes were essentially autonomous. Each, for the most part, went its own way. Parliament might adopt statutes, but they were more often disregarded than observed. There has never been a more literal demonstration of home rule.

While the small local unit, self-governing in most respects, was characteristic of this period (1601–1834), the system had at the start an appreciable impetus from the national government. The development of the Poor Law came at a time in the history of England when there was a growing tendency toward a greater expression of centralized executive power. The seat of this power was the Privy Council. During the closing years of the sixteenth century we increasingly feel the influence of the Council in measures taken to meet unemployment, food shortages, and the need for relief. The Privy Council corresponded to a cabinet. Individual members held authority delegated by the Crown and applied it to the various administrative functions of government.

As early as 1528 the Council asserted itself in relation to the problem of unemployment. The Duke of Norfolk was sent into Suffolk to induce the cloth manufacturers to retain employees whom they were discharging because they feared the effect upon business of the war against the Emperor, Charles V, which threatened to cut off trade with Flanders. From the middle fifties forward, the Council in time of poor harvest frequently fixed the price of grain. It issued orders to the local magistrates looking to the control of vagrancy. After the passage of the 39th Elizabeth, 1597–98, the Council sent instructions by letter to the justices telling them to see to it that the new Statute was carefully carried out.

The greatest exercise of national power in this respect came in 1631. Despite the discussion and attention that had been given to the problem of poverty and the orders hitherto issued by the Privy Council, the parishes had been lax in setting up and administering the new machinery for relief. There was much complaint. Conditions were bad enough to require royal action. In January 1631, Charles I appointed a Royal Commission "for putting in execution of the laws and statutes for the relief of the poor, punishment of rogues, and employment of gifts to charitable uses, etc."

The commissioners issued a set of orders and directions to the justices, instructing them to inquire into the operation of the Poor Laws, and to assess and execute penalties for negligence on the part of administrators. The justices were to report to the high sheriff of the county, who was to deliver their reports to the justices of assize. They in turn were to deliver these reports to the Royal Commission.

The commissioners decreed "that the lords of manors and towns take care that their tenants and the parishioners of every town may be relieved by work or otherwise at home and not suffered to straggle and beg up and down in their parishes," and "that the weekly taxations for the relief of the poor and other purposes mentioned in the Statute of 43rd Elizabeth be in these times of scarcity raised to higher rates in every parish, than in times before were used. And contributions had from other parishes to help the weaker parishes." [301a]

The orders and directions of the Commission brought immediate results and for a decade continued to have great influence. Nearly one thousand reports upon the administration of relief were received from the justices and are preserved among the State Papers of England.

While there was great variation in the degree to which the justices carried out the instructions of the Privy Council, there seems to be no doubt that the growing exercise of power by the Council— and most particularly by the Commission of 1631—was enormously influential in stimulating the relief administration provided for by the Poor Law of 1601. Miss E. M. Leonard, who discusses this subject in her *Early History of English Poor Relief*, 1900, concludes from her examination of the reports of the justices and other documents that "from 1631 to 1640 we had more poor relief in England than we ever had before or since." [465a]

One wonders what the course of public assistance in England would have been had this system of national supervision over local units continued. That prospect was closed by the Civil War. The plan of supervision was dropped and was not reëstablished upon the accession of Charles II. After 1639 there were no more reports from the justices. England fell back into a local relief without any more national oversight than that provided by Parliamentary statutes.

Dissatisfaction with the operation of the Poor Laws mounted. Much of the complaint was leveled, and with justification, at the administrative personnel, the appointed overseers of the poor, serving compulsorily but without pay, usually for a term of twelve months. Caustic statements about these officials appear in Parliamentary statutes, as, for example, the 3rd William and Mary, Chapter 11, 1691:

Many inconveniences do daily arise in cities, towns corporate, and parishes, where the inhabitants are very numerous, by reason of the unlimited power of the churchwardens and overseers of the poor, who do frequently upon frivolous pretences (but chiefly for their own private ends) give relief to what persons and number they think fit, and such persons, being entered into the collection bill, do become after that a great charge to the parish, notwithstanding the occasion or pretence of their receiving collection oftentimes ceases, by which means the rates for the poor are daily increased.

Many churchwardens and overseers of the poor, and other persons interested to receive collections for the poor, and other public moneys relating to the churches and parishes whereunto they belong, do often misspend the said moneys, and take the same to their own use, to the great prejudice of such parishes, and the poor and other inhabitants thereof.[34]

Jonas Hanway, writing in 1766, states the case more dramatically:

What is said by the late ingenious and humane Dr. Hales of spirituous liquors, may be applied to the conduct of some parish officers within the bills of mortality: he says, "Of all the miseries and plagues incident to human life, none are more effectually destructive than this, not even those three sore judgments of war, pestilence, and famine, which after having raged for some time cease. But this evil spirit is an unrelenting merciless enemy, that threatens destruction from generation to generation." [455c]

Dr. Burn, whose *History of the Poor Laws* appeared two years before Hanway's book, implies in his discussion of the overseers some of the reasons for their incompetent administration:

It is true, the law provides that they shall be substantial householders. But many a man may be a substantial householder, who is not fit to be an overseer of the poor. And, in fact, the office goes by rotation from one householder to another; some perhaps tenants at rack rent, whose lease expires the next year; others, ignorant and unexperienced; others, not willing to charge themselves, or to disoblige their neighbors; and all of them wanting to get over the office, with as little trouble to themselves as possible; and if any, wiser than the rest, projects anything for the common good, his office expires at the end of the year, and his labor is frustrate.[413d]

The cure of this incompetence was attempted through two kinds of supervision, supervision of the overseers by the members of the vestry and supervision by the justices of the peace. The use of such terms as "vestry," "parish," "churchwarden," which are basic to any discussion of English relief, illustrates the extent to which the organization of the church influenced the organization of local government. Relief administration derived its original set-up from the ecclesiastical structure, the parish being the territorial unit of operation, the churchwardens the lay executive officers sitting as a committee, and the vestry the church council. This administrative structure was used not only for the business of the church but also for secular matters, a development facilitated by the fact that the church itself was a governmental institution supported by taxes.

The vestries were of two kinds: open vestries participated in by all of the tax-paying parishioners, and select vestries composed of persons chosen by the parishioners or elected by the vestry itself, which became in this instance a self-perpetuating body. The open vestry was the earlier type. At its meetings, among other business the needs of persons applying for assistance were discussed, and once a year, "or as often as it shall be thought convenient," to quote the 3rd William and Mary, Chapter 11, 1691, the relief rolls were called over and a new list of eligibles was prepared.[34]

The effect of this procedure was to put the overseers, who sat as members of the vestry, under immediate and constant pressure. They were subject to the demands of special interests, and favor rather than need was often the basis upon which the decision to grant or not to grant relief was made.

The select vestries were established in 1819 under the 59th George III, Chapter 12, being composed of elected householders, the clergy, the churchwardens, and the overseers.[45] The overseers were ordered under this law to conform to the instructions of the body thus established. The result was the same as in the open vestries.

The second way of supervising the overseers, supervision by the justices of the peace, was equally unsatisfactory. The basic Poor Law of 1601 gave the justices considerable power. It was then established as their duty to select yearly "four, three, or two substantial householders" who, with the churchwardens, were to act as overseers of the poor. The overseers were to carry on their activities "with the consent" of the justices. They were also to render an annual financial accounting to the justices.[30]

Additional powers were given the justices by the Act of 1691, which cited the incompetence and malfeasance of the overseers. This Statute, after providing for the annual review of the relief rolls by the vestry, enacted that no other persons except those thus approved should be granted relief unless by authority of one justice of the peace residing within such parish or, if none be there dwelling, in the parts near or next adjoining, or by order of the justices in their respective quarter sessions, except in cases of pestilential diseases, plague, or small pox.[34]

The justices interpreted this Statute as giving them the power to originate grants of relief, not merely to authorize such action upon request of the parish officials. They employed their powers so unwisely that in 1722 the Law was amended to provide that the justices should not order relief until oath had been made to "A reasonable cause or ground for having such relief" and that the applicant had appealed for relief "at some vestry or other public meeting of the said parishioners, or to two of the overseers . . . and was by them refused to be relieved and until such justice hath summoned two of the overseers of the poor to show cause why such relief should not be given." [37]

The weakness of the system lay in the authority granted the magistrates to overrule the overseers in any individual case but without any responsibility for administrative operation. As long as this threat of review existed, the overseer would be tempted to make his decisions with an eye to the possible subsequent action of the justices of the peace, whose knowledge of the circumstances of the case was inevitably slight and superficial. The effect of this form of magisterial supervision is evident from the tactfully devastating criticism of these officials in 1834 by the *Report from the Commissioners for Inquiring into the Administration and Practical Operation of the Poor Laws:*

Admitting, as we are anxious to admit, the general integrity and intelligence of the magistracy, and the importance of their services in the administration of justice, we yet cannot doubt that there are to be found among more than two thousand persons some exceptions to the general character. But we believe these exceptions to be rare, and that in a great majority of instances—so great as to form the general rule—the magistrates have exercised the powers delegated to them by the Poor Laws—not wisely, indeed, or beneficially, but still with benevolent and honest intentions, and that the mischief which they have done was not the result of self-interest or partiality, or timidity or negligence, but was in part the necessary consequence of their social position, and of the jurisdiction which was confided to them, and in part arose from the errors respecting the nature of pauperism and relief which prevailed among all classes at the time when the allowance system and the scale were first introduced, and still appear to prevail among the majority.[305g]

Dr. Burn's remedy for the corruption and maladministration of the overseers was a system of executive supervision. His plan, as developed in his *History of the Poor Laws*, was to place them under the direction of a paid district or regional superintendent:

Let there be a general *superintendent* over a certain number of parishes, as the justices in sessions shall find most convenient. Let the overseers collect the poor rate, but let them be under the direction of their superior as to the disposal of it. . . .

The said overseer should be, not a person of the most eminent rank and dignity; for it is not to be supposed that such persons will sufficiently attend. He should not be of the lowest rank, lest something of authority should be wanting. In general, a person about the degree of a *high constable* seemeth the most proper; and the high constable himself, in some hundreds, perhaps might be appointed, with a reasonable addition to his salary: for it is essential to the execution, that such persons have salaries. People may talk as much as they please, about serving the public for nothing. Many public spirited men, no doubt, there are in the nation; perhaps there were never more than in this present age. But this sort of men is not always the most active; and it is certain the business of the world is done by another sort of people. From the highest subject to the lowest, no man chooses to serve for nothing. Nor is it reasonable they should. Therefore this overseer must be paid.[413e]

Thomas Gilbert did not believe that any form of supervision would cure the overseers. His Act of 1782 took the administration of relief away from them, leaving them, as far as public assistance was concerned, with the sole duty of providing the funds. The actual work of relief was carried on by salaried guardians of the poor, general supervision being placed in the hands of a visitor, an over-all executive officer appointed by the justices from three nominations made by the guardians. Both Mr. Gilbert and Dr. Burn were active magistrates, and it is not surprising, therefore, that they endowed the justices not only with the powers of appointment but with authority on complaint to order relief.

Granted that the overseers proved to be an incompetent and often irresponsible group of officials, their position was almost impossible. Subject to the pressure of the vestries and the dictation of the justices, they could not call their jobs their own. In such a situation a hodge-podge of administrative procedure was inevitable, some overseers going ahead regardless of the legal checks upon them relying on the preoccupation of the magistrates with other affairs, and some steering by whatever wind of opinion from the vestry or the justices seemed to come their way. Aside from the fact that the overseers were a discontinuous group compelled to serve without compensation, the basic weakness of the system was the power of the justices to overrule in an individual case. Such power placed in the hands of persons outside an administration, and therefore without any organizational responsibility, would under the best circumstances be fatal to the operation of any system of relief.

Throughout the 233 years that followed 1601, there was persistent advocacy of larger administrative units as a way of securing a more effective public assistance. This plan was urged both because it was felt that the larger the task the greater would be its attraction to persons with executive ability, and because the increased numbers of persons served would make possible a classification of need and the development of appropriate types of institutions.

The beginning of this movement toward greater operating units may be said, omitting certain developments in London, to have been the statute authorizing the creation of a corporation within the city of Bristol. In 1696 the overseers in nineteen parishes were superseded by this corporation, with a board of governors charged with the responsibility of public assistance, outdoor and indoor, for the whole city. This board maintained an employed staff, and established workhouses and administered relief as already described. (See Chapter VI) By 1712 thirteen towns had followed the example of Bristol, setting up city-wide boards of guardians in place of the parish system.

The Statute of 1722, which empowered the overseers to refuse relief to persons who would not enter the workhouse (see Chapter VII) and permitted the farming out of the poor to contractors, also provided for the voluntary combination of parishes for the purpose of establishing workhouses. Again in 1782, when Thomas Gilbert succeeded in obtaining the first modification of the Act of 1722, he based his program upon the creation of unions of parishes. The effect of these various efforts to establish wider areas of operation was to prepare the way for a movement away from the extreme of localism represented in the Statute of 1601.

To the development of methodology in relief, the contribution of the years between 1601 and 1834 was meager. There was some effort to use registration as an administrative procedure, i.e., the listing of the names of those receiving assistance. This practice is apparently almost as old as organized relief. Luther and Vives included it in their programs, and the Poor Law required it when in 1531 begging was licensed. From this time forward the recording of the names of the needy was an established procedure. Related to it was the practice of badging the poor.

The Statute of 1563, 5th Elizabeth, Chapter 3, provided that, if a parish had more poor than it could relieve, the justices were empowered to authorize begging within the county, the persons so licensed being required to wear badges on the breast or back. Thomas Firmin, in his *Proposals for Imploying the Poor*, 1678, describes the practice of badging:

The parish, having called over all their poor people, and appointed work for those that are able, have thought it convenient to give a badge, with the three first letters of the parish's name upon it, to such, and only such, as they found incapable of any labor, by virtue of which badge they are permitted to go into the parish at such an hour of the day, and receive such broken bread and meat as their neighbors have to give; who also have promised to give it to these, and to no others; for by this badge, which is made of blue and yellow bayes (baize), pinned upon their sleeve or breast, they are known to the inhabitants to be those very persons whom the deputy, common-council men, and churchwardens, have judged fit to receive such charity. And I know not why anybody should be offended, that the parishioners should invite their poor neighbors once a day to come to their houses, to receive such bread and meat as they are willing to bestow; neither would I have these poor people go under such a dishonorable name as beggars, but to be called invited guests.[437b]

A further description of badging, with the reason assigned for it, is contained in the 8th and 9th William III, Chapter 30, 1697:

And to the end that the money raised only for the relief of such as are as well impotent as poor, may not be misapplied and consumed by the idle, sturdy, and disorderly beggars, be it . . . enacted . . . that every such person as from and after the first day of September, 1697, shall be upon the collection, and receive relief of any parish or place, and the wife and children of any such person cohabiting in the same house . . . shall upon the shoulder of the right sleeve of the uppermost garment of every such person, in an open and visible manner, wear such badge or mark as is herein-after mentioned and expressed, that is to say, a large Roman P, together with the first letter of the name of the parish or place whereof such poor person is an inhabitant, cut either in red or blue cloth, as by the churchwardens and overseers of the poor it shall be directed and appointed.[36]

What we have come to look upon as a method of deterring people from applying for relief would thus seem to have arisen as an administrative procedure. Later, badging did come to have a punitive connotation, but apparently it started as a way of indicating who was entitled to receive assistance and was related to the system of licensed begging. The calling of the relief rolls in the parish assembly, or the publishing of these lists, probably originated in the same intention, that is, as a means of ascertaining from the parishioners who was and was not in need of relief. While later these devices were used in the spirit of deterrence, they seem, like badging, to have started as crude attempts at method in administration.

That a system of investigation and related procedures might be developed as a means of determining who should and who should not receive relief was not indicated in the Law of 1601 and is not emphasized in the two centuries of administration that followed. The compulsory services of unpaid overseers for yearly or even briefer terms prevented the accretion of informed experience. As the eighteenth century advanced toward the nineteenth, the practice of employing paid assistant overseers increased; but basically and almost universally the administration of relief was in the hands of the appointed unpaid overseers whose primary interest was elsewhere. Relief was in effect nobody's job. It was like service on a jury, an occasional obligation of citizenship, not at all anything to be thought of as a career with implications of study and competent performance. It is therefore not surprising that, in determining eligibility for relief, the tendency was to rely upon devices such as the refusal to grant assistance outside the workhouse rather than to develop a method of interviewing and investigation.

This, according to Sir George Nicholls, was in part the purpose of the 9th George I, Chapter 7, 1722, authorizing overseers to deny relief to persons not willing to enter the workhouse. Nicholls definitely indicates that the Statute was intended as a means of ascertaining whether the applicant for help was actually in need. He refers to

the insufficiency of individual judgment for deciding upon the claims and representations of applicants, whether they are actually and unavoidably destitute, or that destitution is simulated and unreal—whether if existing, it was occasioned by idleness or vice, or was owing to circumstances beyond the applicant's control. On these points the insufficiency of personal judgment seems in the present act to be tacitly admitted, and an attempt is made to relieve the parish authorities from a portion of their responsibility, by enabling them to offer lodging and maintenance in the parish houses, which if the applicant should refuse he will be no longer entitled to relief of any kind.[481b]

It was not until the nineteenth century that systematic investigation began to be practised in England, and then only here and there. The issue did not reach the point of quality in skill or in procedure. It seldom got beyond the question of honesty in operation.

Thomas Ruggles, writing in 1793, favored outdoor relief because he thought it less subject to maladministration than the workhouse.

It will be found on inquiry, that the money distributed in the weekly list forms no very material proportion of the expenses of a parish; and in the distribution of money there is no room for lucrative jobs, no knavish contracts for furnishing the various articles of consumption; and the overseer keeping a fair account can have no profit; and possibly as money is the common representative of all necessaries of life, so it is the greatest, most convenient, and best appropriated relief to the individual. It somewhat, in its universality of use, resembles Boniface's ale—"A poor man and his family may eat it, drink it, and sleep upon it." [490a]

Sidney and Beatrice Webb in *English Poor Law History*, reviewing the situation from the vantage of a century and a third later, place the administration of relief prior to 1834 in the setting of the times; and, though they find it inefficient and corrupt, they see it to be no worse than any other area of government before the second half of the nineteenth century:

The inefficiency of the methods of relief can be paralleled only by the corruption of its administrators. There was no end to the fraud that was practiced. Every workhouse was a center of embezzlement and almost continuous theft. The overseers had to be specifically restrained by statute from paying the poor in base coin. . . . The receipts extorted from the fathers of illegitimate children were systematically embezzled; the food ordered for the workhouse inmates was habitually stolen; every contract was shamelessly jobbed, and every contractor practiced the art to an extent and with an audacity that is today unbelievable, of giving short measure and inferior quality.

It would, however, be unfair, to judge the Poor Law administration—even that of no more than a hundred years ago—by twentieth century standards of honesty and efficiency. The parish officers of the first quarter of the nineteenth century were apparently no more corrupt and no less efficient than nearly all the unreformed Municipal Corporations. . . . We do not feel sure that the masters of workhouses excelled in embezzlement the colonels of army regiments; or that the stealing of food in Poor Law institutions was more prevalent than that which Cobbett vainly sought to expose in the feeding of the troops. The workhouses were neither more cruel nor more demoralizing than the corporation prisons; and neither of them were ever quite so bad as the hulks for convicts maintained by the national government in the Thames and Medway. The fact is that, even a hundred years ago, not only were the requirements of hygiene unrecognized, but the science and art of administration was still so far non-existent that, on any but the smallest scale, neither honesty nor efficiency was possible. The necessary technique had not been devised. There was practically no audit of cash, let alone of stores, materials and products. There was no check on individual accounting. There was, indeed, not even any deliberately constructed system of bookkeeping which would automatically reveal what was going on. The very idea of official inspection as a regular instrument of administration had not been born.[506a]

In view of the then primitive state of all governmental operation, it is not surprising that the Poor Law between 1601 and 1834 should have had nothing to contribute to method in relief administration. In addition to being the creature of its times, it carried the handicap of too small a unit of operation and a discontinuous officialdom.

X

HAMBURG AND MUNICH

To make vicious and abandoned people happy it has generally been
supposed necessary, first, to make them virtuous. But why not reverse this order? Why not make them first happy, and then virtuous? If happiness and virtue be inseparable, the end will be as certainly obtained by the one method as by the other; and it is most
undoubtedly much easier to contribute to the happiness and comfort
of persons in a state of poverty and misery, than, by admonitions
and punishments, to reform their morals.

> BENJAMIN (THOMPSON) COUNT OF RUMFORD,
> *Essays, Political, Economical, Philosophical,* 1796.[500a]

DURING the years in which England was engaged in her unfortunate experiments with the allowance, the roundsmen, and the
labor rate, elsewhere other approaches were being made to the problem of poverty. In Hamburg and in Munich systems of public assistance had been developed which were operating to the satisfaction
both of their administrators and of the communities which they
served.

The work in Hamburg was described for the benefit of contemporary opinion by one of the leading spirits in the enterprise, Baron
Kaspar von Voght, first in 1796 in a *Letter to Some Friends of the
Poor in Great Britain,* and again in 1817 through a republication of
the original pamphlet under the auspices of a group of nine Eng-
lishmen, who for this purpose had obtained the permission of the
author.

The plan, which was perhaps the most comprehensive of its time,
was financed by funds secured through taxation and through philanthropic contributions. Baron von Voght tells how the contributions
were obtained and how the project was developed and carried out:

Every inhabitant in rotation went round weekly; collecting among his
neighbors; and the most respectable of our inhabitants made it a point to
collect in person.

The town, after an average calculation of the number of poor in the several parts, was divided into sixty districts, containing each a nearly equal number of poor.

To each district three citizens were chosen for three years; and the number of wealthy and respectable men who offered themselves for the severe task they were to undergo, will forever furnish a bright page in the annals of civic virtue in Hamburg. . . .

For the use of the above named one hundred and eighty gentlemen, whom I shall call overseers, very ample instructions were published.

[These instructions were issued and the work was planned and directed by a central board composed of five senators and ten other persons—later the number was increased—chosen for life.]

Actual relief was the first object; for we were all convinced of the barbarity of preventing beggary when provision for real want is not previously prepared; but at the very moment that this provision was secured, measures were taken to prevent *any man from securing a shilling which he was able to earn himself.* . . .

Our overseers had printed interrogatories, which they were to propose to each poor family. The answers were written upon the white column of the page, and verified by a personal visitation, and the evidence of their neighbors, and many queries were formed to discover the average earning of each member of the family; but this was not a point made easily. *Few answers were sincere.* . . . The state of health was determined by a visit from a physician and a surgeon.

We now began to make an exact calculation of what each pauper wanted for bare subsistence; we went down as far as two shillings a week; but in the course of our investigation respecting the earnings of 3500 families, we were astonished to find that we were still above that sum with which a considerable part of our poor could make a shift to live.

It was our determined principle to reduce this support lower than what any industrious man or woman in such circumstances could earn; *for if the manner in which relief is given is not a spur to industry, it becomes undoubtedly a premium to sloth and profligacy.* . . .

Six-sevenths of our poor being women and children, we fixed upon [the spinning of flax as a means of employing them].

We could now safely offer relief to all sorts of poor, because we had it now in our power to make them comply with the only condition required, that they should use toward their support all the exertion they still were capable of. Accordingly the overseers went through their districts, and asked in all such mansions as could be supposed to harbor want, if the inhabitants stood in need of support. The question to all such poor as wished for relief, and were able to spin, was whether they did earn by their work one shilling six pence a week? For experience had taught us, that many poor lived upon that sum; and we knew enough of our poor to suppose that one shilling six pence avowed earning something more.

If the answer was affirmative, the pauper stood not in need of weekly assistance. If it was negative, we gave him work which afforded him one shilling six pence a week. . . .

Men and boys [were employed] in making rope yarn, picking oakum, or cleaning the streets and mending the roads at four pence a day. . . .

Old age and incurable diseases, sickness, and the difficulty of supporting a numerous family, were evils which also called for assistance. For the first we provided a hospital; and in some cases gave to individuals the money which the boarding in the hospital would have amounted to.

Five physicians, five surgeons, and as many midwives were appointed, one for each twelve districts, who upon the request of the overseer . . . went immediately to the lodgings of the patient, if he was not able to appear . . . at the physician's or surgeon's house. . . . The physician prescribed not only the diet . . . but he informed the overseer of what money he thought necessary for supplying the want of labor, and the extraordinary expenses. . . .

Wherever children under six years of age were in this unhappy situation [i.e. in homes where "misery and drunkenness" existed], *we intended to board them in the houses of the better sort of poor*, and many a good motherly woman we found, who became an excellent nurse.

In other cases, we allowed the mother from six to twelve pence a week for each child; and we are now busy in preparing in every parish a warm room, and bread, milk, and potatoes in plenty, where such parents as go out to work may deposit their children during the day, and thus prevent any obstacle to their own industry, or to that of their elder children.

We determined to oblige them to send all their children from six to sixteen to school, in which they shall work two thirds of the time, and the remainder of it be instructed in reading, writing, casting accounts, religion and church music.

We determined . . . that to no family any relief should be allowed for a child past six years: but that this child, being sent to school, should receive not only the payment for his work, but also an allowance, in the compound ratio of his attendance at school, his behavior, and his application to work; which amounted to an average of twelve or eighteen pence a week, exclusive of other premiums. . . .

An allowance was made for lodging; but as this is paid every six months, and the pauper receives his allowance weekly . . . we reduced, therefore, twenty-four pence (the weekly allowance) to twenty pence and paid his rent to his landlord.

These were the principal elements in the program which Baron von Voght described. He testified to its success:

For the last seven years . . . hardly a beggar has been seen in Hamburg. . . . We not only did much towards the relief of the poor, but . . . we gained some steps towards the more desirable, yet but slowly attainable end, the *preventing some of the causes of poverty*.[503a]

The program at Hamburg was started in October, 1788. A little more than a year later (January 1790) Munich, a city of sixty thousand, had inaugurated a system of relief which, while not so comprehensive as that in Hamburg, contained many of the same features. Here, too, employment was made one of the focuses of the plan. The originator of the administration in Munich was that amazing American, Benjamin Thompson, who in his range of interests came closer to Benjamin Franklin than any other person of his generation. Born in Massachusetts in 1753, he had entered the British army at nineteen years of age and had been sent to England, where he remained during the American Revolution. In 1784, "with His Majesty's gracious permission," he entered the "service of his Most Serene Highness the Elector Palatine, Reigning Duke of Bavaria . . . arranging his military affairs, and introducing a new system of order, discipline, and economy among his troops."[500b] In 1791 he was made a count of the Holy Roman Empire, taking his title (Rumford) from the home of his American wife, who died the following year. It was in 1790 that Thompson, now commander-in-chief of the general staff of the Bavarian army, became interested in the problem of relief through a plague of beggars so serious as to call for the use of the military for its elimination.

Count Rumford describes the situation in the first volume of his *Essays, Political, Economical, and Philosophical,* which is largely devoted to a discussion of his work in Munich.

So numerous were the swarms of beggars in all the great towns, and particularly in the capital, so great their impudence, and so persevering their importunity, that it was almost impossible to cross the streets without being attacked, and absolutely forced to satisfy their clamorous demands. And these beggars in general by no means such as from age or bodily infirmities were unable by their labor to earn their livelihood; but they were for the most part, stout, strong, healthy, sturdy beggars, who, lost to every sense of shame, had embraced the profession from choice, not necessity. . . .

These beggars not only infested all the streets, public walks, and public places, but they even made a practice of going into private houses, where they never failed to steal whatever fell in their way, if they found the doors open, and nobody at home; and the churches were so full of them that it was quite a nuisance, and a public scandal during the performance of divine service. People at their devotions were continually interrupted by them, and were frequently obliged to satisfy their demands in order to be permitted to finish their prayers in peace and quiet. . . .

They had recourse to the most diabolical arts, and most horrid crimes, in the prosecution of their infamous trade. Young children were stolen from their parents by these wretches, and their eyes put out, or their tender limbs broken and distorted, in order, by exposing them thus maimed, to excite the pity and commiseration of the public. . . .

Some of these mothers were so void of all feeling as to expose even their own children, naked, and almost starved in the streets, in order that, by their cries and unaffected expressions of distress, they might move those who passed by to pity and relieve them. . . .

Count Rumford based his efforts to combat this evil upon two premises. The first was that "in order to clear the country of beggars . . . it was necessary to adopt general and efficacious measures for maintaining and supporting the poor." The program "for maintaining and supporting the poor" centered in the establishment of what Count Rumford called a "military workhouse," military not, however, in its operation but in its product. It was designed as a center of manufactory of clothing for the army. With such an outlet for his goods, Thompson was able to offer work to anyone who was capable of employment. Related to the workhouse was a system of districting and inquiry, administered by volunteer workers, not unlike that developed in Hamburg. Payments both of wages and of relief grants were in cash.

As a means of operating on his second premise, which involved making people happy in order that they might then become virtuous, Count Rumford "considered what circumstance in life, after the necessaries, food and raiment, contributes most to comfort, and I found it to be cleanliness." He then tells how he went about making "the poor and unfortunate people . . . really comfortable."

A large and commodious building, fitted up in the neatest and most comfortable manner, was now provided for their reception. In this agreeable retreat they found spacious and elegant apartments, kept with the most scrupulous neatness; well warmed in winter; and well lighted; a good warm dinner every day, gratis; cooked and served up with all possible attention to order and cleanliness;—materials and utensils for those who were able to work;—masters, gratis, for those who required instruction;—the most generous pay, *in money*, for all the labor performed; and the kindest usage from every person, from the highest to the lowest, belonging to the establishment.

Here, in this asylum for the indigent and unfortunate, no ill usage, no harsh language, is permitted. During five years that the establishment has existed, not a blow has been given to anyone; not even to a child by his instructor.

As the rules and regulations for the preservation of order are few, and easy to be observed, the instances of their being transgressed are rare; and as all the labor performed is paid by the piece; and not by the day; and is well paid; and as those who gain the most by their work in the course of the week, receive proportional rewards on the Saturday evening; these are most effectual encouragements to industry.

As soon as the plan was ready for operation, the campaign for arresting the beggars and inducting them into the new system was begun. Count Rumford set an example to his men by making the first arrest himself. The beggars were taken to the town hall where they were registered, informed about the plan for their rehabilitation, and then dismissed to go to their own homes with instructions to report at the workhouse the next morning.

The awkwardness of these poor creatures, when they were first taken from the streets as beggars, and put to work, may easily be conceived; but the facility with which they acquired address in the various manufactures in which they were employed, was very remarkable, and much exceeded my expectation. But what was quite surprising, and at the same time interesting in the highest degree, was the apparent and rapid change which was produced in their manners, in their general behavior,—and even in the very air of their countenances. . . .

The melancholy gloom of misery, and air of uneasiness and embarrassment, disappeared by little and little from their countenances, and were succeeded by a timid dawn of cheerfulness, rendered most exquisitely interesting by a certain mixture of silent gratitude, which no language can describe.

It was not only the beggars who were thus helped but "others who never were beggars."

Many persons of distinguished birth, and particularly widows and unmarried ladies with very small fortunes, frequently send privately to this house for raw materials,—flax or wool,—which they spin, and return in yarn.

Work was supplied to people both at the institution and at home. The dinners at noon which were provided for the workers were also offered to needy unemployable individuals who could come to the military workhouse. Other persons unable to work were granted relief in their own homes. For those too infirm to take care of themselves and without relatives to look after them, a special house was provided.

Count Rumford felt that his program had solved the problem of beggary and destitution. The people of Munich confirmed his opinion.

Will it be reckoned vanity, if I mention the concern which the poor of Munich expressed in so affecting a manner when I was dangerously ill?—that they went publicly in a body in a procession to the cathedral church where they had divine service performed, and put up public prayers for my recovery—that four years afterwards, on hearing that I was again dangerously ill at Naples, they, of their own accord, set apart an hour each evening, after they had finished their work in the Military Workhouse, to pray for me? [500c]

Count Rumford's system of relief and work, like that of Hamburg, was financed through a combination of funds secured from the public revenues and money obtained through private contributions.

The emphasis and the space which he gave in his book to the description of the military workhouse tends to obscure the basic similarity of his organization to the one developed by Baron von Voght. Both programs were in the continental tradition. They were logical descendants of the plans of Juan Luis Vives and the citizens of Ypres. The municipality was the unit of administration. A central body with executive power divided the city into districts and utilized volunteers to visit the homes of those in need, making the necessary inquiries and providing the appropriate relief. This system of districted visitation under an overall supervision was typical of European methods just as the workhouse and the independently operated parish were typical of English administration. At Ypres the system was in its earliest stages; at Hamburg it appears in a much more developed form; and half a century later it attracted attention anew at Elberfeld, in Germany, whence its influence spread to the United States as well as to England.

Hamburg in 1796 offered the most thorough and the most comprehensive program of its time, with a relief grant developed out of a study of thirty-five hundred families and a system of assistance that included employment, aid to dependent children, child placing, day nurseries, and educational provision. The theory of minimum relief at Hamburg was not unrelated to the principle of less eligibility which England was later to establish in its Poor Law reform of 1834, but the plan was not administered in the punitive way that characterized public assistance in England. At Munich, Count Rumford, in philosophy and practice, was far ahead of his generation, with his belief that the way to virtue was through happiness, his reliance upon few rules as contrasted with the extensive regulations of the English workhouses, and his avoidance of punishment.

Count Rumford's description of his program had an extensive circulation in England. His *Essays*, first published in 1796, had run into five editions by 1800. Malthus and other English thinkers were familiar with his work. So, too, with the plan which had been developed in Hamburg. It had an interested English audience and was reviewed by official eyes. The nine men who sponsored the reprint of 1817 addressed their pamphlet to George Rose, M.P., then President of the Board of Trade. None of this attention with respect either to Hamburg or Munich had any perceptible influence in reforming the English Poor Laws. English legislators and administrators were not prepared to exchange the workhouse for the systematic organization of the community that the continental pattern presupposed. They did not take foreign systems into consideration when planning their future program. The commissioners who in 1832 were appointed to inquire into the administration and practical operation of the poor laws did not begin their formal study of relief abroad until they were almost ready to issue their Report, and by the time that the foreign data had been assembled and published in a folio of nearly one thousand pages, the Poor Law of 1834 was already a statute of the realm.

Buried in the bulky volume of foreign communications, appearing too late to be of any value at the time, was an interesting comment about relief in the Bavaria of Count Rumford by Lord Erskine, His Majesty's Minister to that country:

The great and important object is attained of giving relief and support to the aged, helpless and sick, and finding work in workhouses or at their own homes, at a moderate payment, for those who cannot otherwise obtain it; for which purpose a register is to be kept by the guardians of the poor of all those persons who are in want of work, and who are therefore either a burden upon the parish, or are likely to become so, as also a list of those who wish to employ workmen, in order to endeavor to arrange between them the terms of employment; and that this object may be the more easily attained, the directors are required to be in continual communication with the overseers of public works, the masters of manufactories, with individual proprietors, and societies; and that where there are a quantity of hands capable of work, they are to be passed into that part of the country where they are most wanted.[305Aa]

Forty years after the publication of the *Essays* of Benjamin Thompson, Bavaria was still carrying out his measures for "maintaining and supporting the poor." More than that, it was operating a public employment bureau nearly a century in advance of the establishment of the English labor exchanges and the United States Employment Service.

XI

THOMAS CHALMERS

To the theory of charity it might almost be said that since Aristotle and St. Paul nothing has been added until we come to the economic and moral issues which Dr. Chalmers explained and illustrated.

SIR CHARLES S. LOCH,
Charity and the Social Life, 1910.[466a]

WHILE the interest which Baron von Voght and Count Rumford had aroused in the relief plans of Hamburg and of Munich was still current, the attention of people who were concerned about the problem of poverty began to be attracted by the teachings and the activities of the Rev. Dr. Thomas Chalmers in Scotland.

Dr. Chalmers went beyond the writers and the administrators who had preceded him in the discussion of the Poor Law. They had chiefly been advocates of specific projects or reporters about enterprises they had conducted or observed. He formulated a philosophy and evolved a method. Whereas previous discussion had often been engaged by operative devices, as for example the workhouse, or individual aspects of relief like settlement, he first created a theory about the helping of people in need and then translated it into a practice. What he presented had more resemblance in organization to the systems at Hamburg and Munich than to developments in England; but his philosophy and his method were essentially his own, growing out of his own experience and his own thinking and used by him to open a new approach to the administration of relief.

Thomas Chalmers came of a middle-class Scotch family. His father and both his grandfathers were merchants, his great-grandfather and his great uncle clergymen. He was one of fourteen children born within a span of twenty-two years. Although his father's business was prosperous, there was reason for care in conserving the resources of so large a household, and Thomas Chalmers was brought up in an atmosphere of thrift, good management, self-reliance, and independence. Anstruther, the seaport in which he was born, was a small town, and he had all the opportunity that such an environment gives to know people intimately in their ways of life.

Before his twelfth birthday he had entered the University of St. Andrews, and before his sixteenth he had enrolled as a student of divinity.

An illustration of the quality of his character, his courage, and determination derives from his first venture in university teaching. While his chief studies were theological, his enthusiasm in those days was mathematics. At the age of twenty-two he was appointed assistant in that subject at the University of St. Andrews. Because he lectured with a vividness which was foreign to the dull methods of his professor, he was dismissed at the end of the term on the ground of inefficiency. That summer he was ordained as minister of the parish of Kilmany, which was within easy travel of St. Andrews. Whereupon, in the autumn, he returned to the University and started classes of his own in the town. Despite the opposition of the faculty, he soon was conducting not only three classes in mathematics but also one in chemistry. At the end of the year his ability and his success as a teacher were conceded by everybody.

His love of mathematics and chemistry broadened to include astronomy; and later he moved into the field of political economy, in 1808 publishing a book on that subject. For more than half of his years at Kilmany, his real interest seemed to lie in these areas of activity.

His ministry at that time is described by Dr. Hanna as having been

unpopular and ineffective, his church but poorly attended, and his private ministrations followed with but trifling effects. . . . But the great change came, and with it a total alteration in the discharge of all parochial duty. From a place of visible subordination, the spiritual care of his parish was elevated to the place of clear and recognized supremacy.[454a]

This change came about through one of those profound religious experiences that have been the mainspring of many great spiritual leaders. It started during a time of severe illness. He was then twenty-nine years old. When after months of sickness he recovered his health, his "effort," again quoting Hanna, "was to prepare for an eternity felt to be at hand, by discharging aright the duties of time."[454b] These duties meant for him an undivided devotion to preaching and pastoral visitation. It was this pastoral visitation that gave substance to his philosophy and practice of relief.

But it was his preaching that brought him fame, and in 1814 at the age of thirty-four he was called to the Tron Church in Glasgow, one of the most important in the city. His eloquence in the Tron pulpit and his published sermons and other writings added to his growing reputation, and he soon came to be regarded in England as well as in Scotland as one of the foremost divines of his time. His biographer quotes this description of his preaching:

Suppose the congregation thus assembled—pews filled with sitters, and aisles, to a great extent, with standers. They wait in eager expectation. The preacher appears. The devotional exercises of praise and prayer having been gone through with unaffected simplicity and earnestness, the entire assembly set themselves for the treat, with feelings very diverse in kind, but all eager and intent. There is a hush of dead silence. The text is announced, and he begins. Every countenance is up—every eye bent, with fixed intentness on the speaker. As he kindles the interest grows. Every breath is held—every cough suppressed—every fidgety movement is settled—everyone, riveted himself by the spell of the impassioned and entrancing eloquence, knows how sensitively his neighbor will resent the very slightest disturbance. Then, by-and-by, there is a pause. The speaker stops to gather breath,—to wipe his forehead—to adjust his gown, and purposely, too, and wisely, to give the audience, as well as himself, a moment or two of relaxation. The moment is embraced,—there is a free breathing—suppressed coughs get vent—postures are changed—there is a universal stir, as of persons who could not have endured the constraint much longer—the preacher bends forward—his hand is raised—all is again hushed. The same stillness and strain of unrelaxed attention is repeated, more intent still, it may be, than before, as the interest of the subject and of the speaker advance. And so, for perhaps four or five times in the course of a sermon, there is the relaxation and the "at it again" till the final winding up.[454c]

Chalmers' eloquence was not confined to the pulpit, nor were his writings exclusively devoted to theology. He covered a wide range of interests, never losing his liking for mathematics, chemistry, and astronomy. The latter supplied material for some of his most famous sermons. He entered actively into the discussion of ecclesiastical policy and organization, advocated the emancipation of the slaves in the British colonies, and spoke before lay and clerical audiences in support of the restoration of civil rights to Catholics.

His greatest act of courage came during the closing years of his life in his fight for self-government of the established Church of Scotland. When Parliament decreed that the civil authority had the right to determine the appointments of clergymen instead of the presbytery, Chalmers led the movement of secession, led it actually and literally on one of the most dramatic occasions in religious history. On May 18, 1843, more than four hundred ministers and a still larger number of elders, delegates to the General Assembly of the Church of Scotland, withdrew from the hall in which they had been convened, taking this way of asserting their belief in the supremacy of the church in its own affairs. One of the two men at their head as they left the General Assembly was Dr. Chalmers, and it was he who was elected the first moderator of the Free Church of Scotland.

Dr. Chalmers' initial experience in the pastorate introduced him to the material out of which he began building his philosophy and method of relief. For some months before he went to Kilmany he served as assistant to the clergyman of another parish which, though rural, included a considerable manufacturing population.

It was in this parish that he first met with relief from public funds. Kilmany, where he became clergyman the next year, relied entirely on private charity; and more than a decade later when, after his great spiritual change, he became devoted to the temporal as well as the religious necessities of his parishioners, he wrote to his brother-in-law comparing the two parishes to the disadvantage of the former:

I spent some months in a parish in Roxburghshire, before I came to Kilmany. The poor rate had been introduced from England; and I saw as much poverty and more depravity of character than I hope I shall ever witness in these northern climes. The same population were supported at about six times a greater rate than they are in this neighborhood. [And he adds] Mr. Malthus' theory upon this subject would have carried me even without examples.[454d]

This was written in February 1814, in his last year at Kilmany, but it was his appointment to the Tron pulpit in Glasgow, a city which exhibited almost all the things about relief to which he objected, that provided the precipitant for his philosophy and method. Glasgow not only had public relief; it also had a central relief fund formed by contributions received from church collections in the various parishes. Chalmers was as opposed to the charitable fund as he was to the one from taxation:

Now, one evil consequence of thus uniting all the parishes of a town under the authority of one general board, is that it brings out to greater ostensibility the whole economy of pauperism, and throws an air of greater magnificence and power over its administration. . . .

The imagination of a mighty and inexhaustible fund is not more sure to excite the appetite, and so to relax the frugal and providential habits of its receivers, than it is sure to relax the vigilance of its dispensers.[417a]

In addition to disapproving the existence of these public and private funds for relief, Chalmers objected to the custom by which the same person acted as almoner and as religious adviser.

The Rev. S. Humphreys Gurteen, who introduced the charity organization movement (Chapter XV) to the United States, cites Chalmers upon this subject in a quotation which I have not been able to verify: " 'Your ladies,' he [Chalmers] said to the people of his parish, 'go about among the poor with a tract in one hand, and a shilling in the other. How can the eye be single?—it will keep veering from the tract to the shilling.' " [449a]

Another defect from which Chalmers felt Glasgow suffered, as compared with rural Kilmany, was the diffuse and impersonal character of its religious life. The hearers of the Tron Church came from every part of the town, crowding out—because they were able to pay more for their pews—the people of the neighborhood. The clergy were so overwhelmed by demands for appearances at civic occasions and other public activities that they had no time to visit their parishioners. Chalmers had been able to know every one of the seven hundred and fifty souls in Kilmany. He felt lost in the Tron parish with its more than eleven thousand persons.

He began to cast about for a way of "assimilating a town to a country parish," [417b] and he found his solution in trying to develop in and for his people what today we would call a parish consciousness, adopting in Glasgow the methods he had pursued in Kilmany. He determined to visit every family in the Tron parish. This he actually succeeded in accomplishing. In each of the neighborhoods into which he went, arrangements were made for an evening meeting to be held in a local school or other building where the people on whom he had called might hear him speak. He also established Sabbath schools for the children in various parts of the parish. It was precisely what on a smaller scale he had done in Kilmany after his great spiritual change. There was one addition. While he made at least one personal contact with every family in the parish, he introduced an extended use of the laity for subsequent visitation and for teaching in the Sabbath schools.

This experience in parochial activity confirmed for Chalmers the theory of what he called "locality."

There is a charm in locality most powerfully felt by every man who tries it . . . who has personally attached himself to a manageable portion of the civic territory. . . .

He will soon become sensible of the strong additional interest that he acquires, in virtue of having a small and specific locality assigned to him. When the subject on which he is to operate, thus offers itself to his contemplation, in the shape of one unbroken field, or of one entire and continuous body, it acts as a more distinct and imperative call upon him to go out upon the enterprise. . . .

The very visibility of the limit, by constantly leading him to perceive the length and breadth of his task, holds out an inducement to his energies, which, however difficult to explain, will be powerfully felt and proceeded on. There is a very great difference, in respect of its practical influence, between a task that is indefinite, and a task that is clearly seen to be overtakeable. The one has the effect to paralyze; the other to quicken exertion.[417c]

Chalmers saw locality as also having advantage and meaning for the people who were served as residents of the same neighborhood. He illustrated the superiority of their experience by comparing it with that of an audience attending a dramatic performance, as against the same people "reading the composition at home" when the total impressions "were not half so powerful as when within the infection of one another's feelings, they sit together."

When contiguous families hear the same minister on the Sabbath, or come within the scope of the same household attentions on other days, there is between them, through the week, a prolonged, and often a cherished sympathy, which, were the families widely apart in distant places of the town, would have no operation.[417d]

Consistent with this feeling about parish life was Chalmers' confidence in the judgment of the parishioners. His belief in the "just perception of truth on the part of a home-bred peasantry" helped him to support the right of a congregation to exert the veto over a candidate nominated to be its clergyman. He believed in the soundness of the judgment even though the people might be "unable to assign the principles or reasons" for it. He cited in this connection the advice reported to have been given to a man on commencing his duties as judge. "Trust to your own good sense in forming your opinions; but beware of attempting to state the grounds of your judgments. The judgment will probably be right; the argument will infallibly be wrong."

And Chalmers added: "I would take the verdict of a congregation just as I take the verdict of a jury, without reasons. Their judgment is what I want, not the grounds of their judgment." [454e]

He carried his belief in his parishioners still further, feeling that not only were people prone to undervalue the judgments of a "home-bred peasantry," but that they also tended to underestimate the capacity of the poor to provide for themselves:

There is a far greater sufficiency among the lower classes of society than is generally imagined; and our first impressions of their want and wretchedness are generally by much too aggravated; nor do we know a more effectual method of reducing these impressions than to cultivate a closer acquaintance with their resources, and their habits, and their whole domestic economy. [417e]

It was these resources that Dr. Chalmers felt were stopped by the presence of public funds for relief.

The first of these resources—he speaks of them as "innumerable fountains and refreshing rills"—was "situated among the habits and economies of the people themselves"; the second was the "kindness of relatives"; the third "the sympathy of the wealthier for the poorer classes."

But there is still another fountain that we hold to be greatly more productive even than the last. . . . In the veriest depths of unmixed and extended plebeianism, and where for many streets together, not one house is to be seen which indicates more than the rank of a common laborer, are there feelings of mutual kindness, and capabilities of mutual aid, that greatly outstrip the conceptions of a hurried and superficial observer. . . .

Such is the recoil of one human being from the contemplation of extreme hunger in another, that the report of a perishing household, in some deepest recess of a city lane, would inflict a discomfort upon the whole neighborhood, and call out succor, in frequent and timely forthgoings, from the contiguous families. . . .

When the people are left to themselves, they, in the first instance, by their own economy, would prevent the great majority of that indigence which now meets the dispensations of pauperism; in the second instance, the care of individuals for the aged and helpless of their own kindred, would, operating in each separate circle of relationship, work a mighty reduction on the territory of want; in the third instance, a still greater reduction would be effected by the more copious descent of liberality from the wealthier to the poorer classes; and to complete the wholesome process, internal charity among the poor themselves would fill up the many countless vacuities which escape the eye of general observation. We cannot affirm, that never, in any instance, would there be a remainder of want unprovided for; but we are strongly persuaded, that it would fall infinitely short of the ministrations of legalized charity.[417f]

Four years after Chalmers came to the Tron pulpit he had an opportunity to demonstrate his theories about relief. A new parish was organized, St. John's, and he was invited to take it. He stipulated that he be given full control over the administration of assistance. Instead of transmitting his church collections for relief to the central treasury of the presbytery, he asked that he be allowed to keep them and apply them at his discretion to the needs of the destitute. Although the new parish was one of the poorest in the city, he undertook to make no demands upon the general city-wide church fund, and in addition to refer to the Town Hospital (the institution through which public indoor and outdoor relief was administered) no new applications and no family currently maintained by his church funds. The parish would take care of its own but would be protected from having to support new, i. e., non-resident, families moving into its territory.

Chalmers' program having been accepted, he proceeded to put it into effect. He divided the parish of more than eight thousand persons into twenty-five districts. Then, following his theory of separating the spiritual from the temporal, he reintroduced the office of deacon, which had been discontinued, and gave to it the responsibility of providing for all new applications for assistance. Families already receiving relief he left to the elders, allowing them for this purpose to draw upon the money received at the Sunday-morning collections. These were contributed chiefly by the people who came from all over the city to hear the great preacher. He expected the deacons to rely upon the money collected at the evening service, which was almost exclusively attended by the people of the neighborhood, "the most plebeian parish in the city." [422a]

Under this plan the relief activities of the elders would diminish, since they would be receiving no new applications, while those of the deacons would increase. The drafts upon the morning collections would gradually lessen, and ultimately the whole cost would be met by the evening collections. There would be no transfers of families from private to public funds, so that if the program succeeded the local residents would, in the end, carry the whole burden of poverty in their parish.

The deacons, the chief administrators of relief, were almost entirely recruited from outside the neighborhood and were drawn from among people of larger means, occupying more advantaged positions than were represented by the parishioners of St. John's. This was also in harmony with Dr. Chalmers' theories. He accepted with conviction

the inequalities of condition in life. . . . It would require the violence of a perpetual stress on the spontaneous tendencies of every society in the world to repress or overbear them. The superiority of one man to another in certain outward circumstances of his state is not artificial but natural; and the consideration in which the occupiers of the higher state are held is natural also. . . .

People of humble estate are most feelingly and gratefully alive to the notice of those whom Providence has placed in a more elevated station than their own; and never does this principle stand more demonstrably forth as a real ingredient in the constitution of our nature, than in the superior charm of those recognitions or personal kindnesses which descend from the occupiers of a higher sphere on the children of poverty and toil. Even a passing smile of courtesy on the street is not thrown away, but has in it a certain influence or power of graciousness; and this is enhanced tenfold, when any son or daughter of affluence enters the houses of the poor. . . .[420a]

Out of the simple elements of attention, and advice, and civility, and good-will, conveyed through the tenements of the poor, by men a little more elevated in rank than themselves, a far more purifying and even more gracious operation can be made to descend upon them, than ever will be achieved by any other of the ministrations of charity.[417g]

Chalmers thus made difference in social status a contributory element in his program of administration, but he did not stop with general statements of principles. He endeavored to translate his theory into method; he prepared his deacons for their work by careful instructions. There already existed as applicable to their use directions which he had written for the elders of the Tron parish. In addition he issued specific statements about how the work was to be done, supplementing them with personal letters and conferences and with regular monthly meetings of his volunteer staff.

Chalmers believed that the deacon must be clear about his task, and be prepared to recognize and acknowledge what it involved.

By office and designation he stands out as the dispenser of the alms of the church. This is his known business; and he cannot though he would disguise it. . . .

Let him therefore make no mystery of his profession as administrator of the church alms among the families of his district; but openly proclaim the system on which he means to acquit himself of its duties. Let there be a full understanding on this matter between him and them.[420b]

The system which the deacon was to follow is indicated in what Chalmers called the "Directory of Procedure":

When one applies for admittance through his deacon, upon our funds, the first thing to be inquired into is, if there be any kind of work that he can yet do, so as either to keep him altogether off, or as to make a partial allowance serve for his necessities; the second, what his relatives and friends are willing to do for him; the third, whether he is a hearer in any dissenting place of worship and whether its session will contribute to his relief. And if, after these previous inquiries, it be found that further relief is necessary, then there must be a strict ascertainment of his term of residence in Glasgow, and whether he be yet on the funds of the Town Hospital, or is obtaining relief from any other parish.

If upon all these points being ascertained, the deacon of the proportion where he resides, still conceives him an object for our assistance, he will inquire whether a small temporary aid will meet the occasion, and state this to the first ordinary meeting. But if, instead of this, he conceives him a fit subject for a regular allowance, he will receive the assistance of another deacon to complete and confirm his inquiries by the next ordinary meeting thereafter, at which time the applicant, if they still think him a fit object, is brought before us, and received upon the fund at such a rate of allowance, as upon all the circumstances of the case, the meeting of deacons shall judge proper. Of course [Chalmers added in explaining his method], pending these examinations, the deacon is empowered to grant the same discretionary aid that is customary in other parishes.[418a & 417h]

Chalmers supplemented these general instructions with individual supervision and advice, such as that contained in the following letter addressed to one of his deacons shortly after the commencement of the enterprise:

Be kind and courteous to the people, while firm in your investigations about them; and just in proportion to the care with which you investigate will be the rarity of the applications that are made to you. The evidence for residence is had either by the receipts of rents from landlords, or by oral testimony, whether of these landlords or of creditable neighbors; the evidence for income, by inquiring of the people who furnish

them with work. . . . In times like the present, the burden is not all trans-
ferred from the poor to the rich, but is shared between them; it should
be a compromise between the endurance of the one and the liberality of
the other. N.B.—If drunkenness be a habit, this in itself is an evidence of
means, and the most firm discouragement should be put upon every application in these circumstances.[454f]

Three years before writing this letter he had delivered an address
to a group of young men who were added to the number of elders
in the Tron Church as a means of helping him in the parish work.
What he had said at their ordination—and as his discourses were
almost always written, they were available for repetition on other
occasions—was applicable also to the deacons at St. John's:

I ask if there be not room enough in a man's character for the wisdom
of the serpent along with the gentleness of the dove? That we may ward
off the undeserving poor, is it necessary to put on a stern and repulsive
front against all the poor who offer themselves to our observation? The
way, I apprehend, is to put forth patience and attention, and to be in the
ready attitude of prepared and immediate service for all cases and for all
applications in the first instance; to conduct every examination with
temper and kindness,—and surely it is possible to do this and at the same
time conduct it with vigilance. . . .

Your people will not like you the worse that they see you acting in a
sound, judicious, and experimental way with them. They know how to
appreciate good sense as well as we, and they admire it, and they actually
have a liking for it.[454g]

In describing his methods, Dr. Chalmers employed case illustrations
like the following:

A family of six lost both parents by death; there were three children
unable to provide for themselves and the other three were earning wages.
On an impression that they were not able to maintain themselves, application was made by them to their elder for the admittance of the three
youngest into the town hospital, where at the average of in-door pension-
ers, their maintenance would have cost at least 20 pounds a year. He
remonstrated with them on the evil of thus breaking up the family; on
the duty of the older to see after the education and subsistence of the
younger branches; and on the disgrace it would bring to them, by con-
signing their younger brothers and sisters to pauperism. He assured them
that they would find comparatively little difference in the sum which it
required to maintain them when they all remained together, and offered
them a small quarterly allowance so long as they should feel it necessary,

would they try the experiment of keeping together, and helping on each other to the best of their ability. They gave way to this right moral suasion, and application for the stipulated quarterly sum was only made twice. Thus, by a trifling expenditure, a sum at least fifty-fold was saved to the town hospital. But the worth of such management to the habit and condition of the family cannot be estimated in gold.[303a]

For nearly four years, from the beginning of the work on October 1, 1819, Dr. Chalmers supervised the administration of relief at St. John's. Later in reviewing the experience, he told a committee of the House of Commons that "the success of the system greatly outstripped my own expectations." [303c] During this period only twenty new applications were accepted from a population of over eight thousand. In addition, the parish had been able to take over the maintenance of all individuals who had previously been under the care of the Town Hospital, and there was enough money left to make possible an appropriation from the funds in the hands of the elders toward the endowment of a parish school.

The plan was continued under Dr. Chalmers' successor—he left Glasgow to take the chair of moral philosophy at his alma mater, the University of St. Andrews—and in 1833, E. C. Tufnell, one of the assistant commissioners of the Royal Commission for Inquiring into the Poor Laws, after studying the work reported: "The system has been attended with the most triumphant success for thirteen years; it is now in perfect operation, and not a doubt is expressed by its managers of its continuing to remain so." [421a]

Nevertheless, four years later the program was abandoned. From the explanations advanced by Dr. Chalmers, by his successors, and by other participants in the enterprise, it is possible to arrive at the reasons for this action. The experiment covered only a small part of the city while elsewhere the old system of public relief, together with the central fund for church relief, continued. The people of the parish were taxed for relief even though public funds were not spent in their section of the town, and at the same time they were expected to make charitable contributions. The system had little sympathy from the existing public officials, who thought that it implied a criticism of them, "as if," said Dr. Chalmers, "we had charged them with laxity and carelessness in the administration of a public trust." [422b] Many of the church officials in neighboring parishes felt the same way. These three things in combination then—the difference from other congregations, the double demands of taxation and contribution, and the unfriendly officialdom—were too much for the isolated parish.

There is not the least doubt [wrote one of the deacons to Dr. Chalmers] that as the scheme did not receive the countenance which we all thought it well deserved, both from the authorities and the sessions generally, we were discouraged and did give it up.[421b]

Another reason for the discontinuance of the enterprise lay in a fact at which Dr. Chalmers had hinted in his testimony before the Committee of the House of Commons in 1830:

There is in one respect a very great precariousness; for let two or three only of the agents relax their management by a very little, such is the inherent power of the increase in all systems of public charity which are carelessly conducted, that it would be in the power even of these few to overset the experiment.[303b]

The deacons who served at St. John's had other interests than relief which were primary with them, and they had nothing of the sort of backing that goes with professional association. It is not surprising that in the face of official criticism they should have given way.

Dr. Chalmers' contribution to the development of relief was far greater than that of any of the preceding or contemporary leaders in this field. He took the negative philosophy of laissez faire and gave it a positive turn. He had a basic respect for the poor and an underlying kindliness and sympathy in spite of his belief in the natural superiority of the upper classes. His method of investigation and of districted coverage was far in advance of the cruel and wholesale device of the workhouse and the slipshod administration of the allowance in support of wages and the other forms of English outdoor relief. He substituted the exercise of personal influence for the application of penal measures. There was no English experience that—measured according to current criteria, which looked largely to the reduction in expenditure for outdoor relief—was able to approach the record of St. John's parish.

On the other hand, with all the kindliness that characterized the Glasgow experiment, the method of Chalmers often became a contest in endurance. How much could the poor man's family bear before the sympathies of the deacon would force him to recommend assistance or before the local public would become sufficiently concerned to help? Moreover, Chalmers, like the rest of his generation, in emphasizing the personal factors in destitution, wholly overlooked the social-economic causes of distress.

It is not, however, by individual items of theory or practice that the value of Dr. Chalmers' work must be judged. His contribution went beyond any single points of policy or operation. It consisted in the development of a whole system for dealing with the problem of distress, a system based upon philosophy and principle and extending into every operative detail. What Dr. Chalmers brought to the administration of relief was methodology.

His contemporaries were apparently not interested in profiting by what he developed. Later, fifty years after the beginning of the experiment at St. John's, the London Charity Organization Society built its program largely upon his theories and procedure. The movement thus started spread, throughout the English-speaking world, the concept of method which he had created. The particular elements of the system that Chalmers introduced subsequently changed. The concept of methodology, however, as applied to relief remained, paradoxically entering the very area to which Dr. Chalmers had always been opposed—the area of governmental operation. It is this concept that represents Chalmers' contribution to the administration of assistance.

XII

THE REFORM OF 1834

Have you seen the book published by the Poor Law Commissioners? If you have not, let me send it to you. Often you have complained how little of the state of a people is to be learned from books; much is to be learned of it from that book, both as to their physical and spiritual state. . . . I regard this inquiry with satisfaction. . . . It has been more honestly and more ably performed than anything which has been done under the authority of government since I remember.

Letter to THOMAS CARLYLE from
JOHN STUART MILL, May 18, 1833.[477a]

DURING the three-quarters of a century of hard times for agricultural labor that started about 1760, taxes for relief had risen steeply. The increase between that date and 1784 had been 60 per cent. By 1801, after Speenhamland, expenditures as compared with 1760 had trebled. In 1818 they were over six times the amount in 1760. This was the peak, but in 1832, with the population of England doubled, relief cost five and one-half times what it had cost in 1760.[481c]

The burden fell unequally. The increase in England's wealth from 1760 to 1834 was chiefly in manufacture and related fields, whereas the taxes for relief were paid by householders and other occupiers of property. The system by which each parish was responsible for its own destitute involved an additional inequality. The places where there were many poor were seldom the places where there were many rich, and the communities with the greatest need were often the communities least able to pay the cost of meeting that need.

An additional source of dissatisfaction to the taxpayers was an apparent deterioration in the quality of labor. This deterioration was blamed upon relief, although there were in reality other and more influential factors. What enthusiasm could a man be expected to exhibit in life and in work who had been deprived by enclosure of his use of the commons; who had thereby been obliged to give up his flock of geese and his cow; who no longer had a strip of land which he could cultivate; and who had no access to wood and other sources of fuel which he had been accustomed to finding on the wastes, or to the game which had formerly played a part in his diet? Add to this a system of settlement laws that in effect imprisoned him within his parish, giving him little chance to look for better things—and what in the way of initiative could one expect? Only indifference could be anticipated as the response to wages so low that they must be supplemented by public relief. Least of all could enthusiastic energy be looked for in the man on relief who was let out by the parish instead of being free to contract for his own services. As one farmer remarked, "While the laborer was half-pauper and half laborer, he was like a man with two masters, and could do justice to neither." [321a]

On top of the long years of dissatisfaction with the administration of the Poor Laws, there came the theories of a new school of economists. In 1776 Adam Smith published his *Wealth of Nations*, giving enormous impetus to the doctrine of laissez faire, a doctrine admirably suited to the convenience of the rising manufacture of Great Britain, that asked for nothing better than to be let alone to get the profits made possible by the new age of the machine. Coupled with this was a philosophy which placed its weight against the existing provision of relief for the poor.

In 1786 Joseph Townsend, a clergyman, published anonymously a little book which he called *A Dissertation on the Poor Laws by a Well-Wisher to Mankind*:

It is the quantity of food which regulates the number of the human species [he said]. . . .

Nations may for a time increase their numbers beyond the due proportion of their food, but they will in the same proportion destroy the ease and comfort of the affluent, and, without any possible advantage, give universality to that misery and want, which had been only partial. . . .

By establishing a permanent community of goods, and neither increasing the quantity of food, nor limiting the number of those who are to share it, they divert the occasional surplus of national wealth from the industrious to the lazy, they increase the number of unprofitable citizens, and sow the seeds of misery for the whole community; increasing the general distress, and causing more to die for want, than if poverty had been left to find its proper channel. . . .

There is an appetite, which is and should be urgent, but which if left to operate without restraint, would multiply the human species before provision could be made for their support. Some check, some balance is therefore absolutely needful and hunger is the proper balance; hunger not as directly felt, or feared by the individual for himself, but as foreseen and feared for his immediate offspring. Were it not for this the equilibrium would not be preserved so near as it is at present in the world, between the numbers of people and the quantity of food.

It seems to be a law of nature, that the poor should be to a certain degree improvident, that there may always be some to fulfill the most servile, the most sordid, and the most ignoble offices in the community. The stock of human happiness is thereby much increased, whilst the more delicate are not only relieved from drudgery, and freed from those occasional employments which would make them miserable, but are left at liberty, without interruption, to pursue those callings which are suited to their various dispositions, and most useful to the state. As for the lowest of the poor, by custom they are reconciled to the meanest occupations, to the most laborious works, and to the most hazardous pursuits; whilst the hope of their reward makes them cheerful in the midst of all their dangers and their toils.

The fleets and armies of a state would soon be in want of soldiers and of sailors, if sobriety and diligence universally prevailed: for what is it but distress and poverty which can prevail upon the lower classes of the people to encounter all the horrors which await them on the tempestuous ocean, or in the field of battle? Men who are easy in their circumstances are not among the foremost to engage in a seafaring or military life. There must be a degree of pressure, and that which is attended with the least violence will be the best. When hunger is either felt or feared, the desire of obtaining bread will quietly dispose the mind to undergo the greatest hardships, and will sweeten the severest labors. The peasant with a sickle in his hand is happier than the prince upon his throne.

Upon this philosophy Joseph Townsend based his plan for reform of the Poor Laws. He advocated decreasing the fund for public relief by nine-tenths, perhaps eliminating it altogether.

Unless the degree of pressure be increased, the laboring poor will never acquire habits of diligent application, and of severe frugality. To increase this pressure, the poor's tax must be gradually reduced in certain proportions annually, the sum to be raised in each parish being fixed and certain, not boundless, and obliged to answer unlimited demands. This enormous tax might easily in the space of nine years be reduced nine-tenths; and the remainder being reserved as a permanent supply, the poor might safely be left to the free bounty of the rich, without the interposition of any other law. But if the whole system of compulsive charity were abolished, it would be still better for the state.[501b]

Joseph Townsend was a person of consequence in England, but he was outstripped in influence by another clergyman, the Rev. T. R.

Malthus, who set forth and developed similar theories in his *Essay on Population*, first published in 1798. Malthus' fear that agriculture would be unable to support an accelerating population and his belief in the inevitability of reliance upon the three great checks upon the increase of the people—famine, war, and pestilence (later he included moral restraint)—had a profound effect upon thinking about the Poor Laws.

Relief, he believed, by spreading the existing supply of provisions over the whole population only tended to increase the numbers of the poor, ultimately raising the cost of food, reducing therefore the net income of the independent worker, and impoverishing "that class of people whose only possession is their labor." His estimates about the future increase of population in England were proved to be incorrect by actual facts as developed in later years, and his skepticism about the productivity of the earth was unwarranted; but this did not prevent the intellectual leaders of the time from having their ideas colored by Malthusianism.

Meanwhile, in the agricultural communities, the poor themselves had something to say about their plight. They saw enclosure on the one hand and the introduction of threshing machines and like equipment on the other hand, taking their living away from them. Toward the close of 1830 they turned to rioting in a number of the rural districts. Crops were burned and property was destroyed. England had, at about the same time, gone through other disturbances in the battle for the extension of the suffrage, which finally resulted in the Reform Bill of 1832 giving the vote to the business and professional classes.

The fear of revolution was immediate in the minds of the government. The very same group that came into power to extend the franchise to the middle classes turned with severity upon the laborers. The rioting was met with the sternest punishment—execution, deportation, and imprisonment. Then in February 1832, just after the King had indicated to the House of Commons his readiness to create enough peers to force the electoral Reform Bill through the House of Lords, the government announced the appointment of a Royal Commission for Inquiring into the Administration and Practical Operation of the Poor Laws.

The Commission was determined to reform the administration of relief and in particular to stop the allowance in support of wages. It immediately embarked on one of the most extensive, effective, and dramatic pieces of social investigation ever to have been carried on in

Great Britain. The study continued through two years. The Commission sat at least once every week and fed its deliberations with schedules, records, and reports of every kind, and with the findings of a corps of investigators who went through England and Wales inquiring into the administration of relief. The evidence was obtained

from every county and almost every town, and from a very large proportion of even the villages in England. It is derived from many thousand witnesses, of every rank and of every profession and employment, members of the two Houses of Parliament, clergymen, country gentlemen, magistrates, farmers, manufacturers, shopkeepers, artisans, and peasants, differing in every conceivable degree in education, habits, and interests, and agreeing only in their practical experience as to the matters in question, in their general description both of the mode in which the laws for the relief of the poor are administered, and of the consequences which have already resulted from that administration, and in their anticipation of certain further consequences from its continuance.[305h]

The reports of the investigators, when published, occupied thirteen thousand printed pages; but the commissioners did not allow the mass of information to prevent the public from getting the facts. In 1833 they issued a book of some four hundred pages entitled *Extracts from the Information Received by His Majesty's Commissioners as to the Administration and Operation of the Poor Laws*. This was the book which John Stuart Mill recommended to Thomas Carlyle in the letter quoted at the head of this chapter. The following year the final report appeared. The material was selected and presented with regard for the general reader, and there is scarcely a page which is not arresting in its interest. There was great reliance upon case illustrations, direct quotation from witnesses, and dramatic statement. Not only was the study the largest undertaking in social investigation up to its time; its report was also one of the most widely, and, in relation to its purpose, most profitably read of public documents.

The commissioners began by summarizing in one sentence the result of all their studies:

It is now our painful duty to report, that in the greater part of the districts which we have been able to examine, the fund, which the 43rd of Elizabeth directed to be employed in setting to work children and persons capable of labor, but using no daily trade, and in the necessary relief of the impotent, is applied to purposes opposed to the letter, and still more to the spirit of that law, and destructive to the morals of the most numerous class, and to the welfare of all.[305i]

This conclusion the commissioners backed with the full weight of the testimony they had assembled.

This testimony was primarily directed to the able-bodied laborer in receipt of relief. Other types of need were scarcely mentioned. The case against him was marshaled, among other devices, through parallels like the following:

In the pauper's habitation you will find a strained show of misery and wretchedness; and those little articles of furniture which might, by the least exertion imaginable, wear an appearance of comfort, are turned, as it were intentionally, the ugliest side outward; the children are dirty, and appear to be under no control; the clothes of both parents and children, in nine cases out of ten, are ragged, but evidently are so for the lack of the least attempt to make them otherwise; for I have very rarely found the clothes of a pauper with a patch put on or a seam made upon them since new; their mode of living, in all cases that I have known (except and always making the distinction between the determined pauper and the infirm and deserving poor, which cases are but comparatively few) is most improvident. Whatever provisions I have found, on visiting their habitations, have been of the best quality; and my inquiries among tradesmen, as butchers, chandler's shopkeepers, etc., have all been answered with— "They will not have anything but the best."

In the habitation of the laboring man who receives no parish relief, you will find (I have done so), even in the poorest, an appearance of comfort; the articles of furniture, few and humble though they may be, have their best side seen, are arranged in something like order, and so as to produce the best appearance of which they are capable. The children appear under parental control; are sent to school (if of that age); their clothes you will find patched and taken care of, so as to make them wear as long a time as possible; there is a sense of moral feeling and moral dignity easily discerned; they purchase such food, and at such seasons, and in such quantities, as the most economical would approve of.[305j]

There is an abundance of statement in similar extravagant vein. A distinction is repeatedly drawn between the person receiving relief and the independent laborer, to the discredit of the former. That the economic situation of the latter might be superior was not emphasized, nor was there recognition of the whole complex of social conditions which made the life of the pauper more difficult than the life of any other class in society. The evil was held to emanate from the relief rather than from the situation, which was the occasion of relief.

The workings of the allowance in support of wages, the system of roundsmen, and the labor rate (see Chapter VIII) were set forth in such a way that none could doubt the evils of these methods of assistance. The failure of employment by the parish was described. The existence of much imposition and fraud was revealed, all witnesses expressing skepticism about correcting this difficulty through any system of administration involving the use of a staff of officials.

Thus, George Huish, assistant overseer of the parish of St. George's, Southwark:

In such a parish as ours, where we administer relief to upwards of 2000 out-door poor, it is utterly impossible to prevent considerable fraud, whatever vigilance is exercised. . . .

One man to every twenty would be required to watch the paupers living out of the parish, and one man to watch every 100 living within the parish; which is an expense of inspection which could not be borne. Suppose you go to a man's house as a visitor; you ask, where is Smith (the pauper)? You see his wife or his children, who say they do not know where he is, but that they believe he has gone in search of work. How are you to tell in such a case, whether he is at work or not? It could only be by following him in the morning; and you must do that every day, because he may be in work one day, and not another.

Suppose you have a shoemaker who demands relief of you, and you give it to him on his declaring that he is out of work. You visit his place, and you find him in work; you say to him, as I have said to one of our own paupers, "Why Edwards, I thought you said you had no work?" and he will answer, "Neither had I any; and I have only got a little job for the day." He will also say directly, "I owe for my rent; I have not paid my chandler's shop score; I have been summoned, and I expect an execution out against me, and if you stop my relief, I must come home," (that is, he must go into the workhouse). The overseer is immediately frightened by this, and says, "What a family that man has got! It will not do to stop his relief." So that, unless you have a considerable number of men to watch every pauper every day, you are sure to be cheated. Some of the outdoor paupers are children, others are women; but taking one with another, I think it would require one man's whole time to watch every twenty paupers.[305k]

[Comment the editors of the Report:] From the preceding evidence, it will be seen how zealous must be the agency, and how intense the vigilance, to prevent fraudulent claims crowding in under such a system of relief. But it would require still greater vigilance to prevent the bona fide claimants degenerating into impostors; and it is an aphorism amongst the active parish officers that "cases which are good today are bad tomorrow, unless they are incessantly watched." A person obtains relief on the ground of sickness; when he has become capable of returning to moderate work, he is tempted, by the enjoyment of subsistence without labor, to conceal his convalescence, and fraudulently extend the period of relief. When it really depends upon the receivers whether the relief shall cease with its occasion, it is too much to expect of their virtue that they shall, in any considerable number of instances voluntarily forego the pension.[305l]

The possibility of adapting to the field of public relief the methods of inquiry and administration that Thomas Chalmers had originated in Glasgow a few years before—which, whatever their limitations, were certainly to be preferred to the workhouse—was apparently not considered by the commissioners of 1832–34, nor did they conceive the kind of relationship between the person on relief and the relief official that would lead the individual when no longer in need to report the change in his circumstances. Instead, they placed their reliance upon procedures such as that indicated in the following testimony:

However diligent an assistant overseer, or an officer for inquiry may be, there are numerous cases which will baffle his utmost diligence and sagacity; the only test of those cases is making their condition more severe than that of the lowest class of laborers who obtain their livelihood by honest industry.[305m]

Having revealed the weaknesses of the existing system and having expressed doubt about any remedy through the use of an administrative personnel, the report described the operation in certain parishes of a device that seemed to promise a solution of the problem. This device was the workhouse.

In the decade before 1832 there had been a revival of interest in a program similar to that which had been adopted in 1722, but under more efficient management. This plan as established in the parish of Southwell had been expounded in 1822 by Sir George Nicholls, then an overseer of that parish, in *Eight Letters on the Management of the Poor, by an Overseer*. Nicholls credited his ideas to the Rev. Robert Lowe, who had introduced the workhouse in the parish of Bingham. These and similar experiments had enormous influence upon the commissioners. *The Extracts from the Information Received by His Majesty's Commissioners* indicate the methods of Mr. Lowe:

Knowing that it was impossible to refuse relief according to the practice and custom of the country, he devised means for rendering relief itself so irksome and disagreeable that none would consent to receive it who could possibly do without it, while at the same time it should come in the shape of comfort and consolation to those whom every benevolent man would wish to succor—the old, infirm, idiots and cripples.

For this purpose he . . . refused all relief in kind or money, and sent every applicant and his family at once into the workhouse. The fare is meat three times a week, soup twice, pudding once, milk porridge five times.

Surely no man . . . who applies for charity has a right to complain of being placed in a clean and comfortable house, of having a good bed to sleep on, and such fare every day as I have described above; and had Mr. Lowe stopped here, matters would not have been much mended. But the applicant who entered the workhouse "on the plea that he was starving for want of work" was taken at his word, and told that these luxuries and benefits could only be given by the parish against work, and in addition that a certain regular routine was established, to which all inmates must conform. The man goes to one side of the house, the wife to the other, and the children into the school-room. Separation is steadily enforced. Their own clothes are taken off, and the uniform of the workhouse put on. No beer, tobacco, or snuff is allowed. Regular hours kept, or meals forfeited. Every one must appear in a state of personal cleanliness. No access to bed rooms during the day. No communication with friends out of doors. Breaking stones in the yard by the grate, as large a quantity required every day as an able-bodied laborer is enabled to break. . . .

The monotony, the restraint, the want of stimulants, the regularity of hours, are irksome to the pretended pauper. He bethinks himself of liberty and work, and work he will find, if there is a job undone in the parish or neighborhood within a day's walk. No man stood this discipline for three weeks. After a struggle which lasted a few months, the paupers of Bingham gave the matter up. The inmates of the workhouse dropped from forty-five to twelve, who were all either old, idiots, or infirm, and to whom a workhouse is really a place of comfort.[304a]

The commissioners are almost ecstatic about the vitalizing effect of the system upon the persons to whom it was applied. They quote J. W. Cowell, one of the assistant commissioners:

When the relief, though adequate, has been rendered ineligible—new life, new energy is infused into the constitution of the pauper; he is aroused like one from sleep, his relation with all his neighbors, high and low, is changed; he surveys his former employers with new eyes. He begs a job—he will not take a denial—he discovers that every one wants something to be done. He desires to make up this man's hedges, to clear out another man's ditches, to grub stumps out of the hedgerows for a third; nothing can escape his eye, and he is ready to turn his hand to anything.[305n]

A subsequent comment which concludes a description of the workhouse at Falmouth shows that the commissioners also believed that they had found in the institution a way of determining eligibility for relief. The italics are those of the report.

Into such a house none will enter voluntarily; work, confinement, and discipline, will deter the indolent and vicious; and nothing but extreme necessity will induce any to accept the comfort which must be obtained by the surrender of their free agency, and the sacrifice of their accustomed habits and gratifications. *Thus the parish officer, being furnished an unerring test of the necessity of applicants, is relieved from his painful and difficult responsibility; while all have the gratification of knowing that while the necessitous are abundantly relieved, the funds of charity are not wasted upon idleness and fraud.*[305o]

With the backing of such statements and accompanying evidence, the commissioners now proceeded to set forth and to apply a principle which was to dominate the administration of relief for the next seventy-five years.

It may be assumed, that in the administration of relief, the public is warranted in imposing such conditions on the individual relieved, as are conducive to the benefit either of the individual himself, or of the country at large, at whose expense he is to be relieved.

The first and most essential of all conditions, a principle which we find universally admitted, even by those whose practice is at variance with it, is, that *his situation on the whole shall not be made really or apparently so eligible as the situation of the independent laborer of the lowest class.* [Italics mine]

Throughout the evidence it is shown, that in proportion as the condition of any pauper class is elevated above the condition of independent laborers, the condition of the independent class is depressed; their industry is impaired, their employment becomes unsteady, and its remuneration in wages is diminished. Such persons, therefore, are under the strongest inducements to quit the less eligible class of laborers and enter the more eligible class of paupers. The converse is the effect when the pauper class is placed in its proper position below the condition of the independent laborer. Every penny bestowed, that tends to render the condition of the pauper more eligible than that of the independent laborer, is a bounty on indolence and vice.[305p]

This was the pronouncement that inaugurated the famous doctrine of *less eligibility*, the theory that throughout the nineteenth century and into the twentieth controlled the approach of English government to the relief of destitution. Under this theory the assistance provided for the person in need must be such as to cause his condition to be less desirable, less satisfactory—in the words of the Report of 1834, less eligible—than the condition of the lowest-paid laborer who was not in receipt of relief. Less eligibility was here established as an administrative formula.

A beginning of applying this principle was made in the first recommendation of the report:

That except as to medical attendance, and subject to the exception respecting apprenticeship hereinafter stated [The parish gave indirect relief to poor families by placing out their children as apprentices. Further study of this subject was recommended.], *all relief whatsoever to able-bodied persons or to their families, otherwise than in well regulated workhouses,* i. e., places where they may be set to work according to the spirit and intention of the 43rd of Elizabeth, *shall be declared unlawful,* and shall cease in manner and at periods hereafter specified; and that all relief afforded in respect of children under the age of 16, shall be considered as afforded to their parents.[305q] [Italics mine.]

The workhouse was thus defined as the mechanism through which the doctrine of less eligibility would be carried out. It was the device through which the life of the family on relief would be made less satisfactory than that of the lowest-paid independent laborer. The poor were now to live under the shadow of an institution which became essentially penal.

Speaking at Maidstone three years after the passage of the Poor Law amendment, Disraeli summed up the program in one sentence: "It announces to the world that in England poverty is a crime." [479a]

The report in its first recommendation had turned for a solution of the problem of relief to the past, adopting, with nineteenth-century modifications, the system of a century before. The second recommendation, however, faced toward the future:

We recommend the appointment of a central board to control the administration of the poor-laws with such assistant commissioners as may be found requisite; and that the Commissioners be empowered and directed to frame and enforce regulations for the government of workhouses, and as to the nature and amount of relief to be given and the labor to be exacted in them, and that such regulations shall, as far as may be practicable, be uniform throughout the country.[305r]

Additional recommendations gave this central board power to combine parishes for the establishment and management of workhouses; to promote the provision of a paid, permanent, local personnel for relief administration; to set up qualifications for such personnel; to recommend candidates and to remove parish officials who might prove to be unfit; to appoint its own personnel; to establish a system of uniform accounting; to prosecute local relief officials guilty of misappropriation of funds and other maladministration; to report annually to one of the principal secretaries of state with an account of its proceedings and recommendations for improvements, accompanied by appropriate bills for introduction into Parliament.[305s]

These recommendations, all of which were subsequently enacted into law, represented a major revolution in the administration of public assistance, and, except for the authority exercised in a much less organized way by the Privy Council of the sixteenth and early seventeenth century, comprised a new concept in governmental operation in relation to the care of the poor. After more than two hundred years of the most extreme form of localism, England thus set herself in the direction of national supervision and of larger administrative units.

When one thinks of the jealousies and fears of national authority existing in any local community, these recommendations of the Commission of 1832–34 and their translation into law become the more amazing. It was an indication of the extent of the universal dissatisfaction of the public with the administration of relief and an evidence also of the skill of the commissioners in interpreting their program.

There were additional recommendations by the Commission looking to the simplification of the laws of settlement, making certain changes in those relating to illegitimacy and suggesting further study of the question of apprenticing of children by the parish as a means of relief; but the basic recommendations of the report were those calling for (1) the refusal of relief to the able-bodied except through the workhouse, and (2) the establishment of the central board with its powers as already indicated, in particular the authority to effect combinations of parishes for the operation of workhouses.

Larger operating areas would make classification possible. The report suggested four categories:

1. The aged and really impotent
2. The children
3. The able-bodied females
4. The able-bodied males. Of whom we trust that the two latter will be the least numerous classes. It appears to us that both the requisite classification and the requisite superintendence may be better obtained in separate buildings than under a single roof. If effected in the latter mode, large buildings must be erected, since few of the existing buildings are of the requisite size or arrangement, and, as very different qualities, both moral and intellectual, are required for the management of such dissimilar classes, each class must have its separate superintendent.[305t]

The report placed the burden of destitution upon the shoulders of the individual. Poverty was regarded as essentially an indication of moral fault in the person requiring relief. He was held very little short of exclusively responsible for his condition.

Whatever inquiries have been made as to the previous condition of the able-bodied individuals who live in such numbers on the town parishes, it has been found that the pauperism of the greater number has originated in indolence, improvidence, or vice, and might have been averted by ordinary care and industry. The smaller number consisted of cases where the cause of poverty could not be ascertained rather than of cases where it was apparent that destitution had arisen from blameless want.[305u]

The idea of a social obligation was not conceived in the thought of the times. The total absence of anything of a positive nature in the report of 1834 was noticeable even to its authors, as is evident from the words with which they conclude their recommendations:

It will be observed, that the measures which we have suggested are intended to produce rather negative than positive effects; rather to remove the debasing influences to which a large portion of the laboring population is now subject, than to afford new means of prosperity and virtue. We are perfectly aware, that for the general diffusion of right principles and habits we are to look, not so much to any economic arrangements and regulations as to the influence of a moral and religious education. . . . But one great advantage of any measure which shall remove or diminish the evils of the present system, is, that it will in the same degree remove the obstacles which now impede the progress of instruction, and intercept its results; and will afford a freer scope to the operation of every instrument which may be employed for elevating the intellectual and moral condition of the poorer classes.[305v]

The extent to which this philosophy was the philosophy of the times and the degree to which the commissioners had rallied public opinion to the program they had built upon it are indicated by the fact that all their basic recommendations were translated into law. The report was signed on February 20, 1834. The bill embodying its program was introduced in Parliament on April 17 and passed on August 13, receiving the Royal Assent the following day.[49] August 14 is a day of significance in the history of governmental attempts to deal with the problem of insecurity: August 14, 1834—the recommendations of the Royal Commission's Report are enacted into law; August 14, 1935—the President of the United States signs the Social Security Act; August 14, 1941—the President of the United States and the Prime Minister of England sign the Atlantic Charter.

The Report of 1834 stands as an illustration of the success of a Commission that knew what it wanted and knew how to get what it wanted. The commissioners were determined to put an end to outdoor relief for the able-bodied, and to do away with, or at least to curb, parish administration of assistance through the substitution of larger local units combined with a national system of supervision. This they accomplished in a study that concentrated upon the point to be proven. Through an astute use of the printing press and of country-wide yet intensive contacts by their investigators and interviewers, they convinced a public already more than open to conviction of the desirability of the program they proposed.

XIII

A NEW ADMINISTRATION OF RELIEF

Said Egremont, slightly smiling, "but, say what you like, our Queen reigns over the greatest nation that ever existed."

"Which nation?" asked the younger stranger, "for she reigns over two."

The stranger paused; Egremont was silent, but looked inquiringly.

"Yes," resumed the younger stranger after a moment's interval. "Two nations; between whom there is no intercourse and no sympathy; who are as ignorant of each other's habits, thoughts, and feelings, as if they were dwellers in different zones, or inhabitants of different planets; who are formed by a different breeding, are fed by a different food, are ordered by different manners, and are not governed by the same laws."

"You speak of—," said Egremont, hesitatingly.

"The Rich and the Poor."

BENJAMIN DISRAELI, *Sybil*, 1845.[434a]

THE combination of popular interest and civic leadership which had swept the recommendations of the Poor Law Report into speedy legislative enactment continued to exert its stimulating influence during the period in which the organization provided for in the new Statute was being established. On August 23, 1834, nine days after the bill became law, the three Poor Law commissioners forming the central supervisory board were appointed. The same day they chose the secretary and assistant secretary of the Commission.

All five appointees—the three commissioners and the two secretaries—represented a high degree of competence and intelligence. Two of the commissioners were broadly informed about the subject of relief. Thomas Frankland Lewis, with at that time twenty-two years of service in the House of Commons, had been an active and leading member of a committee of the House on the Poor Laws in 1817, the most important committee on the subject prior to the Royal Commission of 1832–34. Sir George Nicholls, retired sea captain and bank manager, had for two years been an overseer of the poor. As author of *Eight Letters on the Management of the Poor*, he had established himself in public estimation as an authority upon the subject. The third member, John George Shaw-LeFevre, was a career man in government with those intellectual and cultural attainments which, when in strategic position, greatly advance the character of public policy and operation. The secretary, Edwin Chadwick, was co-author with Nassau W. Senior of the Report of 1834; and the assistant secretary, George Coode, a young barrister, was later to publish an important contribution to the subject of settlement. The party in power had recognized the importance of the Commission's task and had selected the administrators with regard only for their ability. This policy was also applied to the appointment of the whole professional staff which, remarkably enough in those days of almost universal patronage, was left entirely to the central board.

By December 1, 1834, the board had secured the nine assistant commissioners—a few months later increased to fifteen—which it had been empowered to employ.[321b] The calibre of these assistant commissioners and the similarity of their service to what in state and federal relief administration in the United States would be called "field representatives," is indicated by Sidney and Beatrice Webb who speak of

these ten to twenty well-paid gentlemen—with liberal traveling expenses but without a uniform, and without honorific status of any kind, without any executive duties or any nominal authority, but merely spending their whole time in quietly journeying from one Union to another; annually visiting, sometimes more than once, the ordinary meetings of each Board of Guardians; frequently conferring privately with the Clerk, and occasionally with the Chairman or other influential member; inspecting the Workhouse and the Separate School or other Poor Law institution of each Union; never giving orders but everywhere explaining and advising, discussing problems and smoothing out difficulties. . . coming to the Unions, not as executive officers of superior rank—not even as officers of the same Authority as that to which the Clerk to the Guardians or the Workhouse Master owed their appointments—but merely as consultants and visitors, entitled to advise just as they were authorized to enter, but not empowered to give any order whatsoever, and not even to institute proceedings for breaches of the law.[507a]

With the help of this personnel the newly appointed commissioners quickly accomplished the bulk of the task of combining parishes. Within three years 13,264 parishes, 90 per cent of the number to which the law in this particular applied, had formed themselves into 568 unions.

Equally speedy was the reduction in expenditures for relief which accompanied the introduction of the new administration. By 1837, the cost of public assistance had been cut by more than one-third as compared with 1834, the last fiscal year before the new law went into effect.[481c]

The period during which these reductions took place was for the most part one of good times. Nevertheless, there is reason to believe that the program inaugurated by the Poor Law commissioners was to a large extent responsible for the decrease in the relief rolls. The Second Annual Report of the Commissioners states the case:

There are persons who imagine that the prosperous state of the country would have gone far to produce the results we have exhibited without the aid of the new law. . . . We do not deny that the progress of the change we have described has been highly favored by the prosperous condition of the manufacturing districts, by the cheapness of provisions, and by the general demand for labor. . . . But it must not be forgotten that in whole districts, whilst provisions were as cheap as they have ever been of late years, and whilst the demand for employment was progressive, pauperism nevertheless continued to increase. The application of the measures at different periods of the two last years, at times when employment has been slack, and in places where distress has been the subject of loud complaint, has been attended with the usual average of beneficial results, results differing only in degree.[322a]

All experience in relief administration would substantiate the claims of the Poor Law commissioners. Into a period of better times they had introduced a new factor. That new factor was a concept of administration based on formulated policies. The punitive and repressive aspect of these policies was not new. That had existed for years—indeed almost universally throughout almost all the history of relief. What the Poor Law commissioners did was to translate current attitudes and standards into concrete principles and procedures according to which the appropriate officials acted. Their administrative devices may have been both cruel and crude as in the case of the workhouse; they may have been, in relation to the circumstances, sound, as in the shift from the allowance in support of wages. The essential point so far as the effect on the relief rolls is concerned was the emphasis upon careful administration and, as has been indicated, upon the formulation of policy and procedure. That the commissioners should have come into power immediately after years of hit-or-miss, slovenly, and even dishonest operation made all the more possible a dramatic result.

The Commission had, as a basis for commencing operations, the mandate of the report of 1834—the principle of less eligibility and no relief to the able-bodied outside the workhouse. The new law itself was not specific. It merely gave the central board authority to make rules and regulations. This left the real decision with the commissioners and they immediately found themselves in a dilemma, which twelve years later they describe:

While a wide discretion with respect to the control of relief has been vested in the commissioners, a great discordance of opinion prevails in the public, even in Parliament, as to the manner in which that control ought to be exercised. . . .

The Commissioners have been placed between two extreme opinions with respect to the manner of framing their regulations.

On the one hand, it is held that the main object of the Poor Law Amendment Act is the extinction or repression of outdoor relief generally and not merely of outdoor relief to the ablebodied, with the consequent diminution of the expenditure from the poor's rate; and that the Commissioners ought to proceed to the accomplishment of this end with little regard to public opinion.

On the other hand, it is asserted that the existing law and the regulations made under it have gone much too far in the limitation of outdoor relief to the ablebodied, have effected too great a reduction in the amount of pauperism and the expenditure for the relief of the poor, *and have thereby deprived the poorer classes of a vested right in the property of the rate-paying part of the community.* [Italics mine.]

The Commissioners have pursued a middle course equally removed from each of these extremes. They have considered the main object of the Legislature, in passing the Poor Law Amendment Act, to have been the extinction of the *allowance* system or the system of making up the wages of laborers out of the poor's rate. With this view their regulations respecting the limitation of outdoor relief have been almost exclusively confined to the ablebodied in health, and these regulations have been issued particularly to the rural unions; inasmuch as it was in the agricultural counties, and not in the large towns or manufacturing districts, that the allowance system was most prevalent, and led to the most dangerous consequences.[309a]

The commissioners began the program upon which they had thus determined by issuing to individual unions the following instructions about relief:

Firstly. No relief shall be given in money (except in cases of sickness or accident) to any ablebodied male pauper who is in employment (the same not being parish work), and in the receipt of earnings; nor to any part of his family who shall be dependent upon him, or for whose relief and maintenance he shall be liable.

Secondly. If any ablebodied male pauper shall apply to be set to work by the Parish, one half at least of the relief which may be afforded to him or to his family shall be in kind.

Thirdly. One half at least of the relief which may be afforded to widows or single women, not being aged or infirm, shall be in kind.[321c]

While these instructions were being issued, the commissioners were actively extending the system of workhouses. In the first three years they had authorized the erection of more than two hundred of these institutions and in addition had recommended the renovation and enlargement of a number of the existing establishments.

The policy of the Commission was simple and clear. Outdoor relief would be forbidden to able-bodied men. Assistance granted in return for parish work, or to women who were not aged and infirm, would be made less eligible by being given in kind. As rapidly as a sufficient number of workhouses could be developed, the chief reliance for the practice of the principle of less eligibility would be centered in them. They were to be operated in such a way as to make the condition of the person obliged to seek assistance less satisfactory than that of the independent laborer. The theory and its application were stated by the commissioners as follows:

The fundamental principle with respect to the legal relief of the poor is, that the condition of the pauper ought to be, on the whole, less eligible than that of the independent laborer. . . .

In order, therefore, to carry the above-mentioned principle into effect, it is necessary that the pauper should be relieved, not by giving him money or goods to be sent or consumed in his own house, but by receiving him into a public establishment. But a public establishment, if properly arranged necessarily secures to its inmates a larger amount of bodily comforts than is enjoyed by an ordinary independent laborer in his own dwelling. For example, an inmate of a well appointed union workhouse lives in rooms more spacious, better ventilated, and better warmed; his meals are better and more regularly served; he is more warmly clad, and he is better attended in sickness than if he were in his own cottage. . . .

The only expedient, therefore, for accomplishing the end in view, which humanity permits, is to subject the pauper inmate of a public institution to such a system of labor, discipline, and restraint, as shall be sufficient to outweigh, in his estimation, the advantages which he derives from the bodily comfort he enjoys.[307a]

The proposal of the original Commission of Inquiry in 1834 had been for a classification of inmates, preferably through the erection of separate buildings. As we have seen, four categories were suggested: (1) the aged and really impotent, (2) the children, (3) the able-bodied females, (4) the able-bodied males.

This suggestion the Poor Law commissioners disregarded. They did not establish separate buildings but put everybody—young, old, feebleminded, ill, able-bodied, and mentally diseased—into the same structure. At the same time, applying a penal discipline, they broke up the family, assigning its members to separate parts of the institution.

The able-bodied man who asked for relief was told that the only way in which he and his family could be assisted was through the workhouse. The boys between seven and thirteen years of age were sent to one ward; the girls to another; the father and his sons above thirteen years went to one dormitory, and the mother and the girls over thirteen to a different dormitory; children under seven were kept in a nursery, the mothers being "permitted to have access to them at all reasonable times." Finally if there were grandparents in the home they would be sent to the wards reserved for aged and infirm, the husband and wife being of course separated.[321d]

Under this system of having one building for everybody it would be difficult to achieve the situation described in the report of 1834 as being in force at Bingham, where the workhouse had been administered so that it might be a

means for rendering relief so irksome and disagreeable that none would consent to receive it who could possibly do without it, while at the same time it should come in the shape of comfort and consolation to those whom every benevolent man would wish to succor—the old, infirm, idiots and cripples.[304a]

The Poor Law commissioners apparently disposed of this dilemma by leaning on the side of the "irksome and disagreeable" for everybody, old as well as young, infirm as well as able-bodied. Their theory, as stated, was that

If the condition of the inmates of a workhouse were to be so regulated as to invite the aged and infirm of the laboring classes to take refuge in it, it would immediately be useless as a test between indigence or fraud.

It would no longer operate as an inducement to the young and healthy to provide support for their latter years or as a stimulus to them, whilst they have the means, to support their aged parents and relatives. The frugality and forethought of a young laborer would be useless if he foresaw the certainty of a better asylum for his old age than he could possibly provide by his own exertions; and the industrious efforts of a son to provide a maintenance for his parents in his own dwelling would be thrown away, and would cease to be called forth, if the almshouse of the district offered a refuge for their declining years, in which they might obtain comforts and indulgences which even the most successful of the laboring classes cannot always obtain by their own exertions.[307b]

While the commissioners were not willing to relax the penal discipline of the workhouse in favor of the aged and infirm, they did not in the early years of the administration attempt to apply the principle of less eligibility in dealing with old people who were receiving relief in their own homes.

The procedure followed in general by the central board was to negotiate with individual unions on the basis of announced policies. Orders were issued union by union, prohibiting assistance to the able-bodied outside the workhouse and covering the other items of the program. These individual orders were later consolidated in what was called the Outdoor Relief Prohibitory Order. This Order, dated December 21, 1844, provided that

every able-bodied person, male or female, requiring relief from any parish within any of the said unions shall be relieved only in the workhouse of the union, together with such of the family of every such able-bodied person as may be resident with him or her, and may not be in employment, and together with the wife of every such able-bodied person, if he be a married man, and if she be resident with him.[101]

The Order lists 465 unions to which it applies, not far from 90 per cent of the total number of unions then organized. The prohibition, however, was not so complete as might appear. The Order contained exceptions as, for example, in the case of "sudden and urgent necessity," "sickness, accident or bodily or mental infirmity," "where such person being a widow shall be in the first six months of her widow-hood," "where the widow has a legitimate child or children and no illegitimate child born after her widowhood." [101]

The provision that where "sudden and urgent necessity" developed, the regulation compelling assistance through the offer of the work-house might be disregarded, was the safety valve in the program as far as the able-bodied were concerned. It offered a way out for those parts of England, chiefly the urban and industrial areas, where the workhouse proved to be most unpopular and where public opinion was strong enough to modify the actions of the commissioners who did not attempt to treat all England and Wales alike, but instead ad-justed the imposition of their policies to the particular territory in-volved and to the conditions of the times.

The economic improvement that had taken place in 1835 and 1836 when the Commission got under way began to shade off in 1837, and headed down to a deep depression in 1842 with widespread distress. The workhouse was inadequate to the need. A number of unions ini-tiated, with the reluctant consent of the central board, what became known as the Labor Yard. Here men were employed at various tasks —picking oakum, cutting wood, and breaking stone. They and their families continued to live in their own homes. The amount and char-acter of the work required differed according to the particular unions involved, some calling for light employment and others for the hard-est kind of labor. The plan came into increasing use; and during the first part of 1843, when there was much destitution, forty thousand men were employed in this way.

While the Labor Yard was designed only for emergencies and for the unusual demands of hard times, once it was established it tended to remain, providing a way of avoiding the workhouse. For this very reason the commissioners did not approve of it but were obliged to yield to local demand. They issued to certain unions that preferred a work test outside the institution what was called the Outdoor Labor Test Order. It stipulated that "Half at least of the relief . . . shall be given in food, clothing, and other articles of necessity." No employed person should receive relief. The only employment permitted was that supplied by the guardians of the union.[102]

While this Order presumably applied to unions where the Outdoor Relief Prohibitory Order was not in force, it was also issued to certain unions which were operating under that Order. As time passed the number of these double-order unions increased, bringing a relaxation of the strict and exclusive use of the workhouse. There were unions, particularly in London and other urban and industrial cities, which would not refuse all relief to the able-bodied in their own homes; and for them the commissioners found themselves advocating the provision of work outside the workhouse, a measure about which they were most dubious but which they felt was better than an unconditional relief.

In 1852 an Outdoor Relief Regulation Order was issued for such unions. Under this instruction at least one-half of the relief to the able-bodied must be in food or fuel or in other articles of necessity. The guardians were not permitted to set up a relief applicant in business or to purchase tools for him or to pay his rent. Every able-bodied male receiving relief must be put to work by the union.[103]

The provision, in both the Relief Regulation Order and the Outdoor Labor Test Order, that half of any relief to the able-bodied must be in kind was introduced largely as a form of less eligibility. While it is probable that giving assistance partially in provisions and other articles of necessity was an attempt to make sure that the family received what the commissioners thought it needed, the underlying motive was to make the person who was obliged to accept assistance different from the independent laborer. Relief in kind helped to mark him as pauper. It was hoped that such unattractive relief would reduce the number of applicants.

Despite all these efforts, however, Sir George Nicholls felt that the Poor Law commissioners had been unsuccessful. Reviewing the period from 1840 to 1848, he complained that

With the exception of 1844–45 and 1845–46, in which years some reaction took place, there had been a continual increase in the numbers relieved both in and out of the workhouse throughout the whole period, and that the largest increase had taken place in the last two years. The indoor poor amount only to about one-sixth of the entire number relieved, a proportion the reverse of what was anticipated at the passing of the Amendment Act, 1834, when the extinction of out-door relief was reckoned upon, or at least was expected to be so far reduced as to form the exception, instead of being, as we now see it, rather the rule. . . .

To put an end to out-door relief, or even to reduce it to about an equality with the in-door, became a matter rather to be desired than expected.[481d]

Nicholls, judged by his own standards, was more pessimistic than he need have been. While it is true that relief expenditures in 1848 were only 2 per cent less than in 1834, 1848 was a bad year. A more comparable year would have been 1853, the last year that Nicholls covers in his history; and then the expenditures were 20 per cent less than in 1834 despite an increase of nearly 25 per cent in the population. The principle of less eligibility, reinforced by the workhouse, had paid in pounds sterling if one looks only at the direct outlay for relief. Whether the saving was worth the cost in health and human welfare at a time when the wealth of England was increasing enormously is another question.

The program of the report of 1834 and of the Poor Law commissioners appointed to put it into effect was a stern one. The commissioners paid for their belief in it by suffering great unpopularity and abuse. "They were accused of being heartless tyrants," I am quoting from Nicholls, "unfeeling theorists, 'concentrated icicles'; and were commonly designated as the 'three bashaws of Somerset House.' " [481e] There was bitter opposition from the industrial sections, where the workhouse was spoken of as the "bastille" and where the first attempts to introduce it were met with rioting.

In his *Farmer's Tour through the East of England*, Arthur Young wrote about what he considered to be the poverty-causing evil of tea drinking. He referred to people with whom he discussed this question as being "for or against the poor in their arguments." [509a] The workers of England in the second quarter of the nineteenth century maintained that the Poor Law Commission was "against the poor" and fought it on every occasion. In addition, there were the protests of humanitarians like Charles Dickens, whose *Oliver Twist* appeared serially in 1837 and 1838. His descriptions of the workhouse and its officials, from which most popular impressions in the United States about that institution have been derived, had no apparent effect upon the system. At the time of his death in 1870 the Poor Law was commencing a revival of the strict measures which had been inaugurated a generation before.

The opposition to the commissioners was not, however, confined to labor and the humanitarians. Parliament was suspicious. At the start, in 1834, it had been willing to give only five years of life to the Commission. For a generation thereafter it would not grant a continuation of more than five years, and several times the extension was only a year. The commissioners were frequently attacked in the House. There were many Parliamentary investigations, the first being a select committee of the House appointed within two and a half years of the creation of the Commission. This committee reported favorably in 1837 and again in 1838, but that did not stop the debate, which was inherent not only in the policy of the administrators but in the nature of relief itself. That which provides for people who cannot provide for themselves will always be under attack either from those who are "for" or from those who are "against the poor in their arguments."

It was power as well as policy that people opposed in the commissioners. As the first central body to supervise local relief authorities, the Commission was mistrusted and feared. There was much talk about the dangerous centralization of control. For a long time the commissioners were not allowed to employ and pay the auditors who were to inspect the books of the boards of guardians which it was the duty of the Commission to oversee. All general regulations issued to the unions required the approval of Parliament, which was one reason why in the early years instructions were issued to the unions individually.

Capping the difficulties of the commissioners was a struggle inside their own organization. The secretary, Edwin Chadwick, to whom England owed not only much of the Poor Law reform of 1834 but also, through his later activities, the commencement of the whole public health movement, was an uncompromising person who had definite ideas about how the principles of the original Commission of Inquiry should be carried out. He also disagreed with the commissioners in their methods of operation, and he played every political card he knew to change the nature of the activities of the Commission. His attacks and those inspired by recalcitrant boards of guardians frequently entered into the sessions of Parliament.

Under such fire the Commission was greatly handicapped because, unlike most British governmental bodies, it had no official spokesman in the membership of the House of Commons. To achieve this and perhaps also to silence criticism, the commissioners secured their own decease. Parliament legislated them out and in their place, in 1847, established the Poor Law Board—still, however, on a temporary basis —with a president who had a seat in the House and four ex-officio members from the government.[51] The Board never met. It operated as any other department of English national government, with not infrequently one of its successive chiefs a member of the Cabinet.

The Poor Law Board did not exhibit the fire that characterized the Poor Law commissioners, who had taken office while the spirit of reform was about them and who had the enthusiasm of the inaugurators of a new enterprise. The Poor Law Board was content to concern itself with the letter of its mandate. While it had great power, the power was that of rule-making, not that of direct administration. The Board could give orders but it did not have responsibility for carrying them out. That was the task of the boards of guardians of the unions.

Lacking the creative urge with which the Poor Law commissioners had been inspired, it allowed its leadership to lag. Increasingly the local boards of guardians did as they pleased. They required little time after their election to begin to feel jealous of anything that seemed to infringe upon their powers or that seemed to interfere with home rule. This was particularly true of the persons who took office after the first enthusiasm of the movement had passed. The original members of the boards of guardians were often the kind of individuals whose presence gave prestige to the position. Later, as the dramatic edge of the undertaking dulled, people of lesser calibre sought the office for the prestige which it meant to them. They were correspondingly shortsighted in the selection of executive and operating staff, being moved by personal if not political patronage and by their immediate private interest. Whatever the high principles and aims with which some of the boards started, many of them by the middle of the century were no better than the parish overseers whom they had superseded.

The boards of guardians had succumbed to the petty and close-visioned qualities of localism, and the national body had contented itself with little more than a painstaking insistence upon the formalities of procedure. Between these two manifestations of deterioration in governmental administration, local and national, the Poor Law became more and more callous in its application. What in 1852 Robert Pashley had written in his book upon *Pauperism and Poor Laws* as comment upon the recent past, might equally have applied as prophecy of the immediate future:

All the essential evils of our poor laws are still unmitigated, or, at the most, have been very slightly mitigated, by the Act of 1834; and we now find that during the long years between 1834 and 1852, Poor Law Commissioners, and Presidents of the Poor Law Board, have been successively employed in the mere labor of Sisyphus and that the stone which they have been condemned to turn, has become heavier and heavier, with the efforts of each successive year.[484a]

XIV

THE ORGANIZATION OF CHARITY

It is much cheaper and pleasanter to be reformed by the devil than by God; for God will only reform society on the condition of our reforming every man his own self—while the devil is quite ready to help us mend the laws and the parliament, earth and heaven, without ever starting such an impertinent and "personal" request, as that a man should mend himself.

[CHARLES KINGSLEY], PARSON LOT,
"Letters to Chartists," No. 1, 1848.[463a]

As the nineteenth century advanced in its second half, dissatisfaction with the operation of the Poor Law increased. While there were many persons who shared the belief of Sir George Nicholls that the administration of relief was not strict enough, there was a considerable number of people who thought that the Poor Law was unjustifiably harsh.

Some of this feeling expressed itself in an accession of philanthropic activity. Ever since 1834 there had been an expanding but miscellaneous flow of charity, both personal and organizational, stimulated by the desire to save people from the workhouse and the other rigorous features of public relief. In the winter of 1860–61 this charitable flow became a flood.

It was a time of great distress among the poor, particularly in London. The weather was extremely cold, with heavy freezings and snowfalls sufficient to stop many outdoor industries. People who never before had applied for relief were obliged to ask the boards of guardians for help. They were confronted by an inflexible officialdom that conceived no other way of meeting the emergency than through the offer of the workhouse. This, many of the new applicants refused. They preferred, as was reported later to a committee of the House of Commons, starvation to confinement in the prison-like institution.

That part of the public which had long been rebellious against the methods of the Poor Law Board and the guardians was shocked by what it heard and saw. Letters were written to the newspapers, some of which opened their columns to public subscription. Many people sent contributions to the magistrates whose offices were thronged with persons in need, and there was a great amount of direct help by individuals to families whose destitution was brought to their attention. A number of philanthropic agencies were organized, most important among them the London Society for the Relief of Distress which enlisted the services of civic-minded people who wanted to do something immediate and personal to alleviate suffering.

Hardly had the winter of 1860–61 passed than the cotton famine that resulted from the Civil War in the United States began to cause unemployment. It was a special situation affecting most directly those parts of England which were predominantly textile in their manufactories. Not only did it necessitate increased relief expenditures by government, but it called forth large funds in private contributions. In the twenty-eight Poor Law unions where the need was greatest and where the boards of guardians in the three years ending March 25, 1864, had doubled their appropriations, philanthropy more than matched the additional expenditures.

In 1866, after a period of heavy speculation, England sank into a business depression that brought unemployment and serious distress. Again the generously minded responded with gifts of money and personal service. Individual and organizational activity increased, and the Poor Law was dwarfed in the minds of many people when compared with this development of private charity.

Then at the end of the sixties a reaction set in. It began in London where philanthropic activity had been greatest. Just as in the years preceding 1834 there had been dissatisfaction with the administration of the parochial overseers, so now one-third of a century later there was criticism from a large and influential part of the ruling class, not only of the operation of public relief but of the way in which private charity was being managed.

The same lack of system which a generation before the Commission on the Poor Laws had found in parish relief was now discovered to characterize the activities of private charity. The Rev. John Richard Green, author and historian, in an article on pauperism in the East End of London published in the *Saturday Review* of December 28, 1867, described the situation as he saw it from his parish:

The greater number of the East End clergy have converted themselves into relieving officers. Sums of enormous magnitude are annually collected and dispensed by them either personally or through district visitors, nine-tenths of whom are women, and the bulk silly and ignorant women. A hundred different agencies for the relief of distress are at work over the same ground, without concert or cooperation, or the slightest information as to each other's exertions. The result is an unparalleled growth of imposition, mendicancy, and sheer shameless pauperism.[447a]

The parallel with 1834 continues. Then it had been a feeling of the need for national supervision; now it was a desire for some sort of coördination of metropolitan activities. There was also the conviction that the current state of affairs was disregarding the most fundamental laws of society. To the philosophy of laissez faire which still dominated the intellectual life of England, there had come a dramatic reinforcement from the field of natural science. In 1859 Darwin had published his *Origin of Species,* and by the end of the sixties the theory of the survival of the fittest had become a doctrine which many enthusiasts applied to human economy as well as to the biologic world. Was philanthropy only perpetuating weakness and degeneracy?

Translated into a method of dealing with poverty, this meant the less of relief the better. The point of view of contemporary critics is excellently illustrated by the diagnosis to be found in *Pauperism: Its Causes and Remedies,* a book published in 1871, based upon a series of lectures delivered at Cambridge by Henry Fawcett, professor of political economy in the University, a member of Parliament, and later, despite the handicap of blindness, Postmaster General of England.

One chief cause of poverty is that too much is done for those who make no proper effort to help themselves, and thus improvidence in its various forms is encouraged. . . .

Additions are constantly being made to the list of those things which people ought to do for themselves, but which they desire others to do for them. One of the latest examples is the demand, which so many of the working-classes are now making, that parents should not be required to pay for their children's education, but that all schools should be free. It will be found that these demands simply show how many there are who will always try to escape from the responsibility of their own acts. The extent to which they are permitted to do this will in no small degree determine the amount of poverty and misery which will exist in a country.[486a]

The feeling of the times went further than the position thus expressed by Professor Fawcett. To the middle class which dominated

England, poverty was almost a form of sin. Nearly everybody was influenced by the opportunity for material success that a world in full possession of the machine seemed to offer to any man. The entrepreneur who at the beginning of the century had experienced such a remarkable rise to riches was enlisting the resources of other elements in the community. The middle and upper classes and even many of the workers were investing in the stocks of a widely expanding industry.[428a]

Everybody appeared to be making and saving money. The possession of property, real or personal, was widespread enough to be regarded as an evidence of hard work, thrift, intelligence, and character, while its absence was an indication of serious wrong in the individual. The man who had not saved, irrespective of whether he had the means to do so, was classed with the person who was immoral. There was always a reference to the worthy yet unfortunate exception, but it was only the reservation in statement that ordinary prudence demanded, not anything that had very definite reality for the speaker. People were poor because they refused to profit by the abundant opportunities to improve their condition. Thrift and virtue, thriftlessness and immorality were synonymous. To be destitute to the point of having to ask for relief was to be guilty of a defect in character—in short, to be in need of reform.

Paralleling this belief was a strong and growing movement for personal service among the poor. This movement first appeared as an expression of the sympathy which religious and intellectual leaders had felt for the defeated Chartists. When in 1848 the efforts of the workers to obtain the suffrage and an active share in government had collapsed, J. M. Ludlow, a lawyer, a devout churchman, and a social reformer, together with Frederick Denison Maurice and Charles Kingsley, both clergymen of the Church of England, began advocating the spiritual development of the individual and an association with his fellows in coöperative production as the way of securing the improvement in social conditions which labor had unsuccessfully attempted to attain through the achievement of political rights. To this particular philosophy, Maurice in 1850 had given the name Christian Socialism. The enterprises in coöperative production which he and his associates sponsored did not accomplish what their promoters had hoped. Most of them ended in failure after a few years; but the cause of Christian Socialism attracted an influential group of young men to service among the poor. In 1854 Maurice established the Working Men's College in the East End of London. To its faculty came volunteers from campus and from church.

"The teaching," writes his son and biographer, "had been of a kind that many an older well-endowed educational body would have been lucky to secure." It included such men as John Ruskin, Lowes Dickinson, D. G. Rossetti, Burne-Jones, Thomas Huxley, and many other leaders in art, literature, and science. "A continual fresh stream of young men from the University" [476a] followed these pioneers, establishing an avenue of association with the workers. This movement to the East End of London was reinforced by the activities of other individuals who believed in the power of personal influence to help the laboring classes, particularly if that influence was exercised by men and women of superior economic and cultural background. There was a growing number of people who saw a need in society itself for the spiritual benefits that would be derived from a closer association of rich and poor. The two nations over which Disraeli had said the Queen ruled might thus become one.

A decade later, under the spur of the distress of the sixties, there followed in the tradition of Ludlow, Maurice, and Kingsley a young man whose activities on behalf of the poor caught the imagination of England. At the beginning of the distress that followed the business depression of 1866, Edward Denison had volunteered his services as an almoner of the Society for the Relief of Distress. After a few months he felt so strongly the futility of what he was doing that he resigned his volunteer post and went to live in Stepney in the East End of London. Here in the winter of 1867–68 he taught at night in an informal kind of worker's education and also conducted classes in the Bible. He left Stepney to enter Parliament, and died in 1870 when he was only thirty years old.

Despite his youth he exerted a wide influence upon philanthropy. That the son of a bishop of the Church of England should have given up the comforts of his home to take lodgings in the East End gave a special flavor to what he said. His maiden speech in Parliament, his articles in newspapers, and his letters found a responsive audience, extending later to the United States, when his writings were brought together and published under the editorship of Sir Baldwyn Leighton, himself an active exponent of Poor Law reform.

The Rev. John Richard Green, who helped Denison to establish himself in the East End, tells about his work, describing him as a "Brother of the Poor":

The poor soon came to understand the man who was as liberal with his sympathy as he was chary of meat and coal tickets, who only aimed at being their friend, at listening to their troubles, and aiding them with counsel, as if he were one of themselves, at putting them in the way of honest work, at teaching their children, at protecting them with a perfect courage and chivalry against oppression and wrong.[448a]

What Denison saw in 1867–68, and how he felt and thought about it, is indicated in such comments as these:

Now about this East of London. What is so bad in it is, not what "jumps at the eyes," as the French say. No; this summer there is not so very much actual suffering for want of food, nor from sickness. What is so bad is the habitual condition of this mass of humanity—its uniform mean level, the absence of anything more civilizing than a grinding organ to raise the ideas beyond the daily bread and beer, the utter want of education, the complete indifference of religion, with the fruits of all this, viz., improvidence, dirt, and their secondaries, crime and disease. . . .

The people create their destitution and their disease. Probably there are hardly any of the most needy who, if they had been only moderately frugal and provident, could not have placed themselves in a position to tide over the occasional months of want of work or of sickness, which there always must be. And this occasional pressure is what works the ruin. The breadwinner falls sick, or is out of work, for a few months; the home is broken up; the hospital or the workhouse swallows up the family; the thread of life is broken—perhaps they have been removed to a distance from former employers—at any rate life has to be begun again right from the bottom. Is it wonderful that drink and crime levy a large conscription on these wretches while the remnant subside into dirt and deep despondency? . . .

I am beginning seriously to believe that all bodily aid to the poor is a mistake, and that the real thing is to let things work themselves straight; whereas by giving them alms you keep them permanently crooked.

Build schoolhouses, pay teachers, give prizes, frame workmen's clubs, help them to help themselves, lend them your brains; but give them no money, except what you sink in such undertakings as above. . . .

How many thousands of paupers have lived and died, and been buried at the public expense, whom a little friendly advice, a little search for friends or relations, some pains taken to find proper work, when the first application to the Board was made, would have lifted out of the mire and set on the rock of honest industry!

I think no one endowed with a moderate amount of common sense and of information can doubt that the time for systematizing charity has come 'or is close at hand. The question is how to do it.[433a]

While Denison was working in the East End of London, one of his contemporaries had begun another attack upon the problem of poverty. That Octavia Hill should have been interested in the poor is not surprising. She was the granddaughter of Dr. Southwood Smith, who had been associated with Edwin Chadwick in the beginning of the public health movement in England and who also with Chadwick had been a member of a royal commission which in 1833 reported on the regulation of child labor. At fourteen years of age she came under the influence of Frederick Denison Maurice and the Christian Socialists. John Ruskin was an intimate friend, and philanthropy was the atmosphere and conversation of her home.

She had become convinced that improved housing might be a means of personal reform for the poor. In 1864, with the financial help of Ruskin, she had begun a project of renovating slum dwellings for the purpose of renting them to families with low incomes. In this connection she organized a corps of rent collectors, believing that this activity would give women of culture an opportunity to help the families of the poor to better ways of life.

She shared with Denison the feeling that the poor were responsible for their poverty:

I believe our irregular alms to the occupant of the miserable room, to the shoeless flower-seller, are tending to keep a whole class on the very brink of pauperism who might be taught self-control and foresight if we would let them learn it. . . .

The street-sellers and low class desultory workers usually remain what they are by choice; a little self-control would raise them into the ranks of those who are really wanted, and who have made their way from the brink of pauperism to a securer place, and one where they are under better influences. Above all is this true of the children.

A little self-control would enable the daughters of most of these people to rise into the class of domestic servants; and their sons, instead of remaining street-sellers, would soon learn a trade or go to sea if they cared to do regular work. We are largely helping by our foolish gifts, to keep them herded together in crowded, dirty, badly-built rooms, among scenes of pauperism, crime, and vice.[460a]

Such was her diagnosis of what was wrong with the poor. She saw the way out in a personal influence applied individual by individual, rich man to poor man.

Charity owes all its graciousness to the sense of coming from a real friend. We want to bring the rich and the poor, the educated and uneducated, more and more into direct communication. . . .

If the poor are to be raised to a permanently better condition, they must be dealt with individuals by individuals.[458a]

Edward Denison and Octavia Hill were only two representatives of the direction in which philanthropic thought was heading at the close of the sixties. The amount of discussion was prodigious and varied. There was the point of view expressed by Sir Charles E. Trevelyan as quoted by Mrs. Bosanquet in her history of the London Charity Organization Society:

Since the beginning of this century the gulf between rich and poor has become fearfully wide. The rich have become richer and the poor poorer. The proposal is to close this gulf and to bring back the rich into such close relation with the poor as cannot fail to have a civilizing and healing influence, and to knit all classes together in the bonds of mutual help and good will.[410a]

There was also the approach indicated in the title of a paper read before the Society of Arts in 1868 by the Rev. Henry Solly, a Unitarian clergyman—*How to Deal with the Unemployed Poor of London, and with its "Roughs" and Criminal Classes*. This paper presented the first of a series of proposals by different people which led in 1869 to the formation of a society, intended to precipitate into action the ideas which the philanthropists of the period were expressing. It was designed to put an end to the charitable chaos described by Richard Green, by Mrs. Bosanquet, and Edward Denison; to promote the coördination of public and private relief; and to provide opportunity for lifting the individual out of his poverty through the services and the personal influence which people in comfortable circumstances might provide for the poor.

The plan as originally proposed included a central registration of all applicants for relief to the public and private social agencies; the establishment of district committees with district offices as a means of promoting coöperation among institutions and individuals in the various neighborhoods of the city; the use of the district committees as centers for the work of volunteer visitors in the rehabilitation of persons seeking relief; provision for the auditing of the accounts of the private charities and an inspection of their annual reports; and a system of financial support for the new organization based upon a contribution of 1 per cent of the annual income of each coöperating agency.

The supervision implied in auditing, in the inspection of annual reports, and in the plan of finance was more than the charities of London were prepared to impose upon themselves, and the Society as it finally commenced included only the system of organized relief and service through district committees heading into a central body. Not even central registration seemed possible. On April 23, 1869, the name Society for Organizing Charitable Relief and Repressing Mendicancy was adopted, and a little later as a short title, Charity Organization Society.

Octavia Hill has left us her contemporary description of the workings of the new society:

First, it has offered to examine, free of all charge, for any one who wants to learn about them, the circumstances and character of applicants for relief. . . . But the Society offers a second advantage; it will give an opinion on the case of an applicant. . . .

A representative from every local charity, a few men conversant with the work of every great metropolitan charity, two or three active guardians, the clergy and ministers of all denominations, or some leading member of their staff or congregations, these should form your district committee. After careful investigation by a skilled paid officer, the case of an applicant for charity, when it comes before such a committee as that, has a fair chance of really effectual treatment. Either some one present will know of work that needs to be done; or, if the applicant's wants can only be met by a distinct gift, then, all the givers or their representatives being present, the gift can after due deliberation be made without chance of overlapping, with certainty that it is sufficient and its object well thought out.[460b]

'The Charity Organization Society looked to Thomas Chalmers as its spiritual ancestor, deriving its philosophy and much of its method from his teachings. It also took considerable support from the continental system of administration. In the seventies, the city of Elberfeld in Germany had replaced Hamburg and Munich in philanthropic attention but its organization of relief was essentially the same. It involved the subdivision of the city into small districts presided over by unpaid visitors, serving in rotation. The service was compulsory for the citizens, although the individual was consulted about his willingness to act. The districting was carried to such a point that on an average the total population from which a visitor might draw his cases was only about two hundred.[435a] Under this plan there had been a great reduction in the number of persons receiving relief. The Charity Organization Society made frequent reference to this combination of district operation and citizen service as an important element in dealing with the problem of individual poverty, using it as an additional argument in support of its own system of dividing the city into neighborhoods.

But it was Chalmers who was the Society's chief source of inspiration. His belief in the deteriorating influence upon the individual of relief from public funds or from any central fund, his theory of the four fountains springing from the natural resources of the poor, his confidence in the power of the rich through personal association to elevate the poor, his method of developing support from and for the applicant for help were all incorporated into the operation of the Charity Organization Society.

The influence of the Elberfeld system upon the Charity Organization Society and also upon public relief may be seen in a description of an experiment by the Society in the parish of Marylebone in London, published in the 1873–74 report of the Local Government Board. The account was written by Octavia Hill, who supervised the work. It had to do with the use of volunteer visitors in providing information about families for the use of representatives of the local board of guardians. Miss Hill's concluding remarks indicate the Society's aims in personal influence upon the poor:

I am myself satisfied that the scheme is capable of a far deeper influence on the condition of the poor, when the volunteers shall rise to the perception that, in dealing with poverty, they must aim at prevention rather than cure; at saving those under their influence from sinking to the Poor Law level, rather than merely obtaining relief for them. Few of my fellow workers have as yet grasped the idea that their best success would be to develop the resources of the poor themselves, instead of letting them come upon the rates, or continue upon them.

I think they rarely set before themselves the desire to find some employment, at hand or far off, which may support the young widow and her children before she has tasted parish bread. I think they rarely press upon the old woman the duty of first trying if the successful son cannot support her, or the daughters in service unite to do so. They have not yet watched the poor closely enough to see that this would be in reality the truest kindness. They forget the dignity of self maintenance, they forget the blessing of drawing the bonds of relationship closer, and dwell only upon the fact that the applicant is deserving—see only the comfort or relief which the parish allowance would secure.

How far they can raise the people by degree above the degrading need of charitable or poor law relief, to be energetic, self-reliant, provident, and industrious, will depend upon the height of their own hope, the patience of their own labor, the moral courage which will teach them to prefer being helpful to being popular, and finally to the temper and spirit of their own homes and lives. For say what we may, if our upper class were to become extravagant, improvident and showy, it would be aped by those below it, even though as surely it would be despised. And if we desire to be the leaders of our poor into the ways of happy prosperity, we must order our homes in exactly the same spirit as theirs must be ordered, in simplicity, industry, and providence.[326a]

This quotation from Octavia Hill may help to indicate the appeal which the Charity Organization Society had for its adherents. In practice, as Miss Hill implied, the Society was not able to realize the goals in personal influence which she envisioned for it. Perhaps Count Rumford was nearer reality when he suggested that instead of trying to reform people it might be easier to make them happy first.

Helping people, as the Society gradually learned, is not an art conferred upon one either by culture or by wealth but is a discipline learned with difficulty. And, of course, the London Charity Organization Society of the nineteenth century disregarded almost entirely the influence of social and industrial opportunity and conditions. The great decline in both public and private relief rolls during the upswing of war manufacture in the 1940's is significant proof of the decisive bearing of general economic circumstances upon the problem of poverty.

In one important respect the Charity Organization Society departed from the system set up by Chalmers and those exemplified in Hamburg, Munich, and Elberfeld. Whereas the work in Scotland and in Germany had depended almost entirely upon unpaid citizens, the London Society developed the employed agent and assigned to him a strategic place. Each considerable district had at least one paid official, responsible for inquiry and for acting as an organizing center for volunteer activity. It was this new element, combined with the concept of methodology as conceived by Chalmers, that provided the means for the accretion of knowledge and skill that has formed the basis of a new vocation. The principles of charity organization thus formulated in London in 1869 spread quickly throughout Great Britain. In 1877 the movement reached the United States and within a few years it had spanned the country, where it played an important part in the development of the methods used in dealing with the problem of destitution. In London and throughout England the new Society soon came to exercise great influence on the administration of both public and private relief.

A little more than half a year after the beginning of the enterprise George J. Goschen, president of the Poor Law Board, issued a minute devoted to the question—"how far it is possible to mark out the separate limits of the Poor Law and of charity respectively, and how it is possible to secure joint action between the two." This minute of November 20, 1869, was the first recognition by government in England of philanthropy as an organized force. References throughout the history of the Poor Law had been made to private charity but never as an organized activity with which to negotiate and to arrive at mutual understandings about policy and program.

From this time forward the Charity Organization Society, as representative of the new philanthropy, had a definite impact upon the operations of government in the field of public assistance. Throughout the remainder of the nineteenth century it was an influence against an indiscriminate relief and for careful administration. Its committees served as recruiting grounds for the membership of the boards of guardians. It gave strong support to the program under which, beginning in the seventies, the central body of the Poor Law undertook to reduce, if not to eliminate, expenditures for relief. For, as might be expected from the writings of Edward Denison, Octavia Hill, and Sir Charles S. Loch, general secretary of the Society from 1875–1914, a quotation from whom appears at the head of Chapter XI, the Charity Organization Society belonged to that section of English opinion which emphasized the personal responsibility of the individual for his economic situation and opposed the further extension of government into the field of relief.

An indication of the place which the Society occupied in this connection may be gathered from a tribute paid to Sir Charles S. Loch on the occasion of his receiving the degree of Doctor of Civil Laws from Oxford University. This tribute which appeared in the *Oxford Magazine* is quoted by Mrs. Bosanquet in her history of the Charity

Organization Society. She precedes it with the comment that "the conception of the Society itself in this quotation is perhaps hardly adequate, but no one will think the appreciation of Mr. Loch's services is overdrawn."

Mr. Charles Stewart Loch is one of the most surprising facts of the present day. Here is a man with no official position, no letters after his name, not even a ribbon, whose name is known everywhere, whose influence is felt everywhere. That he was educated at Glenalmond and Balliol means comparatively little: his life begins with his appointment as Secretary to the Charity Organization Society, and even more, the life of the Society dates from his appointment. He has formulated a principle and created a type. The Society, when he joined it, represented a praiseworthy, if somewhat Utopian effort to bring about cooperation in charitable work, and unity among its workers. It has since become the repository of wise counsels in all matters concerning the relief of the poor. It is widely disliked and universally trusted. Its friends are few and they are voces in deserto, but they win a hearing. That independence is among the most valuable of the goods and chattels that a man possesses; that to wound independence is to do a grievous harm; to foster independence is true Charity; that character is nine-tenths of life; that the State shares with indiscriminate Charity the distinction of being a mighty engine for evil—these and kindred precepts are summed up under the name Charity Organization Society principles.

Now the source and fount of all these is Mr. Loch. He resembles the oracle at Delphi more than any modern institution, inasmuch as to him come all those who are in doubt about their charitable conduct and the effect of action. To all such, from his shrine in Buckingham Street, he gives appropriate answers. More than that, the world outside, or at least the wiser part of it, postpone decision in social matters till Mr. Loch has spoken out.[410b]

Such, as expressed in the person of its greatest leader, was the London Charity Organization Society. Starting as an effort to reform the hodge-podge of philanthropic effort that reached a climax in the sixties, it had by the close of the century become an important influence upon public policy in relation to relief. It epitomized that part of England which opposed any extension of governmental activity in this area and which believed that poverty was essentially the responsibility of the individual and that a request for assistance indicated a need for personal reform. It was in those years a strong advocate of the doctrine of less eligibility and played a strategic supporting part to the central body of the Poor Law in a campaign that, lasting through the nineteenth century, endeavored to reduce to a minimum, if not actually to eliminate, public outdoor relief.

XV

THE CAMPAIGN AGAINST OUTDOOR RELIEF

Almost every proposal which hath been made for the reformation
of the poor laws hath been tried in former ages, and found in-
effectual.

RICHARD BURN, *The History of the
Poor Laws with Observations*, 1764.[413]

THE severe distress in the winter of 1860–61 which started the
chain of events that led to the establishment of the Charity Organization Society was likewise the precipitant of a revival of activity in public relief. The suffering that winter not only brought forth
contributions of money and of philanthropic service, it also aroused
much criticism of the Poor Law for its failure to meet the emergency.
Responding to this criticism, C. P. Villiers, then president of the Poor
Law Board, moved in the House of Commons for a committee of inquiry.

When this committee was appointed with himself as chairman, he
adroitly turned the attack from the central board to the local administration of relief. Most of the findings and recommendations of the
report which appeared three years later were designed to strengthen
the principle of national supervision.

By this time, 1864, the destitution growing out of the cotton famine had necessitated the grant to the Poor Law Board of emergency
powers—notably, authority to approve borrowing by the guardians
for relief and by the guardians and other local authorities for public
works. These additional powers greatly increased the prestige of the
central body.

The guardians, on the other hand, were on the defensive, in part because of the report of Mr. Villiers' committee but even more because
of scandals that had come to light in connection with the treatment
of the sick in the workhouses. Miss Louisa Twining, who since 1853
had been visiting these institutions, latterly with the assistance of a
corps of women, and Dr. Joseph Rogers, whose knowledge of the

problem began with his appointment in 1856 as medical officer of the Strand Workhouse, were exposing to a horrified public the terrible conditions to which patients in the workhouses were subjected. Both had testified in 1861 before the Villiers' Committee. In 1865 the efforts of Miss Twining and Dr. Rogers were reinforced by a volunteer commission appointed by the *Lancet*, a medical periodical. Revelations of insanitary practices, foul rooms, beds by many inches too short for the patients, incompetent nursing—if care by the inmates themselves could be called nursing—and a generally callous and ignorant personnel shocked the country into action. Before the end of the sixties long-needed reforms had been instituted, and the structure of public assistance had been reorganized and had been improved in particular in four important respects.

1. The union instead of the parish was made the taxing area for relief. When in 1834 the combination of parishes into unions had been authorized, only administration not finance had been involved. The bickering among the parishes around the question of settlement had therefore continued. Now all relief costs were paid by the union, and consequently within its boundaries the problem of residence was eliminated.[52] Administration was thereby greatly simplified but, what was even more important, the longest step toward increasing the mobility of labor had been taken since the repeal, seventy years before, of the notorious act of Charles II enabling parishes to remove families on the mere suspicion that they might at some later time require relief.

2. All the unions in London were brought under the supervision of the Poor Law Board. Hitherto, fully one-third of the city had been virtually independent in its administration of relief because of the Gilbert Act and other special laws which had not been repealed in 1834.[56]

3. The sick were declared not to be "proper objects" for the deterrent methods of workhouse administration. District asylums boards were authorized by Parliament as a step toward taking hospitalization out of the hands of the guardians. The greatest development in this respect took place in London, where under a central administration that became increasingly independent of the Poor Law a variety of institutions was gradually established.[53 & 56]

4. The central supervisory body of the Poor Law—at that time the Poor Law Board which since 1834 had existed only on sufferance, its life being periodically prolonged by Parliament never for more than

five years at a time—was made a permanent branch of government.[55] Completing this series of changes, came in 1871 the merging of the Poor Law, the public health service, and certain other activities into the Local Government Board. In this combination, the Poor Law became the dominant element.[57]

The way was now cleared for action. The decade of discussion, investigation, and legislation had put new life and new power into the central body of the Poor Law. An era of reform started, taking the direction once more of a campaign against outdoor relief. This, considering the times, was natural and inevitable. The Poor Law was under the influence of the same trends in thought that had determined the development of the charity organization movement—an aggressive individualism, reinforced by the conviction that the doctrine of the survival of the fittest could be successfully applied to human society. Every man, it was believed, could be the master of his own economic life. Hence, if he fell into poverty it was his own fault. Should he request help, assistance should be administered in such a way that he would never be tempted to ask for relief again—at least of the Poor Law. It was the reincarnation of the spirit of Sir George Nicholls and the commissioners of 1834-47.

The immediate occasion for the war against outdoor relief was the rise in relief expenditures between 1860-61 and 1869-70, an increase of 20 per cent. On December 2, 1871, the Local Government Board opened the campaign with a circular addressed to its inspectorate, pointing out that under the circumstances "measures should be taken, not only to check any further increase, but to diminish the present amount." Its diagnosis of the problem was that in many cases outdoor relief was granted by the guardians "too readily and without sufficient inquiry, and that they give it also in numerous instances in which it would be more judicious to apply the workhouse test."[323a]

In pursuance of this diagnosis the new program to restrict expenditures for assistance was based on a more frequent and broader use of the offer of the workhouse, and, in line with the Goschen minute of 1869 (See Chapter XIV), on a greater reliance upon private charity. Two measures of efficiency were applied in this connection—the first was the ratio of paupers to the general population, and the second, the ratio of the number of persons granted outdoor relief to the number of those receiving indoor relief. The Union of Atcham in Shropshire was held before the other unions as an example, in this respect, of good administration. Here, under the influence of Sir

Baldwyn Leighton, the workhouse test had been applied immediately after the Poor Law reform of 1834. By count, on March 25 in 1836 in Atcham, the proportion of paupers to population was 1 in 13; in 1849, 1 in 44; in 1871, 1 in 62; and in 1872, 1 in 78. On March 25, 1871, there were 138 indoor paupers in Atcham as compared with 119 outdoor paupers, whereas for England and Wales the proportion of indoor to outdoor paupers was 1 to 6.[423a]

Both of these measures—ratio of paupers to population and ratio of outdoor to indoor relief—had been used by Sir George Nicholls and his associates in the Poor Law Commission, but they were now revived with a renewed enthusiasm by the inspectors of the Local Government Board and their like-minded associates on the boards of guardians. Henry Longley, the inspector for London, succinctly stated the goal of the campaign in outlining a program of administrative policy which the Local Government Board published with approval in its third annual report, 1873-74.

"Indoor relief shall be the rule and outdoor relief the exception" was his suggestion.[326b] The categories of need to be provided for in the institution were increased to such a point that in some unions nearly everybody asking aid was offered the workhouse. The Brixworth Union on the recommendation of a committee of its board of guardians announced a policy in 1873 under which wives deserted by their husbands, wives or families of convicted prisoners, single women with illegitimate children, and able-bodied widows with one child only, were refused outdoor relief. In the case of the widow with more than one child, the additional children received the offer of the workhouse.[325a]

The inspectors of the Local Government Board approved such a program as this on two grounds. They argued, to refer again to Longley, that the workhouse was the only way of granting adequate relief. Relief to be efficient must be neither inadequate nor excessive; but one cannot be sure that relief will not be excessive when it is given to a family in its own home. There may be other resources. The only place, therefore, where relief can be efficient is in the workhouse, and Longley cites:

A chairman of a Board of Guardians, addressing a widow with two children applying for a renewal of relief, "If you can't earn enough to keep you with what we give you, you must come into the workhouse, *we don't profess to give you enough to keep you* out of the workhouse!" [326c]

Under such a policy one might think that the population of the workhouse would rise to a point at which the expense would be prohibitive, since family-for-family outdoor relief costs less than indoor relief. But here one of the inspectors of the Board, Edwin H. Wodehouse, advanced an ingenious argument:

A family applies for relief; if they are given out-relief to the amount of four shillings a week, they will be satisfied; if they come into the workhouse, their maintenance will cost ten shillings a week. The economists, therefore, argue, that by giving out-relief they will save six shillings a week. Now the very same Guardians, who have used this argument, have frequently acknowledged to me, that when the workhouse test is offered, it is not accepted in more than one case out of ten. By offering the workhouse then in ten such cases the Guardians would indeed lose six shillings a week in the one case in which it was accepted, but in each of the remaining nine cases they would save four shillings, so that their total gain upon the ten cases would amount to thirty shillings a week.[323b]

This estimated ratio of nine refusals of the workhouse to one acceptance is not hard to credit when one measures it against George Lansbury's description of the general workhouse of the Poplar Union as he saw it in 1892:

My first visit to the workhouse was a memorable one. Going down the narrow lane, ringing the bell, waiting while an official with a not too pleasant face looked through a grating to see who was there, and hearing his unpleasant voice—of course, he did not know me—made it easy for me to understand why the poor dreaded and hated these places, and made me in a flash realize how all these prison or bastille sort of surroundings were organized for the purpose of making self-respecting decent people endure any suffering rather than enter. . . .

Officials, receiving ward, hard forms, whitewashed walls, keys dangling at the waist of those who spoke to you, huge books for name and history, etc., searching, and then being stripped and bathed in a communal tub, and the final crowning indignity of being dressed in clothes which had been worn by lots of other people, hideous to look at, ill-fitting and coarse —everything possible was done to inflict mental and moral degradation.

The place was clean; brass knobs and floors were polished, but of goodwill, kindliness there was none. . . .

Sick and aged, mentally deficient, lunatics, babies and children, able-bodied and tramps all herded together in one huge range of buildings. Officers, both men and women, looked upon these people as a nuisance and treated them accordingly. Food was mainly skilly, bread, margarine, cheese and hard tough meat and vegetables, and occasionally doses of salted dried fish. Clothing was of the usual workhouse type, plenty of corduroy and blue cloth. No undergarments for either men or women, no sanitary clothes of any sort or kind for women of any age, boots were worn till they fell off. The paupers, as they were officially styled, were allowed out once a month and could be visited once a month.[464a]

It is not surprising that people hesitated to go to the workhouse when this was the treatment they could expect. The inspectors and the other leaders in the campaign against outdoor relief, on the other hand, felt themselves to be secure in their position. They offered the "adequate" relief of the institution, knowing that their form of adequacy would be unacceptable to nine out of every ten applicants for relief.

They went even further than this in some unions. They succeeded in achieving what their predecessors in the Poor Law Commission had not attempted. In London, and later in certain other of the larger cities, they instituted the able-bodied workhouse.

The first of these was established in the Poplar Union in London, the poorest district of the metropolis. Here a penal regime was inaugurated with long, hard hours of work at stone-breaking, oakum picking, woodcutting, and corn grinding. The other unions in the city were invited to use the house and to it were sent able-bodied men and women, usually those who were a trouble to boards of guardians. When after a decade of operation the Poplar guardians discontinued the institution, the Kensington Union replaced it with one of its own. Several other cities followed the example of these London unions, and there seems to be no question but that the use of the able-bodied workhouse played an effective part in reducing the relief rolls.

Even so strict a disciplinarian as Longley might have hesitated to apply the principle of making indoor relief the rule, outdoor relief the exception, if there had not been available the resource of private charity and in particular the Charity Organization Society.

"It is, in fact," he wrote, "the very existence of charity which strengthens the hands of the Poor Law administrator in adherence to rule." He saw private charity as a way of escape from the harshness of the workhouse, that is, for those whom he regarded to be worthy:

If . . . the poor be given clearly to understand that out-relief is to be granted only as an indulgence to deserving cases, it may be possible, in time, and when a more complete organization of charity shall have been effected, to relegate such cases as these to the care of charitable agencies.[326e]

He felt that charity was the safer form of assistance. It was less subversive to the character of the recipient:

Relief given as of right must tend to encourage improvidence to a greater degree than that which, being a matter not of right but of voluntary, precarious, and intermittent charity, cannot be so surely anticipated as a future resource.[326d]

Longley apparently did not take into consideration the necessity for a frequent asking of assistance that an intermittent relief would involve, or the effect in breaking down the spirit of independence that the having to ask again and again would entail. Nor did he mention the influence of precariousness upon the individual who had no possibility of self-support within himself, as in the case of the aged, the sick, and the young.

With the workhouse as the test of need and as punishment for the undeserving and with private charity as the prospect for the worthy, Longley and his associates carried their campaign throughout the country. Their efforts were successful. Brixworth Union at the end of its first year reported a reduction in the ratio of outdoor to indoor paupers—12 to 1 at the beginning of the year, 8 to 1 at its close.[326f] Canon William Bury, who led the campaign there, was not satisfied, however. He pointed out in his report that the ratio of 8 to 1 was higher than the average for England and Wales. His determination to do better was rewarded. In 1893 the Brixworth proportions had changed to 3 indoor paupers for every outdoor pauper and a combined total of 76 paupers in a population of 12,186, more than 1,000 less than in 1872, when the combined total was 1,111.[423b] Brixworth had come close to eliminating all relief, both indoor and outdoor.

This policy of persistent reduction in outdoor relief was not, however, carried on without qualms, as Canon Bury's report of March 12, 1874, to the Local Government Board indicates:

It must, however, be acknowledged, that a reform so radical as that which has been described, cannot have been effected without a certain amount of suffering, often endured in silence, escaping therefore the notice of the most careful investigation, and difficult to estimate as it was impossible to prevent. Yet at the same time it should be remembered that such consequences, however much to be deplored, are really due, not to the reform itself, but to the neglect in former years which rendered such reform necessary.[326g]

Canon Bury and his associates usually regarded the pauper not as an individual but as a member of a class, a class afflicted with a disease from which he must be saved.

"The question was," writes Thomas MacKay in commenting approvingly upon the work in Brixworth, "at what rate shall the emancipation of the poor from pauperism be pressed forward?" [472a]

It is true that on many of the boards of guardians were representatives of propertied interests who were there to reduce taxes without regard for the cost which this might ultimately entail, but the leaders of the movement against relief were not imbued by obvious personal considerations of this sort. They were reformers. They were drawn from the clergy, from the universities, and from among the philanthropically-minded. They came of a generation that felt that any form of governmental expenditure and activity was dangerous. Their conscious concern was with the moral character of the destitute—and this they saw threatened by the grant of relief. These were the days, it must be remembered, when anyone was presumed by thrift to be able not only to provide for himself against illness, unemployment, old age, and the other contingencies of life, but even (see the quotations from Octavia Hill) to rise from his present to a higher station in life. In so far as human beings can be disinterested, the proponents of this movement against governmental outdoor relief were disinterested. They were public-spirited persons with a deep concern for the welfare of their country.

It was out of such concern that many unions followed the example of Atcham and Brixworth and that the test of the workhouse was more strictly applied than ever before. While public outdoor relief was not abolished—and the Local Government Board itself at no time announced such a policy—the number of persons cared for by the guardians took a decided drop by the end of the seventies and held this lower level in relation to population through the remainder of the century. Sir William Chance lists the thirteen unions, including Atcham and Brixworth where relief policy was strictest, showing that between 1871 and 1893 the decrease in outdoor relief ranged from 78 per cent in Manchester to 98 per cent in Brixworth. [423c]

The Webbs accompany a tabulation for England and Wales of the "mean aggregate number of paupers, including insane and vagrants," year by year from 1872 to 1908 with this comment:

There seems to be no correspondence whatever between the magnitude of the aggregate of persons in recipt of any of the forms of Poor Relief, and what we know to have been the state of trade and the prevalence of unemployment. Thus, after the boom of 1871–72, trade declined and unemployment increased, until the black misery of 1879 was reached, when the slump seems to have been the most severe of any between 1841 and 1921. Yet the total number of persons in receipt of Poor Relief was in 1877 and 1878 actually lower than in any year since 1849, and even in 1879 the percentage of paupers to population was lower than it had been in any year prior to 1877.[507b]

This would certainly indicate the success of the opponents of public outdoor relief. When relief rolls remain unaffected by the greater need that exists in times of depression, then indeed the possibilities of a program of deterrence have been demonstrated. That the overall period during which this result was accomplished should have been a time of, generally speaking, expanding business, when real wages were increasing, does not alter the essential fact. Nor does the increase in charitable activity, particularly unorganized charitable work, during the seventies, eighties, and nineties detract from the main point. The offer of the workhouse in every kind of economic weather brought the same result. People got along without public outdoor relief who otherwise would have accepted assistance.

What actually happened in the campaign that started in the seventies was an assertion on the one hand by Longley and his fellows of the right of the poor to public assistance and on the other of the power of the state to set the conditions under which that right should be exercised. Whereupon the circumstances of administration were made such as to cause the individual in need to deny himself the right. What the relief authorities in the last quarter of the nineteenth century said was: "Yes, you have the right. Come and use it if you dare."

Whether or not a person in need has a right to the relief which his need occasions would be an academic consideration were it not that the consciousness of this right has a bearing upon the preservation of the essential dignity of the human being who is compelled to avail himself of it. The concept of right can be a means of influencing the person administering and the person receiving in such a way as to make the transaction as little demoralizing as possible to the sense of self-respect of the individual in need. This important element in the right to relief, the program of deterrence of the seventies destroyed.

So far as the able-bodied workhouse was concerned, it was not the able-bodied who were subjected to its stern regimes but—to quote the Minority report of the Royal Commission on the Poor Laws and Relief of Distress 1905–09:

the broken down and debilitated weakling, the man absolutely without an alternative, the genuinely destitute man, who is forced in by starvation, finds the conditions unendurable and takes his discharge, only to be again and again driven in by dire necessity . . . a depressed and feeble, but on the whole a docile and decent, set of men, who need, if they are to be kept off the rates, not penal tasks and penal discipline on an insufficiently nourishing diet, but a course of strict but restorative physical and mental training, on adequate food, and a patient appeal to their courage and their better instincts. . . .

Having discovered that a man is really destitute, what right has the destitution authority to punish him? [317a]

It was not only the discovery of the nature of the clientele of the able-bodied workhouse that caused the abandonment of the institution at Poplar and its successors. Even more influential in the discontinuance of these institutions was the fact that they put themselves out of business. Obviously a test workhouse that operated successfully would be shunned by the able-bodied for whom it was intended. Its facilities would stand empty, and empty rooms are always coveted by administrators who have more of the sick and aged than they can care for. The ill and the infirm would be moved into the vacant space, and then, of course, the institution would cease to be a workhouse for the able-bodied. This was precisely what happened at Poplar. To quote again from the Minority report:

Gradually the numbers of the sick and infirm to be provided for in Poplar forced the guardians to the alternative of either building new institutions or utilizing the partly vacant space at the Poplar Workhouse. They naturally chose the latter course. . . . In 1882 . . . it reverted once more to being a General Mixed Workhouse of the ordinary type.[317b]

While the campaign against outdoor relief was effective in reducing the relief rolls, other aspects of its operation must have been painful to the Poor Law authorities who placed great emphasis upon the importance of safeguarding the morals of the people. I am quoting from Sophia Lonsdale who was a Poor Law guardian in the Lichfield Union.

He [the relieving officer] is probably the best abused man in the parish, and I am not going to say that he may not sometimes be hard. But I should like to ask you whether if you were told lies from Monday morning till

Saturday night you might not get a little hard? That is perhaps one of the great evils of Out-door relief, the really awful amount of lying it causes. It is considered perfectly legitimate by the vast majority of the poor, though of course there are exceptions, to lie to the Relieving Officer, and to cheat and deceive him if they can, although they know, or ought to know, that false statements to the Guardians through their officers are punishable by law.[469a]

Under the pressure of need there is every temptation either directly or indirectly to withhold information or to give incorrect answers, but the deterrent policy wherever it is applied enormously accentuates this attitude. Where the person who administers relief approaches the applicant for assistance in the spirit of punishment and detection, he stimulates an evasive and uncoöperative response. The granting of relief becomes a horse trade in which each party to the transaction endeavors to outwit and outdo the other.

Reliance upon the workhouse as the determinant of eligibility for relief tended to promote also a spirit of perfunctoriness in the boards of guardians. Any committee which attempts to act as a relief-deciding committee is likely to fall into this evil, but undoubtely the availability and use of the test helped to accentuate a stereotyped procedure. "I have heard [writes Sophia Lonsdale,] ten or a dozen applications disposed of in as many minutes with the inevitable result of extravagance or injustice." [469b]

Sir Henry Longley in his report of 1873 records the average length of time devoted by boards of guardians to the making of decisions about relief:

The time occupied in disposing of applications for relief varies widely in different Unions and in different committees of the same Board of Guardians. A record of the time so occupied on sixty-five occasions, in my presence, shows that in seventeen cases applications were disposed of at an average rate of less than one a minute, in twenty-three cases at about the rate of one a minute, in nine at a rate varying from one to two minutes per case, and in the remaining sixteen at a rate of not less than two minutes per case. The maximum of speed appears to have been a rate of four minutes to eleven cases, the minimum rate was three minutes per case.

I mention these figures, however, as matters rather of curiosity than of practical utility.[326h]

This kind of procedure, to which apparently Longley did not object, was symptomatic of the existing status of the art of administration. There is much discussion of principle and purpose in the reports and books of the period in England that ends with the close of the last century; there is little that concerns itself with how to arrive at some understanding of people and the manner in which economic distress influences them in applying for assistance or in accepting and continuing to accept relief. There is almost nothing that relates to how the administrator can take into consideration what the whole experience of being in need means to an individual, and how in interview and otherwise he can determine eligibility for aid in an atmosphere of fair dealing and mutual respect.

If the program of deterrence of the seventies is to be questioned with regard to its effect upon the individuals directly involved, it is likewise to be questioned with regard to its value for the community. The fact that governmental relief costs were reduced does not mean that the cost was not felt in other ways. There is no doubt that there was an increase in charitable expenditures, often such as to foster the very dependence which the Poor Law administrators wanted to avoid. What the effect was upon costs in other areas, as, for example, in policing, in the treatment of crime, and in the expenditures on account of sickness, there is no way of ascertaining. Toward the close of the century England was startled by the extent of poverty and deprivation revealed in the studies of Charles Booth in London and of B. Seebohm Rowntree in York. (See the next chapter). It began to be evident that deterrence in the administration of relief had not solved but had rather contributed to the problem of destitution.

A community can secure in human welfare very nearly what it is willing to pay for. The nineteenth century was not willing to pay because it thought the individual could and should foot the bill himself. On this basis it succeeded in its campaign to reduce expenditures for relief. It took the cash and let the credit go.

XVI

A NEW FERMENT

The origin of the ferment is to be discovered in a new consciousness of sin among men of intellect and men of property. . . .The
consciousness of sin was a collective or class consciousness, a growing uneasiness, amounting to conviction, that the industrial organization which had yielded rent, interest and profits on a stupendous
scale, had failed to provide a decent livelihood and tolerable conditions for a majority of the inhabitants of Great Britain.

BEATRICE WEBB,
My Apprenticeship, 1926.[504a]

DURING the years when the campaign against outdoor relief seemed
to be having its greatest success, the premises upon which the
deterrent administration of the Poor Law had been based were being
subjected to increasing assault. The first attack commenced at the
beginning of the nineteenth century when laissez faire seemed to
dominate all English thought. The leaders of this attack were convinced supporters of individualism and of the principles of 1834—men
like Edwin Chadwick, co-author of the famous report of that year,
and Lord Shaftesbury who was one of the founders of the Charity
Organization Society. These and a long succession of other social
reformers, in their efforts to improve the living and working conditions of the people of England, changed the very concept of government in which they believed and put in its place a new theory which
we now regard as axiomatic and from which present attempts to
achieve social security start.

At the opening of the last century, government as related to the
poor occupied a position essentially the same as it did at the time of
the first Statute of Laborers. It was conceived to be an instrument to
advance the interests of a ruling class. Its chief function toward the
poor was that of policing. This was the reason for relief as expressed
by Sir George Nicholls as late as 1854. On the reverse of the title page
of his *History of the Poor Law* appears this quotation from Charles
Babbage on the *Thoughts on the Principles of Taxation*:

Whenever, for the purposes of government, we arrive, in any state of society, at a class so miserable as to be in want of the common necessaries of life, a new principle comes into action. The usual restraints which are sufficient for the well-fed, are often useless in checking the demands of hungry stomachs. Other and more powerful means must then be employed; a larger array of military or [of] police force must be maintained. Under such circumstances, it may be considerably cheaper to fill [up] empty stomachs to the point of ready obedience, than to compell starving wretches to respect the roast beef of their more industrious neighbors: and it may be expedient, in a more economical point of view, to supply gratuitously the wants even of ablebodied persons, if it can be done without creating crowds of additional applicants.[481f]

Nicholls becomes even more specific in his preface, with a comment which he bases upon a partial quotation from Sir Matthew Hale:

Sir Matthew Hale declares the relief of the poor to be "an act of great civil prudence and political wisdom, for that poverty is in itself apt to emasculate the minds of men or at least it makes men tumultuous and unquiet. Where there are many poor, the rich," he says, "cannot long or safely continue such, for necessity renders men of phlegmatic and dull natures stupid and indisciplinable, and men of more fiery or active constitutions rapacious and desperate." It is accordingly an admitted maxim of social policy, that the first charge on land must be the maintenance of the people reared upon it. This is the principle of the English Poor Law. Society exists for the preservation of property, but subject to the condition that the abundance of the few shall only be enjoyed by first making provision for the necessities of the many.[481g]

Such was the concept of government that dominated not only the Poor Law but every other aspect of life in England at the opening of the last century. The public welfare was the well-being of the few. The many without voice, without the means of education, without the right to organize, found in government little more than "an engine of evil."

The beginning of change came in 1802 and was occasioned by one of the by-products of the administration of relief. This was the system through which the overseers of the poor placed children out as apprentices, paying employers to take boys and girls from poverty-stricken families and presumably teach them a trade. It was a holdover from the days of handicraft which were already passing in the greater part of manufacture.

The use, in spinning, of machinery run by water power greatly increased the desirability of the apprentice system. Mills had to be located where there was water, and often they were built where the supply of local labor was not sufficient. It thus became necessary to import workers. Barracks were erected and here were housed children sent by the overseers from London and other cities. There was no restriction on the hours of employment or on the age—even as low as five years—at which the little boys and girls were sent to these labor camps. Many of them were literally worked to death. In 1802 Sir Robert Peel, the father of the man who was later to become Prime Minister and himself an industrialist, introduced and secured the passage of a bill in Parliament restricting the employment of apprentices to twelve hours a day between six in the morning and nine at night, and forbidding work between 9 P.M. and 6 A.M.[44] At first many of the manufacturers were indignant, feeling that the cotton industry would be ruined; but when they found that the law applied only to pauper apprentices, they ceased to worry and began employing children who lived at home whose parents were not paupers. This became the more possible with the introduction of steam power, which meant that factories could be built wherever there was an adequate supply of labor.

While the new legislation thus lost most of its point, the first small step had been taken toward the establishment of the protection of the workers as a major function of government. Since 1349 the law had been almost exclusively employed to coerce and confine the poor— maximum wages, compulsory service, prohibition of trade unions, restrictions upon movement. The spirit of legislation had been negative. The state had been an instrument of repression. Now government was being used, even though ineffectively, in a different way.

Shortly after the passage of the Law of 1802 Sir Robert Peel was joined in his efforts by Robert Owen. Owen was perhaps the first of the long succession of manufacturers who have found in good wages and good working conditions the possibilities of profitable business. Starting as a poor boy, he made a fortune for himself and his associates in textiles, developing around his mills at New Lanark a model community for the families of his employees.

In 1819 Owen and Peel succeeded in securing a law forbidding the employment of children under nine years of age and restricting the work of children under sixteen years to twelve hours, exclusive of meal times, between 5 A.M. and 9 P.M.[46] The Act was limited to the cotton industry and carried no effective means of enforcement, but the principle of legislation in the interest of the workers had been extended to include not only those who were called paupers but all children.

The ranks of the reformers had by this time been swelled by many accessions, including two farsighted employers, John Fielden, whose cotton manufactory was the largest in the world, and John Wood, a successful worsted spinner. These two men helped to finance a new attack. The campaign in the House of Commons was headed by Michael Sadler, who in December 1831 introduced his ten-hour bill. As chairman of the select committee to which the subject was referred, he brought forward such a succession of witnesses and testimony to the long hours, savage discipline including flogging, and the effect in actual deformity upon the children's bodies of their hard labors, that the memory remained a vivid influence in factory legislation for many years.

In the election of 1832 Sadler lost his seat in Parliament. His associates in the movement against child labor, casting about for a successor, called upon Anthony Ashley Cooper, then Lord Ashley, later Earl of Shaftesbury, to be their leader. Lord Ashley reopened the fight that Sadler had begun and for half a century thereafter was the spearhead of the long series of campaigns for protective laws in industry and related fields. During the struggle which he led in the House of Commons another commission of inquiry was appointed. On it was Edwin Chadwick, who was shortly to become secretary of the Poor Law Commission. It was Chadwick who, with his suggestion of peripatetic inspectors working out from a central office of the national government, put teeth into what became the first effective factory act, that of 1833. This Act prohibited the employment of children under nine years in the textile industry, silk mills excepted. The employment of children between nine and thirteen years was limited to nine hours in one day, forty-eight hours in one week.[48] More important even than the restriction in child labor thus achieved was the establishment of the principle of inspection.

In 1847 came the 10th and 11th Victoria, Chapter 29, establishing the ten-hour day for women and for all persons under 18 years.[50] The movement against child labor was leading the way for the long succession of laws designed to safeguard labor in living and working conditions, to promote sanitation and health, to develop housing, to provide education. These and other measures of social improvement caused the individualistic nineteenth century, by an interesting paradox, to be an era of social reform in which the principle of governmental intervention in the interest of the well-being of the people was soundly established.

A second attack upon the bases of a deterrent Poor Law began to become effective at about the time of the opening of the Local Government Board's campaign against outdoor relief. This was the attack represented by the rising power of labor in industry and politics. In 1867 the extension of the suffrage to householders—owners or tenants —in the boroughs, gave urban labor the vote.[54] The following year with the formation of the Trades Union Congress, the workers began in an organized way to take their place in the forum of national discussion and action.

Labor had started the century with almost no rights at all. Laws passed in 1799 and 1800 forbade under severe penalties any man to "enter into any combination to obtain an advance of wages, or to lessen . . . the time of working," or to urge any one to stop work.[43] Not until 1824—and then thanks chiefly to the genius of Francis Place, exercising what was almost legislative legerdemain—were the Combination Laws repealed. In 1832 the workers had been excluded from the benefits of the Reform Bill which gave the suffrage to the middle and professional classes.[47] Labor had sustained another disappointment in 1834 when the effort to achieve a coöperative society through a grand national union failed. During the decade which ended in 1848, there had been agitation, violent demonstrations, and rioting, approaching at times close to rebellion, aimed to achieve a people's charter involving six points: manhood suffrage, vote by ballot, annual Parliaments annually elected, payment of members of Parliament, no requirement of property qualifications for members, and equal election districts.

When Chartism failed and collapsed, despite the presentation to Parliament of three great petitions—1839 with a million and a quarter signatures, 1842 with three million and a quarter, 1848 with two million signatures—the workers turned their efforts from politics to the improvement of their economic status. They found great opportunity for this in consumers' coöperation which, stemming from the teachings of Robert Owen, gained enormous impetus from the inauguration in 1844 at the Equitable Pioneers store in Toad Lane, Rochdale, of the return of dividend on purchases. A little later, trade unionism commenced emphasizing mutual benefits through insurance against sickness, unemployment, and old age. During the fifties and sixties the upper ranks of labor began in this way to achieve a financial position that won the respect of the rulers of England. At the same time the workers were gaining the kind of experience through association in common projects that made possible the formation of the Trades Union Congress.

The way had been cleared for the next great step in the advancement of labor. When John Bright, the Quaker, who with Richard Cobden had led the battle for the repeal of the Corn Laws, began to campaign for an extension of the suffrage, he found a growing feeling among the ruling class that some concession in this direction was inevitable. The government which finally enacted the Reform Bill of 1867 [54] was appropriately headed by Disraeli, the author of *Sybil: or the Two Nations*, long a critic of the Poor Law.

The year 1867, which gave the vote to the urban workers, marked the beginning of a new dispensation. From this time, labor, with a voice in determining the government of England, would be able to act directly in its own behalf. In 1874 the first trade unionists entered Parliament. In 1884 the suffrage was extended to householders in the rural counties, enfranchising the miners and agricultural laborers.[58] In 1892 labor appeared dramatically in the administration of the Poor Law when George Lansbury, William Crooks, who had been a workhouse boy, and three other socialist-labor members were elected to the board of guardians of the Poplar Union in London. In 1894 the way was cleared for larger labor representation on the boards of guardians by legislation eliminating ex-officio and appointed members and opening the office to any parish elector, irrespective of sex or the ownership of property.[60] Meanwhile the ranks of trade unionism had been increased by the inclusion, during and after the great dock strike of 1889, of unskilled laborers, and in 1899 the Trades Union Congress moved toward the formation in the following year of a labor representation committee of which Ramsay MacDonald became secretary, established to elect labor candidates to public office. By the close of the century a new element had been added to the ruling class of England. The workers were beginning to speak for themselves.

The third of the great attacks upon the bases of the deterrent Poor Law was that of socialism. British socialism received its impetus from the various ideas promoted by the same Robert Owen who had been active in factory reform. He may be said to have developed his theory of society in the effort to solve the problem of relief. Concerned by the suffering and destitution occasioned by the depression that followed the end of the Napoleonic wars, Owen devised a plan for "relieving distress and removing discontent by giving permanent productive employment to the poor and working classes." [482a]

This plan involved the establishment of coöperative communities of producers. Both manufacture and agriculture were to be undertaken in villages which would exchange goods with each other. The labor involved in production was to be the measure of value, and barter the basis of trade. Owen proposed that these communities should provide not only materials but education and other cultural and social facilities for their people. It was essentially an extension of the ideas he had applied for the benefit of the employees in his mills at New Lanark. Underlying this program was his belief, surprising in those days when the individual was held to be exclusively responsible for his economic situation, that "the character of the man is, without a single exception, always formed for him" and that "any character from the best to the worst, from the most ignorant to the most enlightened, may be given to any community, even to the world at large, by applying certain means; which are to a great extent at the command and under the control, or easily made so, of those who possess the government of nations." [483a]

Building upon this theory, Owen extended his program beyond the problem of unemployment to the reorganization of society. In the beginning he appealed to the rich to set up the new order so as to make it possible for a system of coöperation to take the place of capitalism. When this help did not eventuate and when among the working people he found his most enthusiastic support, he turned increasingly to them. From his program there flowed two main streams: the one contributing to the growth of the coöperative movement, the other to the extension of socialist philosophy.

The interest in socialism thus quickened by the ideas of Robert Owen was variously augmented and developed by other leaders who came after him. In 1848 Marx and Engels issued the *Communist Manifesto*—more essay than manifesto—which, with its doctrine of the class struggle and the reform of society through revolution, did not make great progress in England.

In 1848, J. M. Ludlow, Frederick Denison Maurice, and Charles Kingsley, responding to their sympathy for the defeated Chartists, started the movement for social and personal regeneration to which in 1850 Maurice gave the name Christian Socialism. The contacts which they and their associates established with labor, their efforts to promote coöperative associations among the workers, and their sponsorship of education for the working classes laid the foundation for the participation by university men in the labor movement and contributed to the awakening of the clergy to the miseries of the wage-earners. All these things helped to foster a sympathetic relationship between the church and socialist and labor leaders, for which a fertile soil existed in the pietism of a great part of the working class.

"Here one sees a feature which distinguishes the British movement from most of those abroad," wrote in 1937 Clement R. Attlee, during the Second World War leader of the British Labour Party and Deputy Prime Minister in the Churchill War Cabinet. "In no other country has Christianity become converted to Socialism to such an extent as in Britain. In no other Socialist movement has Christian thought had such a powerful leavening influence." [404a]

In the seventies another expression of social and collective action developed with the rise of the Birmingham radicals. Their leader, Joseph Chamberlain, later the great spokesman for imperialism, was mayor of that city in 1873–75. Before, during, and after his incumbency he advocated what, for the times, was a municipal socialism. He saw local government as a means of conducting common services for the community and promoted municipal utilities in gas, water, electricity, and sewage disposal. He built free libraries and art galleries and carried on slum clearance and housing development, thus, on the local level, extending the concept of a government for service. Later as a member of Parliament he sponsored legislation looking in the same direction.

In 1881 Henry Mayers Hyndman, a man of some means, founded the Social Democratic Federation which became an exponent of Marxism. The Federation was small in membership but it was aggressive, and its protests were dramatic. It was active in demonstration whenever issues arose, as in strikes, unemployment, and similar situations.

Less·explosive but fully as active was the movement sponsored by Keir Hardie. An evolutionist rather than a revolutionist, Hardie saw the hope of reform in a self-conscious expression of the aims of labor through political action. In 1893 he founded the Independent Labour Party as a means of promoting this idea, leading ultimately to the fusion of the more conservative socialist and labor interests into what is now the British Labour Party.

All these enterprises—Owenism, Marxism, the Christian Socialists, the Birmingham radicals, the Social Democratic Federation, the Independent Labour Party—successively and variously attacked the theory of government expressed by Nicholls and the other exponents of a deterrent relief. Socialism's most direct and specific challenge to the Poor Law came, however, from the Fabians. Of all the movements directed toward social reform, this organization, founded in 1883, was the most fortunate in its membership. It attracted to itself the most delightful, able, and original body of men and women ever, perhaps, to have been gathered together in a common project, certainly at least in the field of social action.

The Fabian Society started in the discussions of a small group of persons who debated the proposition "that an association be formed whose ultimate aim shall be the reconstruction of society in accordance with the highest moral possibilities." A suggested first object was "the cultivation of a perfect character in each and all." At the meeting on January 4, 1884, when the name "Fabian Society" was adopted, the first proposition was modified to read that "its ultimate aim shall be *to help on* the reconstruction, etc." [485a] The suggestion "for the peaceful regeneration of the race by the cultivation of perfection of individual character"—I am quoting from Bernard Shaw's history of the Fabian Society—was not accepted. "Certain members of that circle," says Shaw, "modestly feeling that the revolution would have to wait an unreasonably long time if postponed until they personally had attained perfection, set up the banner of Socialism militant." [494a]

The adoption of the name Fabian and the inclusion of the words "help on" are indicative of the policy by which the new Society proposed to achieve socialism. Its members supported an evolution, not a revolution, and they undertook to help the process of evolution by discussing, advocating, and sponsoring those next immediate steps in political and social reform that seemed to be related to their ultimate goal.

Shaw was elected to the Society on September 5, 1884; Sidney Webb and Sydney Olivier on May 1, 1885; and Graham Wallas a year later. These four men formed the nucleus of a little group that determined the policies of the organization:

We preached continuously the doctrine of Socialism as a matter of abstract economic and political theory [wrote Sidney Webb, reviewing in 1929 the work of the Society]. But we also set ourselves—and this was the specific feature of the Society's work, in which it stood alone—to detach the conception of Socialism from such extraneous ideas as suddenness and simultaneity of change, violence and compulsion, and atheism or anticlericalism. What helped to do this was our no less practical translation of Socialism into separate projects of social and industrial reform, adapted to the circumstances of Great Britain, which could be carried into effect by separate Acts of Parliament. And as a Society, we welcomed the adhesion of men and women of every religious denomination or of none, strongly insisting that Socialism was not Secularism; and that the very object and purpose of all sensible collective action was the development of the individual soul or conscience or character. It is no small gain that the British Labour Party is the only Labor or Socialist Party in Europe that is not Secularist and anti-religious.[505a]

In pursuance of this policy the Fabians concerned themselves with a long succession of immediate, practical reforms from suffrage for women—"that men no longer need special political privilege to protect them against women, and that the sexes should henceforth enjoy equal political rights" (this plank, needless to say, written by Shaw) to the eight-hour day, the municipalization of the London docks, municipal water, housing, public education, minimum wage, and a multiplicity of other projects.

They held meetings, they issued scores of publications—212 tracts in their first forty years. Individual members entered the field of politics and public administration, and into many other areas of life carried inspiration and ideas derived from the discussions of the Society.

The problem of poverty and the Poor Law was a concern of the Fabians from the start. They issued numerous publications on the reform of the Poor Law, addressed leading questions on the subject to candidates for office, and unceasingly in one way or another attacked existing policies and proposed reforms. The program of the Society as developed through the first twenty-five years of its existence appears in the Minority report of the Royal Commission on the Poor Laws and Relief of Distress to be discussed in the next chapter. The major premise of this report—that the Poor Law be abolished—was essentially and typically Fabian.

Three years after the formation of the Fabian Society, one of England's successful industrialists undertook a study so important in its influence upon social thought as almost to constitute a movement in itself. This capitalist and man of affairs was Charles Booth. In 1886 he began an inquiry into the life and labor of the people in London, reported in a series of publications, the first appearing in 1889 and the last, the seventeenth issued, in 1903.

Booth's study was the greatest representative of the fourth attack upon the principles of 1834. Perhaps "attack" is not the word to describe the vast number of inquiries conducted by Parliamentary committees, royal commissions, and other governmental groups, and even by individuals, which characterize the nineteenth and twentieth centuries just as pamphleteering was the typical expression of the seventeenth and eighteenth centuries. These studies, ranging over a wide variety of subjects relating to every aspect of the life of England, provided a leverage of fact which helped ultimately to upset the established individualism of the times. The data contributed by Booth was the most comprehensive of all the material secured through three-quarters of a century of inquiry, but two other individuals who preceded him exerted through social studies an important influence upon their generations. The first was Edwin Chadwick whose report upon the sanitary condition of the laboring population of Great Britain was not a private enterprise but an official task assigned to him by the Poor Law commissioners to whom he was secretary. That report, however, published in 1842 was so much Chadwick's own study of collected data that it stands as his personal contribution.[308] In it Chadwick, the advocate of the complete responsibility of the individual for his need of relief, set forth the facts which showed how environmental conditions were contributing to the mortality and ill health of the people. As social investigator, he demonstrated what as administrator of relief he was denying, namely, that destitution cannot wholly be charged to the person who must seek help of the state—and gave the initiating impetus to the public health movement in England and in the United States.

The second of the two predecessors of Charles Booth was Henry Mayhew. Mayhew's approach was different from that of Chadwick and Booth. Mayhew was a reporter and journalist. In 1849 he began a series of articles in the London *Morning Chronicle* on "London Labour and the London Poor." These articles, later published in book form, profoundly stirred the philanthropists of their day. Octavia Hill, then a young girl, was so deeply affected by what she read that with the added influence of the essays of the Christian Socialists "she began to think all laughter or amusement was wicked." [475a]

The articles as they appeared in the *Chronicle* were likewise a definite factor in stimulating Frederick Denison Maurice to his part in the activity that gave birth to Christian Socialism. His son and biographer, Frederick Maurice writes:

They presented a picture of misery and destitution. They showed an impotence on the part of the working classes, in many trades at least, to make fair terms for themselves, an utter failure of the principle of demand and supply to regulate with satisfactory results the relations of employer and employed, which startled those who knew most of the poor of London.[476b]

What Mayhew took for his coverage as an individual observer, Booth, forty years later, defined as the field of a study for which he organized a staff and to which he applied the best of the current methods of research. His inquiry into the life and labor of the people in London was the first of modern social surveys.

The situation that impelled Booth to the study of the life and labor of the people in London is described by his wife:

People's minds were very full of the various problems connected with the position of the poor, and opinions the most diverse were expressed, remedies of the most contradictory nature were proposed. The works of Ruskin, the labors of Miss Octavia Hill, the principles and practice of the C.O.S., all contributed to the upheaval of thought and feeling. The simple, warm hearted and thoughtless benevolence of former ages was held up to reprobation. . . . In the opinion of some, the great evils to be met were improvidence and self indulgence. To relieve from the consequences of these was to aggravate the mischief.

Yet another view was held, that the selfishness and vice of low lives was the result of the selfishness and vice of high lives; that the first duty of the rich was to produce among their poorer neighbors the physical condition which alone could render decent existence possible. Good air, more room, better clothes, better food, and similar advantages would exorcise the demon which ran rife.

"Stimulate private charity," said one school. "Relieve the rates. It is the State-paid pauper who is the source of all harm."

"Down with charity," said another set; "the very word has become a degradation. Let the State see to it that the toiling millions are fed and housed as they should be."

"Toiling millions," would be replied, "The people who are in want never really toil at all. They are wastrels, lazy and ill-tempered. No one in England who will work need want."

These various views, and many others, were listened to by Charles Booth, and ever more earnestly did he seek an answer to the question.

Who are the people of England? How do they really live? What do they really want? Do they want what is good, and if so, how is it to be given to them? [409a]

Booth's investigation was a two-way inquiry. He studied people by trades and by the districts in which they lived. He surveyed the conditions under which they worked; the size, construction, and quality of the homes they occupied; and the extent to which over-crowding existed. Hours of labor, rates of wages, unemployment and irregular employment were covered by his investigation. It was a study of the people, not a study of the poor; but it soon developed that the poor formed a large portion of the people. "The result of all our inquiries make it reasonably sure that one-third of the population are on or about the line of poverty or below it." [407a]

Year after year came the reports of his findings, each published volume reinforcing the last until England had a cumulative picture of the life of the people of its metropolis such as had never been presented before. Everything contributed to lend weight to his reports. The quality of the study, its systematic and workmanlike approach, and its scientific method carried conviction from the start, setting an example in research and a standard that influenced and inspired many other subsequent studies. The man himself brought support to his own conclusions because every one knew that he was disinterested. That he was a successful business man, conservative in political philosophy, gave him a hearing from the propertied classes which perhaps he would otherwise not have had; and yet his attitude was such that he won the confidence of reformers like George Lansbury, who had this to say of him:

Charles Booth was not a Socialist, in fact he made his investigations primarily to prove the falsity of Socialism—at least, that is how I understood it. He was, however, the most fairminded of all the social experts, I ever came across. I think he did his work much fairer and more thoroughly than any of those who came after him, and his East London and South-East London investigations are standard works of their kind. [464b]

Booth, however, did not set out to prove anything. He wanted to know, to get the facts; and it was his facts which made his study significant and which worked an enormous change in the minds of many people about the problem of destitution and what needed to be done about it.

A few years later, in 1901, Booth's findings for London were confirmed for a small city by the publication of R. Seebohm Rowntree's study of York. Rowntree reported that "27.84% of the total population of the city, were living in poverty." [488a]

Booth's and Rowntree's facts provided the most effective answer that had yet been made to those who believed poverty to be the fault of the individual, a malady to be cured by the pressure of a deterrent Poor Law. Their findings and revelations about the life of the people in London and in York, along with the vast range of information which the many and varied inquiries of the nineteenth century produced, supplied important evidence about the influence of environment upon the problem of destitution, evidence which was used to good effect by the men and women who felt that government should take a more aggressive part in improving the general welfare.

As the century approached its close, the Poor Law itself began to feel the impact of the congeries of forces that were sweeping England toward social change. The Statute of 1884 which completed the basic extension of male suffrage to the working classes was followed in the next year by specific legislation to remove the disqualification, which prohibited voting in parliamentary and municipal elections, from persons who received medical or surgical assistance or medicine for themselves or their families from the poor rates. [59]

At about the same time a system of work relief was established which was designed to help the workman without subjecting him to the processes of pauperism. In 1886 Joseph Chamberlain, the Birmingham radical, then president of the Local Government Board, issued a circular recommending that the boards of guardians endeavor to arrange with the local authorities for public work in the laying-out of recreation grounds, new cemeteries, new streets, for the paving of unpaved streets, the making of footpaths in country roads, and other forms of spade labor. While this assistance was designed for persons whom "owing to previous conditions and circumstances, it is undesirable to send to the workhouse, or to treat as subject for pauper relief," the distinction in practice broke down and men who had previously been aided by the Poor Law as well as new applicants were helped. A way of circumventing the workhouse had been found. [327a]

Later, in 1905, this program led to the Unemployed Workmen Act which set up an elaborate structure entirely outside the Poor Law, with distress committees administering private and public funds in the interest of subsidized emigration, labor exchanges, and the provision of employment in work colonies and through various municipal enterprises. Persons aided in this way did not lose their right to exercise the franchise.[62] Although in practice this program did not prove to be the solution of unemployment relief that had been hoped for, and therefore was discontinued in 1929, it represented a significant invasion of the domain of the Poor Law.

Chamberlain's great interest as far as the Poor Law was concerned, however, had to do with old age. He and Charles Booth took an active part in agitation toward a provision for old people that would be entirely separate from public relief. Chamberlain advocated voluntary insurance with contributions from the state. Booth supported a pension that could be claimed by all persons irrespective of any test of destitution or merit. Both men were members of the Royal Commission on the Aged Poor which in 1895 reported in hopeless division. The differences between those who were opposed to any aid outside poor relief and those who wanted pensions and insurance, and the inability of the proponents of the various schemes and remedial measures to come to any agreement, prevented the kind of strong recommendation that might have led to legislative action.

One of the suggestions of the Commission, even though it was not unanimous, was subsequently translated into relief policy by the Local Government Board, first in a preliminary statement in 1896 and later and more definitely in a circular letter issued on August 4, 1900. This circular is significant as being the first official recommendation that applicants for relief be not urged to enter the workhouse:

With regard to the treatment of the deserving poor, it has been felt that persons who have habitually led decent and deserving lives should, if they require relief in their old age, receive different treatment from those whose previous habits and character have been unsatisfactory and who have failed to exercise thrift in the bringing up of their families or otherwise. The Board consider that aged deserving persons should not be urged to enter the workhouse at all unless there is some cause which renders such a course necessary, such as infirmity of mind or body, the absence of house accommodations or of a suitable person to care for them or some similar cause, but that they should be relieved by having adequate outdoor relief granted to them. The Board are happy to think that it is commonly the practice of Boards of Guardians to grant outdoor relief in such cases, but they are afraid that too frequently such relief is not adequate in amount. They are desirous of pressing upon the guardians that such relief should, when granted, be always adequate.[328a]

The recommendations of the Local Government Board also provided that in the workhouses persons of sixty-five who "by reason of their moral character or behavior or previous habits" were "sufficiently deserving," should have separate day-rooms and separate sleeping cubicles instead of the dormitory life; privileges in their hours of rising and retiring; increased liberty and facilities for visits from friends; a separate locker with a key but to be opened for inspection; and tobacco, dry tea, and sugar.

In these regulations relating to the treatment of the aged, we see an interesting mixture of the old and the new. There is the emphasis upon moral character as a factor in destitution and the interpretation of failure to save as an evidence of wrong—both postulated upon the theory that the individual was wholly responsible for his economic plight; at the same time there is the departure from the principle of less eligibility in the kind of care offered in the institution and in the recommendation that, at least for the deserving aged, outdoor relief be made the rule instead of, as Longley and his associates had advocated, the exception.

Most dramatic of all the evidences of the influence of social change upon the administration of the Poor Law were the developments in the Poplar Union in London. William Crooks, himself a workhouse boy, and George Lansbury, having been elected guardians in 1892, found themselves with a sizable block of sympathetic members of the Board after the legislation of 1894 had liberalized the electoral qualifications for that office. They instituted a major revolution in the administration of relief in that part of London. The spirit of the new dispensation has been described for us by Mr. Lansbury in his autobiography:

From the first moment I determined to fight for one policy only, and that was decent treatment for the poor outside the workhouse, and hang the rates! This sort of saying brings censure on me and on the movement: it cannot be helped. My view of life places money, property, and privilege on a much lower scale than human life. I am quite aware some people are bad and deceitful. I know this because I know myself. I know people drink, gamble, and are often lazy. I also know that taken in the mass the poor are as decent as any other class, and so when I stood as a Guardian I took as my policy that no widow or orphan, no sick, infirm, or aged person should lack proper provision of the needs of life, and ablebodied people should get work or maintenance. Today everybody agrees with this policy. I also determined to humanize Poor Law administration: I never could see any difference between outdoor relief and a state pension, or between the pension of a widowed queen and outdoor relief for the wife or mother of a worker. The nonsense about the disgrace of the Poor Law I fought against till at least in London we killed it for good and all.[464c]

This was a vastly different language from that of 1834; and the Poplar guardians soon found themselves in conflict with the Poor Law Division of the Local Government Board. A decade or more of struggle finally precipitated an inquiry into the activities of the Poplar Guardians, conducted by J. S. Davy, the chief general inspector of the Board and a strong advocate of traditional Poor Law policy. Among the hundreds of pages of testimony taken at the hearings (which incidentally had no effect in changing the relief philosophy of the guardians), the statement presented by W. G. Martley, secretary of the Poplar branch of the Charity Organization Society, is the clearest expression of the difference between the old and the new.

In those days (i.e. before 1894) the Board had no policy at all, good or bad, the guardians did pretty much what the officers told them to do, and their guiding principles seemed to be the saving of the rates and avoidance of trouble to themselves. . . .

A new era commenced in 1894 when the conditions of election were altered. Guardians of a new type were chosen, and gradually a new policy was formed and developed, the credit of which rests mainly with Mr. Crooks (president of the Board) and Mr. Lansbury. . . .

The first principle of the Poplar policy, as I understood it, is that Society has a duty toward its weaker members, which is not fulfilled by throwing them back on themselves, but requires social action to be taken on their behalf, and the second is that those who seek or need relief are neither better nor worse than men and women in general, and are to be regarded for the most part as victims of an unfair social system, and only in a minority of cases as the authors of their own misfortunes. . . .

I am sure [Mr. Martley then adds on his own account] that the mere refusal of relief will never abolish pauperism so long as the industrial and social causes which produce it remain untouched. It may shift the incidence of the burden, but the burden will remain to be borne by somebody.[313a]

This was, indeed, the testimony of a new era. One hundred years of change in the life of England had begun at last to affect the thinking of men about the problem of poverty. New concepts of government, new forces in the electorate, new ideas about the constitution and purpose of society had started hewing at the bases of the old order. After three centuries of practically unchallenged operation, the Poor Law was meeting a social philosophy that with growing power would attack principles and methods that hitherto had had the authority almost of revelation in the administration of relief.

XVII

THE ROYAL COMMISSION OF 1909

It certainly does not consort with twentieth century ideas to imagine that there is to be a class of hewers of wood and drawers of
water. I want no class of hewers of wood and drawers of water: no
class destined to remain there, and prevented from rising, because
we do not provide for it.

> SIDNEY WEBB in discussion after an
> address to the Association of
> Technical Institutes, 1909.[452a]

B Y the time the twentieth century had advanced halfway toward
the end of its first decade, the battle around public relief had
greatly increased in intensity. The protagonists of the opposing
forces were clearly defined. On the one side was the Poor Law Division of the Local Government Board supported by the Charity
Organization Society; on the other were the Fabians and Labor.
Each side was dissatisfied with the existing state of affairs in relief:
the Poor Law Division because it saw the principles of 1834 being
invaded, the Fabians and Labor because change was not coming fast
enough. Both parties wanted a resolution of the situation. Everybody, therefore, applauded the appointment on December 4, 1905,
of a Royal Commission on the Poor Laws and Relief of Distress.

The work of the much desired Commission soon resolved itself
into a conflict between the two opposing groups. The Poor Law
Division was represented by four ranking officials. The chief inspector, J. S. Davy, was, however, not a commissioner. Associated
with the Poor Law leaders were six members of the Charity Organization Society, notably Sir Charles S. Loch, Mrs. Bosanquet, Octavia Hill, and T. Hancock Nunn. By the time of the completion of
the Commission's report, this combination of Poor Law and Charity
Organization had developed a decided majority with fourteen members. The Minority consisted of four persons—Mrs. Webb, the
Fabian; Mr. Lansbury, Socialist-Labourite; Francis Chandler, Trades
Unionist; and the Rev. Prebendary, later Bishop, H. Russell Wakefield. The work and vigor of the Fabian-Labour attack was chiefly

carried by the Webbs, for the appointment of Mrs. Webb to the Commission obviously and automatically brought the other member of "the firm" into the study. The battle soon defined itself as the Webbs against the Poor Law.

Sidney Webb had long had an interest in the subject of relief. His father had been a member of one of the London boards of guardians. Webb, a Londoner born and reared, had started work when he was sixteen years old. After a short excursion into business, he entered the civil service where he continued from 1878 to 1891. In 1892 he became a member of the London County Council, serving in this capacity for eighteen years, thirteen of which were behind him at the time of the appointment of the Royal Commission on the Poor Laws and Relief of Distress.

As a member of the London Council, he was the inspiration of a whole series of municipal enterprises from the provision of libraries and parks to the development of transportation and the control of electrification. He was the creator and moving spirit of a comprehensive educational system for London through secondary and technical schools up to the University of London. As early as 1890 he had written on the reform of the Poor Law for the Fabian Society, and in 1898 he and Mrs. Webb had started their great study of local government that was to continue for more than thirty years. An interest in the subject of relief was inevitable for him.

Whereas Sidney Webb began his career as a boy who had to get his own education, Mrs. Webb "had entered the field of controversy from the standpoint of big enterprise, party politics and metropolitan philanthropy." [504b]

Her father, Richard Potter, was a business man of large affairs and she had been born into a life where [to quote Mary Agnes Hamilton in *Sidney and Beatrice Webb*]

the whole scale of existence was rich, ample, various and important. Not only did the Potters occupy a series of extensive and expensive houses; they moved, as of easy natural right, in the best circles: those socially distinguished and those moreover politically and intellectually most commanding. Their friends were people at the tops of their respective trees." [452b]

By the time Miss Potter was twenty-five she had tired of London society and had found nothing satisfying to her in the work of the Charity Organization Society, with which for a brief time she was associated as a member of a district committee and as a volunteer visitor. She had in 1884 and 1885 acted as a rent collector in a philanthropic housing project, but it was in the field of social research that she finally found her career.

Why [she asks in *My Apprenticeship*] did I select the chronic destitution of whole sections of the people, whether illustrated by overcrowded homes, by the demoralized casual labor at the docks, or by the low wages, long hours and insanitary conditions of the sweated industries, as the first subject for inquiry? Unlike my sister, Kate, who had toiled for six years as a volunteer rent collector, I was not led into the homes of the poor by the spirit of charity. I had never been moved by the "hard cases" which, as I thought, "make bad law." What impelled me to concentrate on the condition of the people as the immediate question for investigation was the state of mind in the most vital centers of business enterprise, of political agitation and of academic reasoning.

There were, in fact, in the 'eighties and 'nineties two controversies raging in periodicals and books, and giving rise to perpetual argument within my own circle of relations and acquaintances: on the one hand, the meaning of the poverty of masses of men; and, on the other, the practicability and desirability of political and industrial democracy as a set-off to, perhaps as a means of redressing, the grievances of the majority of the people. Was the poverty of the many a necessary condition of the wealth of the nation and of its progress in civilization? And if the bulk of the people were to remain poor and uneducated, was it desirable, was it even safe, to entrust them with the weapon of trade-unionism, and through the ballot-box, with making and controlling the Government of Great Britain with its enormous wealth and its far-flung dominions? [504c]

It is interesting how much the same characteristics of the times that aroused Charles Booth to the making of his study of the life and labor of the people in London should have influenced Mrs. Webb, for it was Booth who provided her with the opportunity she desired. She became one of his investigators—first into the condition of workers at the docks and later into the sweated industries. From this experience with Booth she moved to a study of her own of the coöperative movement, and it was in the course of an effort to gain historical perspective for that enterprise that she made the acquaintance of Sidney Webb. This was in 1890. Toward the end of that year, having completed the study of the Coöperative Movement, she began one of Trade Unionism. At the suggestion of Sidney Webb this was made a joint project, and in 1892, with their marriage, the firm of Webb was definitely established and the long series of their great researches was begun.

Mrs. Webb became a member of the Fabian Society in 1893 but for the next thirteen years was comparatively inactive in that capacity. Edward P. Pease, long the secretary of the Society, says: "The Transformation of Mrs. Webb from a student and writer, a typical 'socialist of the chair,' into an active leader and propagandist originated in December, 1905, when she was appointed a member of the Royal Commission on the Poor Law." [485b]

It was only in England that there could have occurred a conflict about the problem of relief so pointed, so clearly defined, and so basic as that in which the forces of the Poor Law, the Charity Organization Society, and the Webbs now engaged. In the United States, for example, we have had public relief since the days of the colonists, but except for the repercussions of English thought we have had no philosophy comparable to that which in Great Britain was derived from the report of 1834. We have had individuals "for or against the poor in their arguments," and we have had every variety of attitude, prejudice, and concern in relation to the problem of poverty; but we have had nothing that has organized our thinking about relief in the way that England was served by the commissioners of inquiry in 1832–34.

Their report was more than an ordinary document of state. It was a pronouncement, as it were, from Sinai. It established what was almost in the nature of a moral code. It was a doctrine founded in statute. Less eligibility and the offer of the workhouse were the core of a philosophy and a creed against which every subsequent development in relief, through three-quarters of a century, was tested and weighed. Each new proposition was considered in the light of the fundamentals of 1834. They furnished the background for the proceedings of the Royal Commission of 1905–09, pointing the issue, with conservatives and progressives alike measuring their distance from the great report of seventy-five years before.

James Davy, the chief inspector for the Poor Law Division, opened the battle with testimony to his loyalty to the principles of 1834, and in so far as there had been departure from them an advocacy of a return in spirit and in letter.

Early in his examination he accepted without reservation, in response to a question by T. Hancock Nunn, one of the Charity Organization Society members, the principle of less eligibility defined as consisting "first, of the loss of personal reputation, (what is understood by the stigma of pauperism); secondly, the loss of personal freedom which is secured by detention in a workhouse; and thirdly, the loss of political freedom by suffering disenfranchisement." [315a]

Charity, he felt, was better for the poor than public relief because "it does not enter into their calculations; whereas if they know that a state provision is waiting for them, they are tempted to unthrift." [315b]

He [the unemployed man] must stand by his accidents; he must suffer for the general good of the body politic; according to my view, what you have to consider is not this or that pauper, but the general good of the whole community; and the general good of the whole community is, I submit, that every obstacle should be put in the way of a man settling down into the status of a pauper—for pauper he is, whether he is disenfranchised or whether he is not.[315c]

The Webbs, on the other hand, were in complete and unconditional revolt. Their program was the abolition of the Poor Law. Between these two extremes of attitude toward the principles of 1834, an unremitting conflict was waged from 1905 to 1909. In the range of its investigations and in the quality and quantity of its inquiries, the Commission of the twentieth century went far beyond its predecessor. It held 159 hearings, examining 452 witnesses who responded to over 100,000 questions. Special studies were made by a corps of investigators. There were extensive statistical analyses of relief and of many other related subjects, and specialists were called upon for a variety of reports in addition to which members of the Commission themselves undertook particular assignments. Upon completion, the testimony and the researches covered forty-seven published volumes.

When all this had been done the members of the Commission still found themselves in opposing positions. The fourteen members, chiefly drawn from the Poor Law officialdom and the Charity Organization Society, published one report—the Majority report. The remaining four persons, headed by Mrs. Webb, issued another report—the Minority report. The two documents covered 1,600 pages. The division expressed in the two reports lost for the Commission of 1905–09 the quality of pronouncement that the clarity of a single purpose gave to the Report of 1834; yet despite divergent recommendations, there was substantial agreement in their dissent from the principles enunciated by the earlier commission, the Commission for Inquiring into the Administration and Practical Operation of the Poor Law.

What the Majority report stated with qualification and almost reluctantly, the Minority report asserted flatly and without reservation. One suspects that under the pressure and attack of the Webbs, the Majority receded further from the position of 1834 than, left to itself, it would have moved. It did not exhibit the same consistency of purpose that at every point characterized the Minority report. Nevertheless, the total effect of the more than three years of work was to demonstrate that England had at last emancipated herself from the domination of the principles established by the earlier inquiry. The most convincing evidence of this is to be found not in the Minority report, which obviously was the voice of the forces battling the Poor Law, but in the report of the Majority:

It has been impressed upon us in the course of our inquiry that the name Poor Law has gathered about it associations of harshness and still more of hopelessness, which we fear might seriously obstruct the reforms which we desire to see initiated. We are aware that a mere change of name will not prevent the old associations from recurring, if it does not represent an essential change in the spirit of the work. But in our subsequent criticism and recommendations, we hope to show the way to a system of help which will be better expressed by the title of Public Assistance than by that of Poor Law. The general aim will remain, as it always has been, the independence and welfare of the people, but as a means towards that end we desire to introduce into all branches of the work a spirit of efficiency and hopefulness. We think that this object will be made more easy of attainment, and that the work will be more accurately described by a change of title.[316a]

This was, indeed, a departure. The negative tone of the recommendations of 1834 had become in 1909 a positive emphasis upon the importance of facilitating a "system of help." Contrast, also, the findings in 1834 that "the pauperism of the greater number has originated in indolence, improvidence or vice, and might have been averted by ordinary care and industry," [305w] with the reference in 1909 by the Majority report to "modifications and developments in our industrial system which cannot be ignored, and their products and wreckage, when either out of employment or in distress, require a treatment more elastic and varied than the simple method which, eighty years ago, was sufficient to cope with able-bodied pauperism in agricultural districts." [316b] Compare the statement in 1834 that "for the general diffusion of right principles and habits we are to look not so much to any economic arrangements and regulations, as to the influence of a moral and religious education" [305x] with the recommendations of the Majority report in 1909 for a national system of employment exchanges, raising of the standard of the child-labor laws, extension of technical education, regularization of employment, planning of public work to take up the slack in periods of unemployment, unemployment and invalidity insurance, and like measures.

Even more significant of change is the attitude toward the workhouse as a test. This by implication is abandoned. Only a short paragraph is devoted to the subject, and in the recommendations of the Majority report no mention of the test workhouse for the able-bodied is made.

To the general workhouse there is specific opposition—"so long as an institution remains the receptacle for all classes needing relief, and good, bad, and indifferent characters are herded together, so long will the bad be indulged and the respectable suffer." [316c]

The workhouse is found to be unsuitable for the able-bodied:

The only principle which can be defended in the case of the ablebodied is that they should leave the workhouse better fitted to earn their living than when they entered it. . . . But the evidence of the workhouse Chaplains, a high authority on such a point, is emphatic that, so far from this end being reached, the effect of a sojourn in the workhouse is wholly bad. [316d]

Essentially, the change that has taken place as compared with 1834 is that the Majority report has substituted "treatment" for "test." As against the wholesale deterrence of the earlier Commission, it proposes a program directed to the reform and prevention of pauperism in the individual. Outdoor relief is viewed as an opportunity and a means to this end. To abolish it would be unwise not only because this would involve "considerable hardship" and "a feeling of harshness and injustice" in those affected, but also because it

would deprive the administrators of the Poor Law of a method of assistance which may be turned to good account in skillful hands. . . . While we do not disguise the fact that we desire by the reforms we suggest to reduce the present number of cases by a wiser discrimination, we hope also to check the supply of future pauperism by a more constructive policy. . . . [316e]

What we are aiming at is, instead of a system of allowances, granted capriciously and irresponsibly to meet a constantly increasing demand, to substitute a system of careful and varied assistance, in which the "allowance" will be only one of many forms of help, and which will be directly designed to raise the recipients, or where that is not possible the children of the recipients, to a position of independence.[316f]

The concept of treatment has here taken the place of the concept of less eligibility, but not without reservation. Thus, in speaking of the general mixed workhouse the Majority report points out that "it may act as a deterrent in the case of the aged and infirm to whom it might legitimately be a refuge," but adds, "at the same time we think it will be a great misfortune if the aged should be brought to prefer life in the workhouse (under whatever name it may in future be known) to an independent life amongst their own friends and relations." [316g] In other words, what is wanted is not too much but a little deterrence.

The same attitude appears in the discussion of the exercise of the vote by persons receiving relief. While the Majority report recommended that "no disfranchisement should be attached to any form of medical assistance," [316h] it at the same time submitted that "persons who have received assistance other than medical relief for not less than three months in the aggregate in the qualifying year be disfranchised." [316i] Octavia Hill wanted a stricter deterrence than this: "I regret that the recommendations with regard to disfranchisement extend, rather than diminish, the number of those dependent on public funds, who would have votes." [316j]

The program of treatment was to be administered by private charity, supplemented by specialized public institutions for children, the aged, the sick; and industrial and agricultural institutions, labor colonies, and detention colonies for the various categories of the able-bodied. Paralleling a public assistance committee to be developed in every community would be a voluntary aid committee.

Generally speaking, a first application for assistance will naturally be made to the Voluntary Aid Committee. Temporary need due to non-current causes will belong primarily to the sphere of voluntary aid; chronic distress or destitution to the Public Assistance Committee.[316k]

Restoration to independent habits of life should be an ever present consideration in the minds of the various organizations in prescribing treatment. In some cases in which such restoration may seem to be impossible, curative treatment may be effective if undertaken by voluntary organizations having within their ranks persons of experience whose whole lives are given to this work.[316l]

In order to make this plan effective, the Majority introduced a new form of less eligibility:

An essential principle to be observed in connection with Home Assistance to the ablebodied is that it shall be in some way less agreeable than assistance given by the Voluntary Aid Committee. Unless the superiority of the assistance afforded by the Voluntary Aid Committee is in some way secured [the Majority report continues with delightful frankness] it is doubtful whether that Committee will be able to collect voluntary subscriptions for the purpose of helping deserving cases of unemployment. Experience has again and again shown that the charitable public will not contribute to any extent towards a purpose for which they are also taxed or rated. It, therefore, follows that if, as is our desire, cases in the class we are considering should be chiefly dealt with by the Voluntary Aid Committee, it is necessary that the aid given by that committee should confer greater benefits, or have less onerous conditions attached to it than the Home Assistance given by the Public Assistance Committee.[316m]

This proposal for an integration of private charity with public assistance represented the antithesis of everything the Webbs believed, and helped to point the issue between the Majority and the Minority. The Minority report was instant in its rejection of the plan:

To these irresponsible Committees of benevolent amateurs all applicants will apply in the first instance; and in case of refusal of aid, the Public Assistance Committee is to be bound to assist the applicant if at all, "in some way less agreeable" than the Voluntary Aid Committee would have done! We have found some difficulty in unravelling the complicated details of the constitution recommended in this scheme for the administration of an annual expenditure from the rates and taxes of, in England and Wales alone, at least 15,000,000 pounds sterling. What is clear is that the unconcealed purpose of constructing this elaborate and mysterious framework,

"With centric and eccentric scribbled o'er
Cycle and epicycle, orb in orb"

is to withdraw the whole relief of distress from popular control.[317c]

The Minority report is equally downright in its rejection of disfranchisement:

We can see no practical advantage in disfranchising a person because he has received the treatment which Parliament has provided for his case. The evidence goes to show that, so far as disfranchisement has any effect at all, it is a "Test" of the very worst kind; deterring the good and self respecting, and in no way influencing the willing parasite.[317d]

Throughout the Minority statement and program there is none of the reservation about deterrence and less eligibility which we find in the Majority. It vigorously attacks what it calls "the fatal ambiguity about the axiom that the condition of the pauper is to be less eligible than the condition of the lowest class of independent laborers." [317e]

The program of the Minority was founded upon a complete rejection of the Poor Law in philosophy and method. It offered, as a substitute, a concept of treatment but with a different emphasis from that to be found in the Majority report. It proposed that this treatment be carried out by breaking up the Poor Law and reassembling its activities under various existing governmental agencies.

It pointed out that the Poor Law of 1834 was directed to deterrent provision for an undefined pauperism. In three-quarters of a century this provision had taken on specialties. The word "pauper" included individuals at every stage of life and with every form of ailment and need. Institutionally and otherwise, the Poor Law had found itself having to make arrangements for dealing with these various types of distress. It had become responsible for the education of pauper children, for the care of the sick and of the aged, for the maintenance of the feebleminded and insane, and for the employment of the able-bodied. Meanwhile, in the community outside the Poor Law, similar provision was being made for persons who were not classed as paupers—there was care for the sick in public hospitals; there was the Unemployed Workmen Act of 1905; there were institutions for the mentally ill and also for the feebleminded; and in 1908, while the Commission was still at work, there had been enacted outside the Poor Law a system of pensions for the aged.

Why, asked the Minority, should this duplication of activities and agencies continue? Why should not all health activities be carried on by the public health authority, education by the educational authority, and so on? Moreover, these various public bodies had undertaken certain relief operations. The educational system had established school feeding. Free medical care was supplied by the health agencies. Would it not be sound to have these authorities take over responsibility for such relief as was involved for the persons coming under their charge? On this assumption the following program was proposed:

That the services at present administered by the Destitution Authorities (other than those connected with vagrants or the ablebodied)—that is to say the provision for:—

(i)   Children of school age;

(ii) The sick and permanently incapacitated, the infants under school age, the aged needing institutional care;

(iii) The mentally defective of all grades and ages; and

(iv) The aged to whom pensions are awarded—should be assumed under the directions of the County and County Borough Councils, by

(i)   The Education Committee

(ii) The Health Committee

(iii) The Asylums Committee

(iv) The Pension Committee respectively.

That the several committees concerned . . . should . . . provide . . . for the several classes of persons committed to their charge whatever treatment they may deem most appropriate to their condition; being either institutional treatment, in the various specialized schools, hospitals, asylums, etc., under their charge; or whenever judged preferable, domiciliary treatment, conjoined with the grant of Home Aliment [i.e., relief] where this is indispensably required.[317f]

To coördinate these activities the office of Registrar of Public Assistance should be created, charged with keeping a registry of all persons under the care of the various authorities, with assessing the charges to be made for particular kinds of relief and treatment, and with sanctioning the grants of home aliment proposed by the committee concerned with the treatment of the case.

His business [i.e., public assistance registrar] will be limited strictly to the ascertainment of the pecuniary resources of the family—not with any view of preventing the requisite treatment being afforded, for that will already have begun—but in order to ascertain what charge, if any, should be made for it, and upon whom it should be made. He, having no concern with the health or morals of the family, will have no more right than the agent of an insurance company or the assessor of income-tax to do what in a relieving officer excites such resentment, namely pry into the bedroom, cross examine the woman as to her relations with the male lodger, or comment on the cough and expectoration of the delicate daughter—all in order to find a reason for refusing outdoor relief and offering the workhouse instead.[317g]

The Minority report argues for specialization through its proposed categories because

> The combination in a single Destitution Officer of such heterogeneous functions is, in our judgment, fatal to the establishment of an efficient service. Struck by the imperfect qualification of the Relieving Officers for their varied and responsible duties, we asked what had been prescribed in the matter by the Local Government Board, only to find that no qualification whatever was required. Nor could the Inspectors or the Clerks to the Boards of Guardians suggest to us any qualification or training that could advantageously be insisted on for the office as it at present exists. "There is no standard," explained to us one of the inspectors, "there is no college of Out-relief, there is no faculty." [317h]

The theory underlying the treatment which the Minority proposed to substitute for the principle of less eligibility and the way in which this treatment would be applied is indicated in the following quotations from their report:

> We now come to what appears to us the worst feature of the Outdoor Relief of today. With insignificant exceptions, Boards of Guardians give these doles and allowances without requiring in return for them even the most elementary conditions. [317i]

> But when the cost and trouble of providing for the several members of the family when destitute fall upon the committees which have, as part of their ordinary duty and machinery, the periodical visitation of the home, irrespective of destitution, these committees will have the families continuously under observation. Is the child unfed at school? A member of the Children's Care Committee calls to ascertain the cause. At every birth, at every death, at every occurrence of notifiable disease, the officer of the Health Committee becomes acquainted with the circumstances of the household. Thus, the several Committees of the Town Council . . . will be perpetually doing whatever may be necessary to maintain the family intact, to encourage those members of it who are striving to keep the home together, and forcibly to restrain any member whose conduct is threatening it with ruin. [317j]

All of the foregoing program of the Minority had to do with the non-able-bodied, the people with whom the report of 1834 had scarcely concerned itself. For the able-bodied the Minority proposed separate treatment under a specially established ministry of labor. The new ministry should be responsible for carrying out certain recommended preventive measures—a country-wide network of labor exchanges, the halving through restriction of the existing amount of child labor, the withdrawal of mothers with young children from the labor market, the reduction of the hours of railway, tramway, and omnibus workers. These recommendations, while felt to be desirable on their own account, would, it was believed, create additional jobs for employable adults.

For those who despite these plans would still be out of work, it was further recommended that the ministry of labor, utilizing the trade unions, should provide unemployment insurance over a broadened range of industry. The men who could not qualify for these benefits should be sent for training to day-training camps or residential farm colonies, outdoor relief being provided for their families without the loss of the franchise. Detention camps should be established for persons requiring reformatory measures. The whole program for the able-bodied should be nationally operated.

Both Majority and Minority reports advocated larger areas of administration—national, as above, in respect to labor exchanges, insurance, and similar provisions; county, so far as the administration of relief was concerned. In this the reports carried still further the policy inaugurated by the Commission of 1832–34. The union, despite its administrative lapses, had proved to be a better unit of operation than the parish. It had reduced 15,000 jurisdictions to less than 650. The recommendation by the Commission of 1905–09 that the county and the county borough councils be utilized as the basic territorial unit for relief would reduce the number of local relief administrations by three-quarters and would correspondingly increase the average area covered by any one agency.

From this point, the differences between the two reports became more evident. The Majority saw the existing functions of the Poor Law carried out by public assistance committees appointed by the county borough councils. The Minority wanted these functions assigned to the divisions in the councils responsible for education, health, pensions, and mental disease, with such relief as might be needed to supplement the program for the prevention of unemployment administered by a to-be-created ministry of labor. In this respect the Majority stood for maintaining the status quo of the Poor Law, while the Minority advocated its abolition.

Both Majority and Minority advanced programs involving treatment through appropriate institutions and through the personal activities of the representatives of government. The treatment recommended by the Majority was to be administered by private agencies utilizing the methods of the Charity Organization Society, personal influence individually applied to the rehabilitation of the people seeking assistance. The Minority report built its concept of treatment around the use of the specialist in education, health, pensions, mental problems. There would be a committee in each field capable of meeting every ill from which the person seeking assistance might be suffering.

It is interesting that the Minority report which based its program upon categories of need and specialties of service did not recognize the administration of relief to be a specialty in itself and not something that could readily be disposed of by a system of coördination and approval of grants of aid under the supervision of a registrar of public assistance. A motivating factor in the Minority's proposal was obviously the desire to rid the poor of the stigma of the Poor Law. This phase of the program of the Minority was not emphasized by the Majority because they wanted public relief to be less desirable than private charity, and a modicum of deterrence would, therefore, not be unwelcome.

Viewed from the distance of more than a generation, the differences between the Majority and the Minority seem less significant than their areas of agreement. In three essential respects they were substantially in accord.

First, there was the rejection of the Poor Law of the nineteenth century. Despite reservations designed to give to private charity a priority over public relief, the Majority stood beside the Minority in opposition to the spirit of 1834. While the Minority was against the admixture of private charity with government in principle and in practice, it subscribed to the concept of replacing repression with treatment. The use by both groups of the term "public assistance" indicated the extent to which the doctrine of deterrence had been discarded. The findings of the Commission that reported in 1909 mark the end of the dominance of the Commission that reported in 1834.

Second, there was the agreement upon the county as the area of administration with certain functions to be carried by the national government, and, connected with this, the recognition that persons engaged in such specialized services as those growing out of the Poor Law should be appointed, not elected. As already indicated, the Commission of 1909 was continuing the trend, started in 1834, away from the small local unit toward the larger jurisdiction.

Third, there was the acceptance without debate of a concept not touched upon by the earlier Commission, a concept that indeed was foreign to its philosophy of individualism, revealing the revolution in thought and attitude which separated the two Commissions and the times of which they were a part. This was the principle of prevention and social provision. Prevention as described by the Majority and Minority reports was illustrated by measures, for example, the labor exchange, the extension of the child-labor laws, and the reduction in the length of the working day which would spread jobs and decrease unemployment. Social provision was represented in the recommendations of the two reports for the development of a system of insurance against unemployment and invalidity.

Prevention and social provision and the other recommendations of 1909 were not the creation of the Commission on the Poor Law and Relief of Distress. In their programs the Majority and Minority commissioners were only expressing the trends of their times, divergent though in some respects these trends were. If the Commission of 1834 was unanimous and if its recommendations were immediately effective, it was because there was a current consensus upon which it could draw. If the Commission of 1905–09 was divided in some respects and united in others, it was only reflecting the conflict in the opinion of its times. The nineteenth-century struggle between an uncompromising individualism and the concept of government as a social force was still in the course of being resolved. The Majority and Minority reports reflected that struggle. Their differing recommendations could not result in the sort of immediate legislative enactment that followed the unanimity of 1834; but ultimately change came, and when it came it was revolutionary, creating as far as the Poor Law was concerned a new world that has made the twentieth century different from all of its predecessors in its approach to the problem of poverty.

XVIII

SOCIAL INSURANCE

I do not agree with those who say that every man must look after himself, and that the intervention by the State in such matters as I have referred to will be fatal to his self-reliance, his foresight, and his thrift. . . . If terror be an incentive to thrift, surely the penalties of the system which we have abandoned ought to have stimulated thrift as much as anything could have been stimulated in this world. The mass of the laboring poor have known that unless they made provision for their old age betimes they would perish miserably in the workhouse. Yet they have made no provision; . . . for they have never been able to make such provision. . . . It is a great mistake to suppose that thrift is caused only by fear; it springs from hope as well as from fear; where there is no hope, be sure there will be no thrift.

WINSTON SPENCER CHURCHILL,
speaking at Dundee on unemployment,
October 10, 1908.[425a]

WHILE the Royal Commission on the Poor Laws and Relief of Distress, despite its divided recommendations, was declaring the emancipation of public assistance from the principles of 1834 and was proposing along with an emphasis upon treatment a program of prevention and social provision, Parliament itself was moving in a similar direction, building through a series of legislative acts the approach to a new order of life for the people of England.

The same day—December 4, 1905—on which the Warrant for the Royal Commission had been issued, the Conservative government, which had sponsored the plan for a study of relief, resigned. The next day the Liberals, after having been out of office for more than a decade, came into power. In the general election that took place in January 1906, they received an enormous majority, "the most sweeping reversal of party balance ever experienced in the House of Commons"—397 Liberals as against 83 Nationalists (Irish Separatists) and 157 Unionists. Labor for the first time had an appreciable group, 51 persons of whom 29 were elected as members of the newly-formed Labour party.[448a]

It was a new House, not only by reason of the shift that had taken place in party power but also with respect to the character of its membership. For the first time there had appeared in substantial numbers men who had been chosen because of their sociological ideas. These new men saw government as a means of social change.

The election was the dramatic and decisive revelation of the new forces that had been released by the nineteenth-century's successful struggle for the enfranchisement of the workers. Although, with the extension of the vote in 1884 to householders in the rural counties, affecting in particular the miners and the agricultural laborers, manhood suffrage had been close to universal for two decades, this was the first country-wide expression of a desire of the people for change.

Among the many complex elements that influence an election, two factors were evident as representing in particular the feeling of the working class. The first was a support of free trade as against the movement in the Conservative party toward the tariff and higher prices. The second was the demand that a decision made by the House of Lords in 1901 be reversed. This decision, in compelling the Amalgamated Society of Railway Servants to pay 23,000 pounds sterling in damages for losses sustained by the Taff Vale Railway Company in a strike, had set a precedent which in effect had deprived labor of its ultimate weapon in collective bargaining—the power to refuse to work.[429a] Now armed with the vote, the workers had been able to move toward the restoration of their rights by returning to Parliament candidates pledged to corrective legislation. While the labor delegates as such were greatly in the minority, a substantial majority of the new members of the House of Commons were in favor of this and other reforms.

Representative of the men who pointed the way to social change were David Lloyd George and Winston Spencer Churchill. Lloyd George had become president of the Board of Trade when the Liberals took over the government in December 1905. Two years later, when he was appointed Chancellor of the Exchequer, Churchill was his successor in the Board of Trade. They and their associates were now in a position to translate their ideas into law. Said Lloyd George in a speech at Bangor, January 19, 1906:

I believe there is a new order coming from the people of this country. It is a quiet, but certain, revolution, as revolutions come in a constitutional country, without overthrowing order, without doing an injustice to anybody, but redressing those injustices from which people suffer.[467a]

Again, speaking on September 25, 1906, at Penrhyndeuraeth:

Shame upon rich Britain that she should tolerate so much poverty among her people. . . . There is plenty of wealth in this country to provide for all and to spare. What is wanted is a fairer distribution. . . .

I do not suggest that there should be a compulsory equal distribution of the wealth of this country among its inhabitants, but I do say that the law which protects those men in the enjoyment of their great possessions should, first of all, see that those whose labor alone produces that wealth are amply protected with their families from actual need, where they are unable to purchase necessaries owing to circumstances over which they have no control. By that I mean not that they should be referred to the scanty and humiliating fare of the pauper, but that the spare wealth of the country should, as a condition of its enjoyment by its possessors, be forced to contribute first towards the honorable maintenance of those who have ceased to be able to maintain themselves.[467b]

Winston Churchill was addressing himself to the same purpose:

No view of society can possibly be complete which does not comprise within its scope both collective organization and individual incentive [he said at Glasgow, October 11, 1906]. The whole tendency of civilization is, however, towards the multiplication of the collective functions of society. The ever growing complications of civilization create for us new services which have to be undertaken by the State, and create for us an expansion of the existing services.[425b]

This was the philosophy that now began to express itself in legislation. Within six years a series of laws had been enacted forming a broad attack upon the problem of poverty. First, there was a confirmation and extension of the fundamental rights which the nineteenth century had established for the people of England. The passage of the Trade Disputes Bill, 1906, in effect reversed the Taff Vale decision of the House of Lords and made it once more possible for the workers to operate freely through their trade unions to improve their conditions of employment. The bill provided that in a trade dispute it should not be actionable to induce "some other person to break a contract of employment." It was likewise established as lawful for one or more persons "to attend at or near a house or place where a person resides or works . . . for the purpose of peacefully persuading any person to work or abstain from working." Picketing was thus legalized. Labor was once more able to speak for itself in industry.[63]

On the same day, December 21, 1906, on which the Trade Disputes Act became law, another measure for which labor had pressed received the Royal Assent. This measure came as a by-product of the nineteenth-century's achievement in making the opportunity for education available to the people of England. With attendance at school compulsory and free, there were brought dramatically to notice considerable numbers of children who were so poorly fed that their progress in learning was affected. Here was a fresh introduction to the fact of destitution, and the new forces in Parliament proposed a new method of dealing with the problem thus revealed.

Under the Provision of Meals Act of 1906, the local education authorities were empowered to supply meals where "any of the children attending an elementary school within their area are unable by reason of lack of food to take full advantage of the education provided for them." The school could collect from the parents for the cost of the food; but if the parents were unable to pay, the meals were to be furnished without charge. Moreover, "the provision of any meal under this act to a child and the failure on the part of the parent to pay any amount demanded under the act in respect of a meal shall not deprive the parent of any franchise, right or privilege, or subject him to any disability." [64]

This was a definite invasion of the Poor Law. A method of relief had been established which could be operated outside the jurisdiction of the boards of guardians and which, moreover, did not carry the loss of the vote and the other civic disabilities of pauperism. Initially the new program was not extensive. Subsequently it was applied on a large scale toward meeting the privations suffered by children through the unemployment of their parents, particularly in economically distressed areas. Still later it became the basis of the great expansion in the feeding of children during the Second World War. In 1906 it marked the beginning of a broad development of the social services. There followed in the next five years a series of enactments that charted new or enlarged fields of activity by government on behalf of the people of England. The most important of these were:

1907. The Education (Administrative Provisions) Act, inaugurating medical inspection and "attention to the health and physical condition of the children educated in public elementary schools." [65]

1908. The Old Age Pensions Act.[66]

1908. The Coal Mines Regulation Act, establishing in principle the eight-hour day.[67]

1909. The Labour Exchanges Act,[68] creating a system of labor exchanges that would attack unemployment by increasing the mobility of labor which, through nearly six hundred years, the Poor Law had held—to quote Nassau W. Senior, co-author with Edwin Chadwick of the report of 1834—

in one of the heaviest chains in which a people calling itself free has been bound . . . a scheme prosecuted for centuries, in defiance of reason, justice, and humanity, to reduce the laboring classes to serfs, to imprison them in their parishes, and to dictate to them their employments and their wages.[493a]

1909. The Trade Boards Act which, almost exactly one hundred years after the failure of Samuel Whitebread's attempt in 1808 to pass a minimum-wage law through Parliament, made a beginning in four of the sweated industries of fixing a floor for wages.[69]

1909. The Housing, Town Planning Act (Housing of the Working Classes). This Statute set far forward on its way the movement to secure better homes for the people which Lord Shaftsbury had begun in 1851 with the passage of the first act in this field. The Law of 1909 inaugurated town planning, an important step toward the prevention of congestion. It made it compulsory for local authorities, aided by national loans, to provide for the construction of houses where a shortage was adjudged to exist; and in this and other respects it increased the supervisory powers of the national Local Government Board over the local authorities.[70]

1911. Inclusion for the first time in the civil service estimates of an item for the payment of salaries of members of the House of Commons, thus making service in Parliament possible for the poor man. (Resolution adopted in the House of Commons August 15, 1911.)

1911. The National Insurance Act [Health and Unemployment Insurance.] [71]

Each of these milestones in legislation marked an advance in the development of social security, but the two items that bore most directly upon the problem of want and that pointed away from the Poor Law were old-age pensions and health and unemployment insurance. The idea of governmental action in this direction was not new. In 1772 a bill designed to set up a system in local government through which annuities might be secured passed the House of Commons but was defeated in the House of Lords. As early as 1786 a plan of compulsory insurance against sickness, infirmity, and old age had been proposed.[481h]

Toward the end of the nineteenth century the movement for social insurance was precipitated into legislation by the work of Bismarck in Germany. His efforts over several years had come to a head in 1881 when the Emperor in an address at the opening of the Reichstag "warmly" recommended insurance against accident and sickness, stating at the same time that "those who are disabled from work by age or invalidity have a well grounded claim to greater care from the state than has hitherto been their share."[412a] Legislation providing for insurance against sickness was enacted by the Reichstag in 1883, the employee paying two-thirds, the employer one-third; and against accident in 1884, with the employer carrying the insurance. Invalidity and old-age insurance came in 1889 with employees, employers, and the state contributing toward the pension which, in the case of old age, became due at seventy years.

In England the active campaign for social insurance started toward the end of the 1870's. It was begun by a clergyman of the Church of England, the Rev. William Lewery Blackley. His plan originally was for a combined system of insurance against sickness and old age.

In the year 1878 [he said in describing later his efforts] I published a proposal for the prevention of pauperism by means of a national compulsory insurance by requiring all young persons from the age of 18 to 21 to contribute to a fund, State collected and State secured, a sufficient amount to entitle each contributor, when physically unable to earn wages, to a weekly sick pay of eight shillings and to an old age pension of four shillings per week.[312a]

Canon Blackley's plan—he subsequently became Honorary Canon of Westminster—aroused great interest. The National Provident League was organized to promote his ideas, and a special committee of the House of Commons on National Provident Insurance met in 1885, 1886, and 1887, and devoted a large part of its inquiries and discussions to his program.

Shortly after Canon Blackley's scheme came to general public attention Joseph Chamberlain proposed a plan for voluntary insurance against old age with contributions by the state. There were other suggestions—one for purely voluntary and unaided insurance and one for insurance aided by employers—but the scheme, which in the interest it aroused ranked with those of Canon Blackley and Joseph Chamberlain, was the program advocated by Charles Booth. This program called for a universal pension of 5 shillings a week to each person after reaching sixty-five years of age, paid for out of funds derived from taxes. The pension was to be granted irrespective of need and without any previous contribution by the beneficiary.[408a]

By 1893 the interest in the various proposals for insurance and pensions was great enough to call for the appointment of a Royal Commission on the Aged Poor which engaged in an extensive study of the needs of old people and the plans that had been suggested for providing for those needs outside of the Poor Law. The Commission reported in 1895 in hopeless disagreement. There was a Majority report, with a number of individual reservations, to the effect that personal savings, mutual benefit societies, and the Poor Law were equal to the situation and that nothing more was warranted. During the discussions of the Commission a suggestion was developed in addition to those which had previously been made. This was that a distinction be drawn between the worthy and the unworthy aged poor, and that the worthy be given preferential treatment by the Poor Law. It was this suggestion that in 1896 and 1900 the Local Government Board incorporated in circular letters of instruction addressed to the boards of guardians. (See Chapter XVI.)

Beyond this, nothing in specific action resulted from the work of the Commission, though in 1897 the movement for provision outside the Poor Law against the contingencies of life made an important step forward when Parliament passed the first Workmen's Compensation Law.[61] In 1899 a select committee of the House of Commons on the aged deserving poor reported in favor of a system of pensions to be operated by committees set up in the Poor Law unions. Nothing came of the proposal. One of the members of this committee was David Lloyd George.[314]

Then came the great period of social legislation that started in 1906. Two years later old-age pensions had been placed upon the Statute Books. The basis of the new law was the proposal of Charles Booth—5 shillings a week—modified in two respects. First, a top level of income was fixed above which no one would receive a pension; and second, only the deserving were to be entitled to the benefit. The candidate for the pension could not qualify if he had "habitually failed to work according to his ability and need, for the maintenance or benefit of himself and those legally dependent upon him," unless he had been saving money regularly over a period of years. If he had been convicted of habitual drunkenness, it was left to the court to decide whether he should become ineligible for a pension.[66] Not until 1919 were these provisions eliminated from the law.[75]

The effect of old-age pensions upon the work of the guardians was immediately noticeable. On January 4, 1913, the number of persons seventy years and over receiving outdoor relief was only 6 per cent of the number on January 1, 1910. (Old-age pensions became effective as of January 1, 1909, but until December 31, 1910, any person who had received relief at any time since January 1, 1908, was disqualified for the pension.)

While old-age pensions as adopted in 1908 represented a dramatic step away from the traditional Poor Law, they were still little removed from relief. The means test, though in modified form, still continued to be involved. Only persons with an income of less than 31 pounds 10 shillings a year could receive any stipend; and while the payments were to be made through the post office, they had, as already indicated, the limitations of a moralistic as well as an economic standard.

In 1911 came social insurance against sickness and unemployment. Here Lloyd George took the lead. His particular interest was health insurance, and in this respect he was greatly influenced by his personal observation in Germany in 1908 of the program which Bismarck had introduced. The bill which finally passed Parliament in 1911 was called the National Insurance Act. Part I provided for health insurance; Part II for unemployment insurance.[71]

Aside from the influence of the German legislation, there was precedent for health insurance in the benefits developed by the friendly societies and the trade unions. The trade unions also paid benefits during periods of unemployment, but aside from a short-lived attempt in the Canton of St. Gall, in Switzerland, no nation had ever undertaken to establish compulsory unemployment insurance.

However, on April 29, 1909, Lloyd George, then Chancellor of the Exchequer, in the course of his budget speech announced that the Board of Trade had for six months been engaged in working upon a scheme "which, while encouraging voluntary efforts of trade unions, would extend the advantages of insurance to a larger circle of work-men, including unskilled laborers." [202]

The president of the Board of Trade at that time was Winston Churchill, and the permanent under-secretary was Sir Hubert Llewellyn Smith. It was Sir Hubert Smith who, with the collaboration of Sir William H. Beveridge, worked out the details of the scheme. It was Winston Churchill who on May 19, 1909, announced the intention of the government to adopt the principle of compulsory insurance.[203] Two years of campaigning for the measure followed; and then on December 16, 1911, the National Insurance Act became law. Social insurance had been legislated for England.

Both the health and the unemployment insurance schemes were based upon contributions by the employer, the employee, and the state. Both provided for a specified number of weekly benefits during sickness and unemployment. Participation in the insurance was limited to manual laborers and to persons in other occupations receiving less than a certain amount of wages. Initially the maximum wage was 160 pounds. By 1941 the figure had become 420 pounds.[87] Health insurance was administered through approved non-profit societies organized by friendly societies or labor unions, or as adjuncts of commercial insurance companies. Unemployment insurance was administered chiefly through a national system of employment exchanges.

The number of persons insured under the health part of the Act was large from the start—more than ten million as early as 1913. The number with coverage against unemployment was much smaller in the beginning—reaching two and one quarter million persons.[319a] Eligibility for participation was determined on the categorical principle, through the definition of certain age limits and certain occupations and the requirement of a certain number of payments within designated periods. Less directly than old-age pensions, but most effectively, this system of insurance achieved an attrition of the Poor Law. It prevented many persons from having to apply for public relief.

In 1916 unemployment insurance was extended to include a total of four million people,[72] and in 1920 it was enormously enlarged so that it included two-thirds of the employed people of Great Britain.[76]

In 1925 the principle of insurance was extended to cover the eventualities of old age and death. The Widows', Orphans' and Old Age Contributory Pensions Act of that year provided payments to the widows of insured men and allowances for their dependent children within certain age limits, and allowances for orphans. Insured men and their wives were eligible to receive old-age pensions upon reaching sixty-five years. All manual workers and anyone whose earnings were not in excess of 250 pounds a year [77] (increased to 420 pounds in 1941) [87] could qualify. Contributions were to be paid by employer and employee with the state adding a subsidy, the payments by employer and employee being lumped with those for health insurance. Non-contributory old-age pensions at seventy continued for the insured, but a large area of need had been removed from the application of the means test.

The Act of 1925 as well as the amendments of 1916 and 1920 were only extensions of the principle which had been inaugurated with the National Insurance Act of 1911. In that Act Britain took a step of profound significance in her efforts to achieve social security. In adopting health and unemployment insurance she had applied an innovation only to be compared in importance with the legislation that between 1536 and 1601 established the responsibility of the state for guaranteeing the individual a protection against starvation. A new principle had been introduced in Anglo-Saxon government. Taking inspiration from a fundamental characteristic of English life—the thrift of the people as expressed in the friendly societies, the coöperative societies, and the mutual-benefit features of trade unionism, and utilizing with appropriate modifications the program developed by Bismarck in Germany, social insurance provided a system through which the government aided the people to pool their resources as a means of obtaining security.

Recognizing the inevitability of the major vicissitudes—old age, sickness, widowhood, and, for many people, unemployment—the state undertook to create a fund which would pay to its participants that average amount which, coupled with the individual's own savings, would in a majority of instances carry him through the period of the emergency.

Nothing in our plans [said Winston Churchill, speaking at Leicester in 1909 about the purpose of the new program] will relieve people from the need of making every exertion to help themselves, but, on the contrary, we consider that we shall greatly stimulate their efforts by giving them for the first time a practical assurance that those efforts will be crowned with success.[425c]

The new system was not, like relief, based upon need. Its payments fell due upon the arrival of a previously-agreed-upon contingency and were received in an amount which also had been previously agreed upon. It provided a backlog to which each beneficiary added the proceeds of his own thrift. This was the opposite of relief, where the individual unable to provide for his needs requested the state to make up the difference between his resources and his basic requirements. Under insurance a man remained responsible for his economic situation; under relief the state assumed that responsibility. In relief, the state, in order to discharge its obligations, was compelled to inquire into the resources and circumstances of the applicant. In insurance, where it assumed no obligation for the needs of the claimant, no such inquiry was necessary.

With relief, the beneficiary was restricted to a maximum allowance. Whatever resources he had were deducted from this maximum. Relief acted as a ceiling, and in this respect the freedom of the individual was restricted. Insurance, on the other hand, was a floor to which the beneficiary could add other available income, the proceeds of his savings, and the like. Insurance did not limit his freedom as did relief.

The fund was derived in part from general taxation and in part from contributions by the employer and the employee. This element of contribution helped to emphasize the receipt of benefits as a right, but irrespective of this the system was fundamentally different from relief. The difference was that already pointed out, the difference between the retention by the individual of responsibility for meeting his needs and the assumption of this obligation by the state, the substitution of the right of contract for the right of need.

This was the significance of the great Social Insurance Act of 1911. A quarter of a century before the passage in the United States of the first Social Security Act, that of 1935, England had put on seven-league boots and had taken a giant step forward on the road to security with freedom.

XIX

PUBLIC ASSISTANCE

> You can make your rules as nice as you like, but it is the person who administers them who counts, and the spirit of administration is, after all, the governing factor.
>
> ERNEST BEVIN, Minister of Labour and National Defense, speaking in the House of Commons, February 13, 1941.[212]

ALTHOUGH the social program that began with the start of the Liberal government on December 5, 1905, had profound implications for the future of social security, the actual structure of the Poor Law was not immediately affected. Not until the closing months of the First World War was any basic principle of operation attacked. Then one of the major elements in less eligibility was destroyed. The Representation of the People Act of 1918 which extended the suffrage to women and to men who had not been enfranchised in previous acts included the following clause: "A person shall not be disqualified from being registered or from voting as a parliamentary or local government elector by reason that he or some person for whose maintenance he is responsible has received poor relief or other alms." [73]

Parliament had taken an important step toward establishing in the eyes of the world the fact that in England poverty was no longer a crime. It had removed a barrier that had existed between the Poor Law and many people whose need warranted an application for help.

In the following year, 1919, the national supervision of local relief was placed under new titular auspices. The Local Government Board was abolished and a Ministry of Health was established. Whereas in the old set-up the Poor Law Division had occupied a dominant place, now it was obliged to compete for attention with a congeries of other activities. The new department was responsible not only for public health and sanitation but also for the administration of national health insurance, of the laws relating to housing and town planning, and of certain functions in local government which it had inherited from the Local Government Board.[74] In the sweep of these interests public relief was relegated to a less important position. The problem of destitution was at the time less compelling. Between the Royal Commission of 1905–09 on the Poor Laws and the Relief of Distress and the First World War, applications for assistance remained at a relatively low level, and during the war they fell to new bottoms. In the brief period of post-war prosperity, the demands upon the Poor Law continued to be slight, and in 1919 public relief seemed to require little attention.

Then came the depression of the twenties. By the end of March 1922, the number of persons receiving indoor and outdoor relief was more than three times the number in 1919.[330a] Through the last three quarters of the nineteenth century and up to the twenties the people receiving economic assistance in their homes were the aged, the sick, the widowed, and orphaned. It was these groups which had borne the burden of the old program of deterrence. Except for limited periods of acute industrial distress when special funds and measures, both public and private, came into operation, the able-bodied did not, in any appreciable numbers, receive assistance. The repressive program that had started in 1834 and a world that, whatever its immediate ups and downs, was active in commercial and mechanical expansion, had restricted the problem of relief primarily to those who were incapacitated for the labor market. Now this was all changed. Unemployment, despite the existence of the insurance program, became the major consideration in relief.

For this new problem the administrators of assistance were unprepared. Its impact found them in the trough between two philosophies, neither of which was in control. The old certainties of the Poor Law of 1834 had been unsettled. The Royal Commission of 1905–09 had pointed out that repression was not a solution and had proposed a system of treatment and prevention—the Minority had advocated the abolition of the Poor Law itself. The boards of guardians were beginning to be infiltrated with a personnel which, like George Lansbury, could not "see any difference between outdoor relief and a state pension." The fact that thousands of persons were now receiving benefits during sickness and unemployment and pensions in old age could not help making the thought of payments for relief, even to the able-bodied, less a cause for alarm. For years, moreover—ever since the Local Government Board in 1896 and 1900 had recommended more consideration for the aged—there had been increasing emphasis upon the importance of making relief adequate once the decision to grant assistance had been made. All these shifts in opinion and feeling about relief had their effect upon the way in which England met the great increase in need that began to express itself toward the end of 1920.

The old system was gradually being abandoned, but there had been in the interval little development in method that could provide an administration appropriate to the changes in thought and policy. The Ministry of Health was, after all, only a supervisory body. Its circulars and statements were in effect suggestive rather than imperative; and its rules were broadly construed by the locally elected and locally financed guardians, who had a strong feeling of their own independence as local officials. The old conviction that sent forth the Poor Law inspectors in the campaign against outdoor relief in the seventies and eighties was gone. The guardians, on the other hand, as far as administrative operations were concerned, were functioning pretty much as they had when Henry Longley had timed committee decisions at a maximum of three minutes to the case and a minimum of nearly three cases to the minute.

The Ministry of Health still suggested the use of the workhouse which many of the unions had abandoned.[330b] It also favored work as a test and as discipline—a full week's work required of the person receiving relief irrespective of the amount of that relief, whereas there were unions (Poor Law unions, not trade unions) which believed in paying for work at the going rate of wages, limiting the hours of employment to the number needed to cover the necessary relief. The Ministry questioned the use of relief scales partly because they limited "undesirably the discretion of a Relief Committee; and further, if a scale is once published, there is a grave danger lest the recipients may begin to regard the gift as a right," [329a] and partly because there were local boards which, in employing the scale, did not take into consideration income received by the family that might have been applied in reducing the amount of relief. But the fairness of deducting income in estimating relief needs would depend upon what the maximum-allowed grants were, and the grants seldom touched a bare subsistence level. Often when the boards allocated relief without relation to the resources of the household, they did not do this because of a desire for a less inadequate relief. Frequently it was only a matter of careless administration. On the other hand, there were unions like Poplar in London where there was deliberate effort to increase the standard of relief.

Affecting the way all these items of policy were carried out was, as marked by the Ministry of Health, the absence of careful investigation. Standards of operation were at a low level. Despite the existence of an over-all supervisory body there was every variety of procedure in the 643 Poor Law unions administering assistance in England and Wales. The scales differed from union to union, and so also did the attitude toward the people applying for help. The range was from a use of the workhouse in the strictest sense to no labor test at all, from an attempt to achieve an adequate relief to an adherence to the old repressive policy. The Ministry of Health seems to have occupied a middle position with the boards of guardians going pretty much their own way.

In the face of this confusion of procedure and in the presence of an overwhelmingly justifiable need, the relief rolls rose rapidly from the beginning of the twenties. In the year ending March 31, 1921, expenditures for outdoor relief were 5,793,383 pounds sterling, nearly two and a half times the expenditure in 1914, the year before the beginning of the First World War. In 1922 they had risen to more than 15,000,000 pounds, over six times the expenditure in 1914.[330c]

The need was far in excess of what the more seriously affected unions could meet from their limited resources. The boards of guardians in the poorer districts felt that they should have help from general taxes. The Poplar guardians, covering one of the most poverty-stricken sections in London, were particularly aggressive in this respect; and, at their instigation, the Poplar borough councillors, several of whom were also members of the board of guardians, refused in 1921 to levy taxes toward the requirements of the London County Council. Thereupon the thirty borough councillors, twenty-four men and six women, were committed to prison for contempt of court. There they were held for six weeks until an understanding was reached which ultimately resulted in the charging of relief in London to the metropolitan common poor fund, subject to a scale of maximum relief set by the Minister of Health. In this emergency action, the essential financing of relief passed from the union to the county.[507c]

Even more revolutionary and almost as dramatic was the step taken five years later by the Ministry of Health. Three unions, having been obliged to resort to borrowing, had reached the point of bankruptcy. The National Exchequer had backed their commitments, which continued to rise despite remonstrances from the Ministry of Health. Thereupon, under an act of Parliament which became law on July 15, 1926,[78] the Ministry superseded these boards of guardians—two in 1926, one in 1927—with its own appointees. Thus a national supervisory body actually took over the management of a unit of government normally presided over by officials elected by direct popular vote. At the same time, a campaign of inspection of the case records of the local boards was carried on by the Ministry of Health. This helped to tighten administration. The localism of the early twenties was now meeting an increasing assertion of national authority.

On the other hand, there was a growing feeling of hardship among local taxpayers who were put to disadvantage by the system under which each union bore the cost of its own relief. The inequalities were enormous. There were unions with tax rates seven, twenty, twenty-five times greater than those of other unions where poverty was less.[204]

Fully as dissatisfied as the taxpayers were the unemployed. With the scales and policies in relief varying from union to union, applicants for help frequently thought themselves being discriminated against. The mere fact that a man's residence fell into one union or another made great difference in the way he was treated when he asked for assistance. There were unjustified variations in the amounts of the grants that were made and in the conditions—the use of the work test, for example—accompanying the payment of relief.

Organizationally the unions had long outlived their usefulness. Their functions overlapped those of other local authorities, their boundaries crossed those of other jurisdictions, and the whole system had become administratively a source of waste and inefficiency. The great increase in unemployment during the twenties had dramatized and emphasized an already bad situation.

Toward the close of 1928, Neville Chamberlain, then Minister of Health, introduced a bill changing the whole structure of the Poor Law. This bill, which became law on March 27, 1929, abolished the boards of guardians and turned their functions over to the county (rural) and county borough (urban) councils. These councils had been established during the latter part of the nineteenth century as the largest unit of local administration. As contrasted with the 643 unions, the system of counties divided England and Wales into 145 urban and rural areas.[79]

Under the new law each county and county borough council was to devise its own plans for the administration of the Poor Law, subject to the specifications of the Act and the approval of the Ministry of Health. Relief and related activities were to be directed by public assistance committees drawn from the membership of the county and county borough councils with the addition, where desired, of citizen appointees. This meant that relief administration would follow the general pattern of administration in health, education, and other activities conducted by the councils. The Poor Law had ceased to be a special local unit of government and now took its place with the other functions of the counties. There was this additional provision in the law:

A Council in preparing an administrative scheme shall have regard to the desirability of securing that, as soon as circumstances permit, all assistance which can lawfully be provided otherwise than by way of poor relief shall be so provided.[79]

This was close to making possible the break-up of the Poor Law which the Minority report of 1909 had advocated. Fully as important, however, was the mitigation of the effect of the law of settlement that the extension of the area of administration from the union to the county implied. For 643 jurisdictions, 145 had been substituted; and by that many the number of local wars around the problem of residence had been reduced.

On the same day on which the Local Government Act of 1929 took effect, a new relief order became operative—the Relief Regulation Order, 1930. Its approach to the problem of need was as different from that of the Order which it replaced, the Relief Regulation Order of 1911, as public assistance under the county councils was from the Poor Law administration of the boards of guardians. The 1911 Order had been stated in the traditional negative terms that expressed the principles of 1834: "Except as hereinafter provided, the Guardians of a Poor Law Union shall not afford relief other than institutional relief to any person who is within the union." While the exceptions opened the way to a less deterrent policy, the language and attitude were prohibitive.[104]

The new Order, the Order of 1930, took a positive position: "the Council shall formulate . . . arrangements for setting to work male persons . . . and for training and instructing such men . . . and for their attendance at classes in physical training or of an educational character." [105] The Ministry of Health in its next annual report, in commenting upon this Order, pointed out that "institutional relief is no longer to be regarded as exclusively the appropriate form of relief to the able-bodied." [331a] While the training program was put into effect only to a limited extent, the shift from indoor relief for the able-bodied had been accomplished, and aid was now being given to the unemployed man in his own home.

Reorganized in policy as well as in structure, the Poor Law had at last yielded to the sweep of the times. The recommendation of Majority and Minority reports of the Commission of 1905–09 had been realized. The boards of guardians had been eliminated in favor of the public assistance committees and the unions had given place to the county and county borough councils. The threat of the workhouse had been modified and the emphasis upon deterrence had been discarded. The principles of 1834 had been replaced by the beginning of a new program that was to characterize the relief of the first half of the twentieth century.

XX

THE ASSISTANCE BOARD

Helping every one in need is far beyond the means and convenience of any private person. For a private man's wealth is no match for such a demand. Also a single man's opportunities are too narrow for him to contract friendship with all. Wherefore, providing for the poor is a duty that falls on the whole community, and has regard only to the common interest.

> With the above quotation from Spinoza,
> 1632–77, T. W. Fowle closes his book
> on the Poor Law, 1881.[440a]

WHEN in 1930 the Minister of Health, reviewing in his eleventh annual report the changes that had taken place in the Poor Law, observed that "institutional relief is no longer to be regarded as exclusively the appropriate form of relief to the ablebodied," he was marking with mild and official understatement the commencement of the final stage of the revolution that had been taking place in the principles and measures applied in England to the solution of the problem of individual destitution. In rapid successive steps the country now began to move into a position diametrically opposed to the pronouncement of the Commission for Inquiring into the Administration and Practical Operation of the Poor Laws. One century after the recommendation that "all relief whatever to able-bodied persons or to their families, otherwise than in well-regulated workhouses, shall be declared unlawful," a special service was established to provide outdoor relief for the very people to whom one hundred years before it had been denied.

The immediate occasion of this new development was the failure of insurance to supply the complete answer to need arising from unemployment. Initially it had seemed as if the plan which had been adopted in 1911 might solve the problem. All that would be necessary was an extension of the new system of insurance, supplemented as it was with old-age pensions and the possibility of relief for the relatively few persons who, despite an expanding coverage, might require assistance. This program held without undue strain for seven years, first because of reasonably good conditions in business and later because of the industrial and military activity in the First World War. Then came the post-war depression.

It was preceded by the discharge of large numbers of persons from the army and navy and from munitions and related manufactories. Unemployment insurance, covering only a small portion of the people of England, was obviously inadequate to such a deluge. At the same time the persons who were now being discharged from the military services and the war industries were felt to be entitled to a treatment different from that under the Poor Law. A new device was attempted which was neither insurance nor relief. It was called the Out-of-Work Donation, a flat grant with scaled additional grants for dependents. To be eligible an individual must be "normally in employment," "capable of work," and "unable to obtain suitable employment." It was unnecessary to demonstrate need. The benefits were more than twice as large as those provided through insurance. The employment exchange was the chief administrative agency of the program. The plan took effect November 25, 1918.

The Out-of-Work Donation served to protect the insurance system and local relief from being overwhelmed with applications, but it aroused enormous opposition. The cost—the grant for one adult became 29 shillings a week, with total expenditures in four years of 66,000,000 pounds sterling; the absence of any considerable basis for administrative discretion; the feeling, subsequently proved to be unwarranted, that there was widespread fraud—all operated to put an end to the scheme. It closed officially in 1921, the last individual payment being made December 28 of that year.[318a & 319a]

In the meantime plans for a new program were developed. Britain undertook to meet the problem of assistance to the unemployed by greatly extending the area of insurance. In 1920 the coverage was broadened to include most of manufacture, with twelve million participants.[319a] Unemployment, however, which in numbers and duration far exceeded anything that had been previously experienced or anticipated, found the insurance too narrow for the need. The fund had been built upon the contributions of employees as well as of employers and of the state, and the benefits available to the individual were based upon the number of payments which the claimant had previously made. An actuarial approach had been attempted in accordance with which the period of benefits was defined and limited.

But this system could not solve the problem of the person who though capable of work had not been able to get even a first job, or had not been in a covered industry long enough to make the specified number of payments. It did not help the person who remained unemployed after his insurance benefits had expired, or who, having been unemployed, finally obtained employment but was laid off again before he could qualify for further insurance. To meet this variety of exigencies the insurance system was modified and enlarged, this way and that.

The period during which the insured person might receive benefits was successively extended. A scheme of "uncovenanted" benefits was devised, a benefit in advance of insurance, which assumed that insurance payments by the individual in question would follow when he obtained work. A plan of transitional benefits, i. e., payments to the individual whose period for insurance benefits had expired, was developed which provided practically indefinite grants to the beneficiaries.[414a]

By 1931, on any actuarial basis, unemployment insurance had ceased to be insurance, and the fund had long been insolvent. Drastic reorganization seemed to be necessary. The National Economy Act was passed in that year which gave the government power to issue orders in Council for the purpose of reducing expenditures in various areas, among them unemployment insurance.[80] Thereupon England attempted to return to the actuarial approach, increasing the contributions, reducing the amount of the benefit, and limiting the period of benefit to twenty-six weeks.[462a]

These changes necessitated some provision for the persons whose unemployment continued beyond the twenty-six weeks and who required financial assistance. To meet the situation of these people a system of transitional payments was devised. The payments were to be made from the national treasury, but in contrast to the abandoned transitional benefits they would be conditioned upon need. The task of determining this need was placed upon the recently created public assistance committees of the county and county borough councils.

The new administration began on November 12, 1931. The Poor Law was now responsible for the determination of the need of the unemployed. There were, however, these differences. First, national instead of local funds footed the bill. Second, the man who accepted unemployment relief under this plan of transitional payments was not subject to the "disqualifications in regard to service on Local Authorities statutorily applicable to persons in receipt of poor relief." That is, the unemployment relief did not prohibit the recipients from serving on the county and borough councils and their committees. Here was a right retained which under the Poor Law would have been yielded. Third, there were more liberal policies in the administration of the transitional payments than in other forms of relief. The assistance would be "payable in money and would not be subject to conditions as to test work or advanced on loan." [332a] A year later, November 17, 1932, a statute was enacted, exempting from consideration in the determination of unemployment relief one-half of pensions received on account of wounds or disability, one-half of weekly payments of workmen's compensation, and also certain capital assets including the interest in a dwelling house if occupied as the home of the applicant.[81]

Despite these modifications in the procedure of the public assistance committees, the new plan for the administration of transitional payments to the unemployed did not prove itself. The same variety of attitude and policy that had characterized the activities of the boards of guardians appeared also in the relief administration of the county and county borough councils. The interpretation of law and regulation and the amounts of the grants to the applicants for assistance varied from jurisdiction to jurisdiction, a fact which caused great dissatisfaction. There were also the problems that developed because of the "complete divorce" described by Sir Henry Bucknell Betterton, Minister of Labour, speaking in Parliamentary Debate on November 30, 1933, as existing "between the responsibility of the central authority, which is providing the money, and that of the local authority which disburses it."

Out of the demand for change came a new organization for the administration of unemployment relief. It was based upon the principle, to quote Sir Henry Betterton again:

that there should be, on the one hand, a contributory insurance scheme covering as much of the field as possible, and that outside insurance the State should assume a general responsibility for the relief of the ablebodied industrial unemployed.

It was established as a national organization because, as Sir Henry said:

If . . . unemployment is due to something which is quite without the control of the locality, if it is due to causes which are international or national, then there is every reason why its victims should be treated nationally. . . . I would venture to lay down this rule as axiomatic, that if the responsibility is to be a national obligation, the administration can no longer remain local but must be national also.[205]

The new national organization, legislated into existence by the Unemployment Act of June 28, 1934, was called the Unemployment Assistance Board. It was designed to provide for the unemployed who had exhausted their insurance or who, though ineligible for unemployment insurance, were or had been insured under the Widows', Orphans' and Old Age Contributory Pensions Acts. Its functions as described in the law were:

the assistance of persons . . . in need of work and the promotion of their welfare, and, in particular the making of provision for the improvement and reestablishment of the condition of such persons with a view to their being in all respects fit for entry into or return to regular employment, and the grant and issue to such persons of unemployment allowances.[82]

Like the Poor Law commissioners of one century before, who introduced national supervision in relief, the Unemployment Assistance Board represented an innovation. For national supervision it substituted national administration. Just as the Poor Law commissioners of 1834 were not directly responsible to Parliament, so the Unemployment Assistance Board was one step removed from responsibility to the legislature—in both cases a much criticized feature. The six members of the Board were appointed by the Crown and were not immediately represented in the House of Commons. Their spokesman in this respect was the Minister of Labour, in whose department the Board was placed. The powers of executive action, however, belonged exclusively to the Board.

From it the lines of administration passed directly to an employed officialdom operating throughout Great Britain. In public assistance, on the other hand, the voluntary public assistance committee in each of the 145 counties and county boroughs made basic administrative decisions which were then carried out by their own employed personnel. Under the Unemployment Assistance Board, local interests were served by advisory voluntary committees set up under the law to make recommendations upon policies appropriate to the requirements of their respective communities but not to administer any part of the program. In addition, local review committees—appeal tribunals—before which persons dissatisfied with the decisions of the officials of the Board might have a hearing, were appointed by the Minister of Labour.

The Unemployment Assistance Board began operation in 1935 and soon had established over three hundred offices throughout Great Britain with more than six thousand senior officers and investigating clerks. Differences over the amount of the assistance grants retarded the full assumption by the Board of the relief of the unemployed until after the first part of 1937; but by the end of 1938, the first year of full operation, more than half a million allowances were being paid in Great Britain, with an average individual grant of over 25 shillings a week.

This national system of unemployment assistance soon proved to be a more satisfactory medium of administration than the general relief of the successors of the Poor Law, the public assistance committees of the county and county borough councils; and with the coming of the Second World War the authority of the Board was enlarged to cover a new area of aid. Under the Unemployment Assistance (Emergency Powers) Act, which became law September 5, 1939, the Minister of Labour was empowered to "extend the class of persons to whom an allowance may be granted . . . so as to include . . . persons who are in distress as the result of circumstances caused by the war." [84] The activities of the Board in this respect were steadily increased, including among a variety of other services the payment of "injury allowances" to members of civil-defense organizations suffering from a "war service" injury and to all adult civilians injured in an air raid (this as agent for the Ministry of Pensions) and the payment of compensation for damage to property—furniture, clothing, tools, essential articles of personal use, small retail stocks—where the income of the applicant was 250 pounds a year or less, 420 if he had dependents.

In 1940 the Board received another accession of power. Under an act which became law on March 21 of that year the title "Unemployment Assistance Board" was changed to "Assistance Board." The Statute provided that "the functions of the Assistance Board shall include the functions of granting supplementary pensions" to any person "entitled to receive weekly payments on account of an old age pension, or a person who has attained the age of sixty and is entitled to receive weekly payments on account of a widow's pension." [85]

The increase in responsibility by reason of war services and supplementary old-age and widows' pensions brought the staff before the end of 1941 to fifteen thousand employees [406a] and the number of cases (not individuals) aided to over one million.[334a] Part of this development represented new areas of activity, but there was also involved a transfer from the local public assistance committees of a considerable amount of supplementation for which they previously had had responsibility.

This shift from local to national operation expressed a change in attitude toward the problem of assistance, a change which is illustrated by statements made by the representatives of the Ministry of Health in support of the legislation which in 1940 entrusted to the Assistance Board the supplementation of old-age and widows' pensions.

"It is because in this country, especially in the minds of old people, there still remains the idea of the stigma of the Poor Law," said Miss Florence Horsbrugh, Parliamentary Secretary to the Minister of Health, speaking in the House of Commons.[207] The Minister of Health, Walter E. Elliot, in a previous debate had developed the same thought:

These poor people should not, at the end of their lives, have to suffer the indignity of going before a Public Assistance Committee every week or so to obtain the wherewithal to live. . . .

The practice of the Assistance Board is in many respects more considerate than that of the local authorities.[206]

A year later, March 26, 1941, a further difference in policy between local and national assistance was established in one of the most dramatic and significant steps in the whole history of English relief. On that day the following principle was written into the statutes of the realm (Determination of Needs Act, 1941). "*The resources of members of the household, other than the applicant, the husband or wife of the applicant, and any member of the household dependent on the applicant, shall not be regarded as resources of the applicant.*" [86]

This Statute narrowed the theory of the responsibility of grandparents and parents for the support of children, and of children for the support of parents, which ever since 1601 had been one of the basic considerations of the Poor Law. From 1941 this responsibility in the operations of the Assistance Board would be restricted in principle only to persons dependent upon the applicant at the time of his request for assistance. The parent with whom the hitherto self-supporting son or daughter, now in need of assistance, had been living, or the son or the daughter with whom a parent applying for assistance made his home, were no longer in law a financial resource.

Actually the regulations which implemented the Act did not carry out this principle to its ultimate conclusion. Contributions from self-supporting members of the family living under the same roof with applicant were not wholly excluded. The contributions were, however, limited in amount and scaled according to income. In effect, the son or daughter who was self-supporting but remaining at home was placed upon the same economic basis as a boarder, and so too was the elderly parent living in the household of a son or daughter. Under the regulations of 1941, for example, an employed son having his home with his father and earning 20 shillings or less a week would be required to make no contribution to the family budget. If he earned more than 20 shillings he would be expected to contribute a specified weekly sum scaled up to 7 shillings for the person who earned 55 shillings or more. If, on the other hand, an elderly man should be living in the home of his son, no contribution from the son would be assumed unless the son were earning 6 pounds a week or more. In the latter event the state would grant no assistance in supplementation of the father's old-age pension. Much the same procedure was applied in unemployment assistance.[106 & 107]

While thus the administration of the law tempered somewhat the application of the principle set forth in the Determination of Needs Act of 1941, the new Statute is none the less significant. Its revolutionary nature was the subject of much of the comment in the debate which accompanied the passage of the bill through Parliament. The following quotations indicate how important the speakers in the House of Commons felt the step they were taking to be.

Aneurin Bevan, Labour Party member from Ebbw Vale:
When the system of the relief of the poor was started under Elizabeth the family was the basis because it was the unit of society. It was a purely objective and tangible reality. . . . When the industrial revolution came and the family was dispersed, the family ceased to be a real basis for the administration of assistance. Every Board of Guardians then employed officers to chase relatives of applicants all over Great Britain in order to get them to contribute half-crowns to their families' maintenance. The family thus became an unreal thing. Then the Unemployment Assistance Board had to give up the family and take the household. But there is no such

thing as the household as a unit. It is too intangible, too flexible, too fluid, too ambiguous a unit as a basis.[211]

Ernest Bevin, Minister of Labour and National Defense:
Somebody said the other day that the only thing now left of Queen Elizabeth was one toe sticking out of the ground and that, for the rest, the Poor Law was now buried.[214]

F. W. Pethick-Lawrence, member from Edinburgh East:
This bill constitutes a revolutionary change in the principles which have been adopted for a very long time, dating right back to the days of Queen Elizabeth. . . . It shifts in general and in the main the obligation to look after those who are old or out of work from the family and from the household to the community as a whole. It marks the recognition that to-day unemployment has ceased to be a private affair and is the public concern of the state as a whole.[209]

This departure from the principle that the state should exact contributions from the relatives of an applicant for assistance before determining the amount of maintenance it would provide is only one indication of the distance from which the England of the fourth decade of the twentieth century had moved from the old Poor Law. The creation of the Unemployment Assistance Board (now Assistance Board) marked the beginning of a new form of social security, a system halfway between relief and insurance exhibiting characteristics of both.

Under the old relief, the individual in need could never know certainly what he might expect. He was wholly dependent upon the unpredictable discretion of each local authority. Under the new assistance, while he was not able as with insurance to estimate the payment to which he would be entitled, he had the advantage of a definite schedule, graduated according to the number of members of the family, which represented the range of financial aid available to him. This scale had been submitted to Parliament and was a matter of public knowledge. Related to it were precise definitions of the resources which would or would not be taken into consideration by the Assistance Authority in determining the amount of the grant. What in receipts from pensions, workmen's compensation, insurance, savings or earnings of children or parents would be exempted, was stated in law in regulations or administrative orders. Assistance thus exhibited some of the precision and definiteness of insurance. What was lost for the individual in flexibility was gained in freedom from the danger of rule-of-thumb determinations. Moreover, there was one standard of eligibility as contrasted with the 145 jurisdictions of the public assistance authorities.

The development of national assistance affected the unemployed, the aged and widows, and the war sufferers. Outside these categories local relief as administered by the counties continued, but with a diminishing part in the program of social security. That program at the end of the fourth decade of the twentieth century consisted of three defenses against want: social insurance, the largest; then national assistance; and for those not protected by the first two provisions, public assistance. In organization and in spirit, as related to the problem of human need, the Britain that entered the Second World War was a new and different country from the England that throughout the nineteenth century had been dominated by the principles of 1834.

XXI

THE BEVERIDGE REPORT

You will witness a development of the new mind of England which will make up by its rapid progress for its retarded action.

BENJAMIN DISRAELI, *Sybil*, 1845 [484b]

From Poor Law to public assistance, from public assistance to national assistance, from an assistance service to social security—that is the road that this country should travel as quickly as possible.

ELLIS SMITH, Labour member from
Stoke, House of Commons, March 12, 1942 [215]

ON June 10, 1941, Arthur Greenwood, then the Minister without Portfolio, announced in the House of Commons the appointment of an interdepartmental committee to survey the social insurances and allied services. This was not an ordinary or routine assignment. It was a study that had long been indicated and which came as a result of broad public demand. The conclusions of the inquiry were awaited from its start with nation-wide interest.

For thirty years since the passage of the first insurance act, the Statute of 1911, Great Britain had been expanding, adjusting, and changing its measures and agencies of insurance and assistance. These developments had taken place—to quote a speaker in the House of Commons (Graham White, April 29, 1941)—"not as part of a plan but in response to a variety of political agitations and circumstances." [213] Much had been accomplished. The generation since 1911 had made more progress toward social security than any previous century had seen, but there were gaps, shortages, inconsistencies, and inequities great enough to cause the system to be the object of continuous attack.

There was dissatisfaction with the scattering of the agencies of insurance and assistance through a variety of governmental departments and jurisdictions and the absence of any central planning organization. There was criticism of the inadequacy of the benefits and, particularly with respect to unemployment, that the period of the benefit was not long enough. There were still many people who were not covered and, despite the great distance which assistance had moved from the old Poor Law, the means test remained as the barrier which the uninsured individual and the person with insufficient benefits was obliged to pass when he found himself in need. The means test was a factor in one-third of the benefits and grants paid in 1938–39, this being the division of the provision against insecurity borne by insurance on the one hand and by national assistance, public assistance, and contributory old-age pensions on the other hand.[335a]

During the unemployment of the 1920's, when the hatred of the old Poor Law stemmed from long experience with its policies, there had been the demand for work or maintenance, with insurance as the avenue through which maintenance would be received. The attempt to stretch the existing system to meet that demand had, as we have seen (Chapter XX), failed, and national assistance had developed as a result of subsequent efforts to supplement inadequate insurance benefits and provide a substitute for benefits that had expired. National assistance had represented a great advance beyond the traditional methods of relief, but it still involved the determination of need and had not proved to be the way to security with freedom. The alternative possibility of a basic maintenance not subject to a means test came to receive increasing attention. People in every area and class of British life began to discuss the theory of a national minimum which for a number of years had been a goal of labor and many social reformers.

The position of labor in this respect was expressed in the House of Commons on March 12, 1942, by Ivor Thomas. Every citizen, he said, "has an obligation to work for society as long as he is able, and when he falls out of work for any reason, he has the right to expect a fair rate of remuneration which will enable him to keep up a reasonable standard of comfort and self respect . . . a remuneration," he continued, "which will be his inalienable right not subject to any test of means or needs." [216]

Some such basic level of income for everybody, in or out of work, in sickness or in health, in accident or in retirement, was the subject of interested debate. At the same time there was the call for simplification in the organization and administration of the insurances and assistance. What was wanted was an integrated program. It was a desire strong enough throughout Britain to bring the announcement of the appointment of the Interdepartmental Committee while the country was in the darkest period of the war, facing the imminent threat of invasion, and on the same day on which the Prime Minister reported to the House the details of the loss of Crete.

The Committee was composed of representatives of eleven departments concerned in one way or another with the administration of the insurances and allied services. These persons and the secretary were all members of the civil service, the only individual on the committee not a civil servant being the chairman, Sir William Beveridge.

There could not have been a more appropriate selection for the leadership of this Committee. Sir William Beveridge had worked intimately with Winston Churchill in establishing the unemployment part of the social insurance program that was inaugurated with the legislation of 1911. From 1909 to 1911 he had been director of Labour Exchanges, the national employment service. His book, *Unemployment: A Problem of Industry*,[405a] had been a standard work on the subject from the time of its first publication in 1909. Since 1934, as chairman of the Unemployment Insurance Statutory Committee, he had been at the heart of the insurance system. From 1919 to 1937 he had been director of the London School of Economics, and since 1937, master of University College, Oxford. His reputation as an economist, as an educator, and in the field of the insurances was international.

Since all of the other members of the Interdepartmental Committee were civil servants, Sir William, at the request of the government, undertook the sponsorship of the Report. When it was presented to Parliament at the end of November 1942, his name alone was signed, a tribute to the position occupied by him in Great Britain.

It recalls a social statesman of a century before—Edwin Chadwick, likewise the only signer of a report, that upon the Sanitary Condition of the Labouring Population of Great Britain, which was chiefly responsible for the commencement of the public health movement in England and in the United States. It was Chadwick also who as coauthor of the Report in 1834 of the Royal Commission for Inquiring into the Administration and Practical Operation of the Poor Laws, dominated the thinking of England about relief and the problem of poverty to the end of the nineteenth century.

The Beveridge Report is based upon a review of the existing schemes of social insurance and related services; upon studies made by the governmental departments represented on the Committee and by subcommittees assigned to special topics; upon the work of various commissions and the testimony and memoranda of 127 organizations, together with special consultative services from the International Labour Office. The conclusions, while influenced by the work and discussion of the members of the Interdepartmental Committee, are those of Sir William Beveridge alone.

What he did was to examine the programs and ideas which had been developing and which had been discussed in Britain for a number of years. He sifted out what seemed to be the most appropriate of these operations and proposals and brought them together in a comprehensive and integrated program. One fundamental concept underlies the whole Report. That is the national minimum—a basic income which, irrespective of need or any means test, every citizen of Great Britain will receive in the event of old age, sickness, unemployment, or other vicissitudes, an income toward which he will have contributed and which is his by right of contract. Along with this goes the proposal for the administration of insurance and assistance by one organization, a Ministry of Social Security, with a single contribution by the insured person and a series of benefits built upon one calculated base.

The Report begins with a diagnosis of the causes of want. For this it draws upon surveys made in a number of cities before the war.

From each of these social surveys the same broad result emerges. Of all the want shown by the surveys, from three-quarters to five-sixths, according to the precise standard chosen for want, was due to interruption or loss of earning power. Practically the whole of the remaining one-quarter to one-sixth was due to failure to relate income during earning to the size of the family.[335b]

Starting from this diagnosis, the Report concentrates upon one remedy, the national minimum. The effect of mass unemployment in interrupting income and the essential importance of putting an end to this threat are recognized. The whole Report, indeed, is based upon the assumption that this problem can and will be solved, but the particular goal of the Beveridge plan for social security is conceived as the abolition of want by providing that every individual in Britain shall have a basic income which will supply his essential needs no matter what vicissitude of life he experiences. This aim is to be achieved through the use of the existing pattern of social insurance, supplemented by private insurance and assistance, and accompanied by a system of allowances for every child after the first child irrespective of the income of the family and including the first child where there is an interruption of earnings. Health is held to be so important, both to the family and to the nation, that it is not left to individual arrangement. Instead, the Report makes a fundamental recommendation, stated as an assumption, that a comprehensive national health service be developed which will

ensure that for every citizen there is available whatever medical treatment he requires, in whatever form he requires it, domiciliary or institutional, general, specialist or consultant, and will ensure also the provision of dental, ophthalmic and surgical appliances, nursing and midwifery and rehabilitation after accidents.[335c]

Since the core of the program is the establishment of the national minimum, the floor of income below which no one shall be allowed to fall no matter what casualty he may suffer, the Report sets about to define the basic budgetary needs of individuals and families and then to translate them into money. These needs—health being otherwise provided for—are food, clothing, fuel, light, sundries, rent, and a margin to allow for some "inefficiency in purchasing, and also for the certainty that people in receipt of the minimum income required for subsistence will in fact spend some of it on things not absolutely necessary." [335d]

Taking 1938 as a base, the Report estimates the cost of buying the items in this budget, enough of each to maintain individuals and families at a subsistence level. It endeavors to arrive at a figure which can ultimately be expressed in benefits, a figure that might be universal the country over. Rent, with variations between London and other cities and between urban and agricultural communities, presents the greatest obstacle to this purpose. Because of this, the Report suggests further inquiry into the possibility of a regionalization of contributions and benefits as a way of providing for areas of higher costs. It concludes, however, by fixing upon one weekly budget applicable everywhere.

This for working adults is as follows at 1938 prices:

	Man and Wife	*Man*	*Woman*
Food	13 shillings	7 shillings	6 shillings
Clothing	3 "	1 " 6 pence	1 " 6 pence
Fuel, Light, and Sundries	4 "	2 " 6 "	2 " 6 "
Margin	2 "	1 " 6 "	1 " 6 "
Rent	10 "	6 " 6 "	6 " 6 "
	32 shillings	19 shillings	18 shillings [335d]

For the same items a couple, retired on age, would need 29 shillings 8 pence a week; and children living at home would require for food, clothing, fuel, light, and household sundries, rent not being included, from 5 shillings 4 pence for children under five years to 9 shillings for children of fourteen and fifteen years, with an average for all dependent children of 7 shillings.

Taking $4.90 as the conversion rate of the pound in 1938, 32 shillings a week for a man and wife would be the equivalent of $7.80, with $1.72 for each child at the average of 7 shillings. The higher living costs and the differences in the standard of life in the United States cause a flat translation of this sort to be misleading. The Beveridge budget of 1938 would buy much more in England than the same amount in dollars and cents would buy here. Even without consideration of these differences in cost and living, the Beveridge allowance for 1938 would be substantially greater than relief grants in many parts of the United States.

It is interesting to relate this budget to minimum wages of men in Great Britain. The lowest wage as of 1938 in a number of occupations reported for large towns or important districts by the International Labour Office were those of passenger porters with an average of 43 shillings a week.[336] An I.L.O. compilation of minimum wage rates showed 34 shillings 3½ pence a week for agricultural laborers in England at the end of March 1938,[337a] and twenty-five industries with minimum wages established at 1 shilling an hour or less for a basic 48-hour week as of December 1937—i.e., not more than 48 shillings a week.[337b]

Comparing the Beveridge allowance with these wages, one finds that even the lowest-paid workers in 1938 earned substantially more than the Beveridge subsistence estimate for a single man—19 shillings a week—and more than the minimum requirements—32 shillings—of a man and wife. As soon as children are added the Beveridge budget begins to rise above the income from wages, none of the minimum wages being sufficient for three children. Further evidence of this can be seen in a sample survey of families receiving allowances from the Unemployment Assistance Board, made in the fall of 1938, which showed that if every employable member in each family had been working at his or her normal occupation, instead of being unemployed, the combined wages in one-quarter of the families would have been less than 50 shillings a week.[338] This is in line with the finding of the Report that want is in a large number of instances due "to failure to relate income during earning to the size of the family."

The Beveridge budget, it must be remembered, is designed to meet the bare material necessities. It includes nothing beyond them. The rest it leaves to the voluntary action of the individual through private insurance or savings. Health needs are assumed to be met through the recommended comprehensive system of health services providing medical and nursing attention in every form.

The attempt to establish this budget of 32 shillings for a man and wife as universal for Great Britain manifestly presents great problems when one comes to apply it to individual families. The urban dweller would experience much more difficulty in living within the allowance than his fellow in a rural community. The difference between agricultural wages and the wages in large towns is an indication of what would be involved. On the other hand, by developing one budget applicable the country over Sir William Beveridge enormously facilitated the bringing of the Report to the attention of the public. The plan under which everybody in the same insured class would have the same benefit involved the least possible departure from the existing system and could readily be explained to the people of Britain.

Having defined the budget as of 1938, the Report estimates that after the war prices will hold at a level 25 per cent above 1938 and arrives at a weekly income to be provided, through the plan for social security, of 40 shillings for a man and wife, whether of working age or retired; 24 shillings for a single person, whether man or woman; and on an average 8 shillings for a child. This, then, is the national minimum, and this amount the Beveridge Report proposes to make available to everybody, rich or poor, in the United Kingdom.

Insurance is extended not merely to the employed. The self-employed person, that is the man in business for himself, the student, the housewife, together with every one in agriculture and industry, is included in an expansion of the system of social security to cover the whole population.

Forty shillings for a man and wife, 24 shillings for a single person, become the basic benefit whether the individual is unemployed, sick, or ready to retire.

In order to achieve this national minimum it would be necessary to increase substantially the benefits in force under the system of insurance existing at the time of the appearance of the Report. The unemployment benefit for a single person would be raised by one-fifth and the disability benefit by one-third. The old-age benefits would be more than doubled. The recommendation therefore is that the leveling up of the old-age benefits be undertaken gradually to reach 24 shillings for a single person and 40 shillings for a man and wife in 1965. A premium would be placed upon the postponement of retirement by adding 2 shillings to the weekly benefit for a man and wife, and 1 shilling to the single person's benefit, for each year that the worker remained in his employment. This last is additional evidence of the extent to which the whole Beveridge plan assumes the maintenance of employment after the war.

Not only does the Report recommend that the same basic benefit be paid in unemployment, sickness, disability, and retirement, but also that benefits in sickness and in unemployment carry as long as disability or absence of work continues to be the problem for the insured person. The extension of the unemployment benefit beyond the present twenty-six weeks is contingent upon the individual's being able and available for work as evidenced by his readiness to take suitable employment when offered by the employment exchange. As the time of unemployment lengthens, the interpretation of "suitable work" becomes stricter; and after twenty-six weeks the beneficiary must be willing to take training if he is to continue to receive benefits.

Is this a return to the extended benefits of the 1920's that helped to bankrupt the unemployment insurance fund? The difference is that the present proposal is founded upon a plan in which the benefits are actuarially related to contributions. Always it must be remembered, however, that the estimates are based upon the assumption that mass unemployment can and will be eliminated. Sir William Beveridge expresses the belief that rarely should unemployment for the same person extend beyond six months.

That there should be no limit to the time an individual may receive unemployment insurance, and that there should be no smaller benefit for unemployment than for other contingencies, shows how far England has moved beyond the old days of the punitive Poor Law. The Report does not fear that men on benefit will be loathe to return to work. However, even the lowest wages—see page 232—are nearly 50 per cent greater except in agriculture than the Beveridge allowance for a man and wife and from 50 to 100 per cent greater than the allowance for a single man. In the United States the overwhelming experience with unemployment insurance as with unemployment assistance is that where there are jobs paying decent wages men prefer work to either relief or insurance. Nothing has been more dramatic than the steep falling off of the unemployment compensation and the assistance rolls in the United States since the signing of the Lend-Lease Bill in March 1940, when the country began to move into the labor shortage of a war economy.

In the recommended extension of the insurance system to cover everybody, the self-employed—shopkeepers, farmers, fishermen, professional people, and independent workers of all kinds—are included. For them unemployment is difficult to determine. They become eligible, however, for a training benefit equal to the unemployment benefit with, where needed, special removal and lodging grants. This treatment applies also to students, unmarried women engaged in domestic duties without pay, and persons who have had an independent income. Opportunity for training would, of course, be open to any unemployed person.

The sickness and disability benefit under the Beveridge Report is completely separated from any connection with the administration of the proposed comprehensive health service. The function of insurance is to supply income; the function of the health service is to provide for prevention, treatment, and cure. The Report assumes not only a complete system of medical, surgical, dental, and nursing care throughout the country, but also looks forward to the development of a rehabilitation service for disabled persons starting with medical care and continuing through the post-medical period until the individual's maximum earning capacity has been reached. Rehabilitation, like the health service, is a responsibility of appropriate departments of government other than the proposed Ministry of Social Security.

The disabilities hitherto provided for through workmen's compensation are merged with the sickness and disability benefits, and workmen's compensation as such would cease if the recommendations of the Beveridge Report should be put into effect. The person whose disability resulted from disease or accident in a hazardous industry would for thirteen weeks receive the same benefit that any sick or injured person would receive. After that, however, if his disability was total he would receive, so long as the disability continued, an industrial pension equal to two-thirds of his wages up to a maximum of 3 pounds, but not less than the basic benefit of 24 shillings for a single person, 40 shillings for a man and wife. Special adjustments would be made for partial disability. Should the industrial accident or disease result in death, there would be a lump-sum payment related to wages made to the widow or other person dependent upon the wage-earner. In the case of all insured adults, in or out of industry, there is a funeral grant of 20 pounds, smaller amounts being paid for young persons and children.

The proposals for the merging of workmen's compensation into the general system of insurance represent a logical and inevitable progress from the principle of indemnity and individual-employer liability to that of social responsibility. Employers engaged in hazardous industries would pay a special levy adjusted to meet two-thirds of the excess costs involved in the industrial pensions and grants, but the remaining expense would be assumed by the general social insurance fund. The determination of whether an injury or disease lasting beyond thirteen weeks was due to the connection with hazardous industry, and the amount of the special benefit or lump-sum payment, would be made through administrative processes subject to appeal before a tribunal established for that special purpose.

Another departure made by the Beveridge Report is the establishment of married women in a new and special category.

All women by marriage acquire a new economic and social status with risks and rights different from those of the unmarried. On marriage a woman gains a legal right to maintenance by her husband as a first line of defense against risks which fall directly on the solitary woman; she undertakes at the same time to perform vital unpaid service and becomes exposed to new risks, including the risk that her married life may be ended prematurely by widowhood or separation.[335e]

For married women, therefore, a series of benefits appropriate to their special economic and social status is devised, starting with a marriage grant or dowry of 1 pound sterling for every forty weekly contributions prior to marriage, up to a maximum of 10 pounds. In other words, it is assumed that most women will have been gainfully employed before marriage. Married women whether gainfully employed or not will be entitled to a maternity grant of 4 pounds. If gainfully employed they will receive a maternity benefit, running for thirteen weeks, of 36 shillings a week, this of course conditional upon their discontinuing employment for the whole period. When the husband is unemployed, sick, or disabled, the woman's benefit is contained in the 40 shillings a week granted to married couples and is represented by 16 shillings of this amount. Since as housewife she is not working for wages, she receives no benefit in sickness and obviously she is not subject to unemployment. If, when she is sick, substitute household help is needed the Report suggests that this be supplied as a function of the comprehensive system of health services. At the time of the retirement of the husband, the married woman is covered, as in his unemployment and sickness, by 16 shillings of the 40-shilling benefit. At her death a funeral grant would be paid.

The gainfully employed married woman has the right to choose whether or not she will enter the insurance system by paying benefits. If she does, when she herself becomes unemployed she receives a benefit of 16 shillings as against 24 for the single woman, and, on retirement at sixty, if her husband is below retirement age, the basic 24 shillings.

The married woman who is widowed becomes eligible for the 24-shillings retirement benefit for single persons as soon as she reaches sixty years. If she is less than sixty she receives a widow's benefit of 36 shillings a week for thirteen weeks to cover the period of adjustment to her new status. Thereafter, if she has dependent children, she will receive a guardian's benefit of 24 shillings a week plus an average of 8 shillings for each child. The widow who is of working age and capacity can apply for training and a training benefit, after which, if she has no dependent children, her status as far as the program is concerned will become that of the unmarried woman, eligible for employment. If she has dependent children an adjustment in relation to her earnings will be made in the guardian's benefit. If her husband dies of industrial disease or through industrial accident, she will receive a lump-sum payment related to his earnings.

In divorce, legal or voluntary separation, and desertion, the general principle is that the termination of marriage should result for the wife in the same insurance arrangements as those that accompany widowhood, "unless the marriage maintenance has ended through her fault or voluntary action without just cause." [335f]

Here is one of the few traces of the old judgmental attitude of the Poor Law. Fault in dissolving marriage—leaving out of consideration the difficulty of establishing the fact—has no relation to economic need. The importance of a thirteen-week allowance during a period of adjustment, and of opportunity for training and training benefit, would be as great in divorce as in widowhood; and it is scarcely conceivable that a woman would separate from her husband just for the sake of obtaining thirteen weeks or even twenty-six weeks of benefits.

The situation of the unmarried woman living as wife involves additional complications, but the recommendation is that in the event of the man's unemployment or disability his benefit should be increased as it would be if the person dependent upon his earnings were his wife. The maternity grant might be considered if some plan for previous registration of the status of the woman could be devised, and, if she had been gainfully employed, the maternity benefit would be available. Widow's and guardian's benefits would be paid only to the legal wife, and retirement benefits to the unmarried widow only if the woman had herself been insured.

The administrative difficulties involved in establishing eligibility for widow's benefits where the man and woman were not married may be great enough to justify this decision, but it would seem that the presence of children would make it possible to determine guardian's benefits.

With a few reservations such as this, social insurance under the Beveridge recommendations appears to meet the chief predictable contingencies of life. In addition, there are two parts of the plan for social security which do not operate through insurance but are covered by direct expenditure by the state.

The first is designed to meet the need of people during the period in which the scheme is moving toward full operation and that of those persons who for one reason or another may not be eligible for benefits. Retirement provisions for old age do not reach the basic 24 and 40 shillings until 1965, and in the interval assistance will be required to supplement the benefits of elderly individuals or couples whose other resources are not sufficient to cover their essential requirements. Persons with less than 75 pounds a year will not be insured and most of the benefits depend upon the payment of a minimum number of insurance contributions. There will be persons who by reason of the exceptions in connection with divorce, desertion, and separation, may fall outside the provisions of the plan; and there will be some individuals who will not be eligible for unemployment benefit because they have quit employment without just cause or because they have refused suitable employment. Then, too, there are special needs in diet and care which cannot be covered by insurance. Here assistance paid out of the national exchequer would come into operation.

The Report recommends one system of assistance, replacing the three present forms of relief—national assistance, public assistance, and non-contributory old-age pensions. Under this plan all that remains of the old Poor Law would be wiped out. Public assistance as administered by the counties would be abolished, thus eliminating the settlement laws that have been an obstacle in the way of a decent provision against need ever since the notorious Statute of 1662. There would be one national program of aid wherever insurance did not operate. The system of local provision against want that began to develop in 1536 would come to an end, and the last vestige of the feudal tradition would disappear.

The second part of the plan for social security which does not operate through insurance is a financial provision for children below the years of self support. This the Report discusses as the first of three assumptions upon which the whole plan for Social Security depends, the other two being the comprehensive national system of health services and the maintenance of employment, in particular the abolition of mass unemployment.

The recommendation is that a system of allowances paid from the national treasury be established for every child after the first child in every family in Great Britain, whether employed or unemployed, and irrespective of its income. This program rests on two arguments:

First, it is unreasonable to seek to guarantee an income sufficient for subsistence, while earnings are interrupted by unemployment or disability, without ensuring sufficient income during earnings. Social insurance should be part of a policy of a national minimum. But a national minimum for families of every size cannot in practice be secured by a wage system which must be based on the product of a man's labor and not on the size of his family. . . .

Second, it is dangerous to allow benefit during unemployment or disability to equal or exceed earnings during work. But, without allowances for children, during earning and not-earning alike, this danger cannot be avoided.[335g]

Children's allowances are also advocated because, the Report states, "with its present rate of reproduction, the British race cannot continue" and children's allowances can at least "help to restore the birth rate, both by making it possible for parents who desire more children to bring them into the world without damaging the chances of those already born, and as a signal of the national interest in children, setting the tone of public opinion." [335g] In fixing the allowance, graded according to age, so that it will average 8 shillings per week, the Report takes into consideration the fact that provision in kind is already being made for children through school meals and free or cheap milk.

The allowances would continue up to sixteen years provided the child is attending school on a full-time basis. They would apply to every child after the first when the breadwinner is employed and to all children when for any reason—unemployment, old age, widowhood, sickness—the breadwinner is receiving insurance or assistance. The Report finds that the number of men whose wages are insufficient to the support of two adults and one child is small, and the exclusion of the first child where the wage-earner is employed would involve an estimated savings to the program of nearly 100,000,000 pounds a year. The plan as proposed calls for between 100,000,000 and 110,000,000 pounds annually.

How do the children's allowances differ from the disastrous Speenhamland allowance in support of wages that spread over England beginning in 1795 and that was finally abolished upon recommendation of the Poor Law Commission of 1834? The Speenhamland plan (See Chapter VIII) set a minimum based on the price of bread and scaled according to the size of the family. Where wages were less than this amount the local Poor Law authorities presumably made up the difference. This minimum became in effect a maximum; for what inducement, particularly in a time of surplus labor, was there for an employer to pay even the minimum when he knew that the local authorities would make up out of public funds whatever difference was left between the wages he was paying and the established scale? The Speenhamland system, where it was in effect, applied, moreover, to laborers in the lower-paid employments, and only to them. The children's allowance, on the other hand, would apply irrespective of the grade of employee, from the lowest-paid to the highest-salaried person, but, during employment, only to families where there is more than one child. This fact would prevent it from having any possible influence upon the wage scale.

Irrespective of the difference in method between the allowance in support of wages and the children's allowance, there is the even greater difference in attitude. The Speenhamland plan was born out of the needs and fears occasioned by the French Revolution and the Napoleonic wars, when the spirit of government was that expressed by the Combination Laws. The effort was to keep labor down and to rule in the interest of an owning class. The allowance of those days was interpreted as making possible a ceiling over wages.

The Beveridge Report appears at a time when, with an established system of minimum wage administration, the principle of a floor for wages has been accepted. Sir William only proposes to extend this floor, leveling up the situation of the man with more than one child toward an equality with the man who has no children or only one child.

The children's allowance and the national system of assistance would be administered along with the program of social insurance by one governmental department, the Ministry of Social Security. This would involve taking the various forms of insurance and assistance from agencies where they have been for years. It is a major operation. In Great Britain this plan for a more efficient administration faces an additional problem, special to the development of insurance in the United Kingdom, because it includes the separation of sickness and disability insurance from any connection with commercial insurance.

Health insurance in Britain has been conducted through what are called "approved societies." The scheme was adopted when national insurance was enacted in 1911 because of the existence of large numbers of friendly, (i.e., mutual-benefit) societies and of benefit plans operated by trade unions. Under this system it became possible, however, for industrial insurance companies to establish societies, the operation of which paralleled that of their ordinary business, the same agent often representing both activities. The connection with commercial corporations led many people to subscribe for an industrial insurance much more expensive than the social insurance proposed under the new program. Moreover, under the plan of approved societies the benefits varied with the society. The Beveridge plan would break the connection with commercial industrial insurance, and it is not surprising that the first reservations to the general enthusiasm with which the Report was received came from this area of special interest.

The total program for social security would entail an annual expenditure of 858,000,000 pounds in 1965 when the retirement benefit reaches the basic 24 shillings a week for a single person and 40 shillings for a man and wife. This includes the cost of children's allowances and a contribution of 170,000,000 a year toward the health and rehabilitation services. The bill would be distributed as follows:

Government	519,000,000	pounds
Insured persons	192,000,000	"
Employers	132,000,000	"
Other, chiefly interest	15,000,000	"
	858,000,000	" 335h

What does this mean for the three contributing parties—the government, the employers, the insured persons? The corresponding expenditures for 1938–39 were 342,000,000 pounds. The new program would therefore cost two and a half times what was spent in the last year before the war.

The government's share, 519,000,000 pounds would be 307,000,000 pounds more than the comparable outlay (local and national) in 1938–39. The increase would not, however, be immediate. The Report assumes for the purpose of illustration and estimate that the plan would begin to operate on July 1, 1944, and that the first full year of benefits would be the year, 1945. The biggest item in the program— 300,000,000 pounds for retirement benefits—would not be reached until 1965. On the other hand, the cost of the insurances had already begun to increase when in 1941 the benefits in insurance and the number of participants under the existing program were enlarged. Estimating expenditures in 1945 on this basis the Beveridge plan would involve, over and above what has been contracted for, an additional outlay by the government in that year of 86,000,000 pounds.

It does not seem unreasonable [the Report concludes] to hope that, even with the other calls upon the Exchequer, an additional expense of this order could be borne when actual fighting ceases. The Budget imposes a much increased burden on the Exchequer in later years to provide retirement pensions; this is an act of reasonable faith in the future of the British economic system and the proved efficiency of the British people. That, given reasonable time, this burden can be borne is hardly open to question.[335l]

The Report cites in support of this faith the experience of Britain after the First World War when despite mass unemployment, "the real wealth per head in a Britain of shrunken oversea investments and lost export markets, counting in all her unemployed, was materially higher in 1938 than in 1913." [335m]

The increase in contributions for the employers is less than that for the government or for the insured persons, about twice the 1938–39 expenditures and a little over 50 per cent more than the estimate of payments required under the existing system in 1945. As the contribution is universal and the same for all employers in relation to the number of their employees—3 shillings 3 pence for each male employee, and similarly 2 shillings 6 pence for each employed woman over twenty-one years—no competitive disadvantage would seem to be involved.

The most difficult problem is that which the insured person on the lower-wage levels faces. Every male of twenty-one years or over would pay 4 shillings 3 pence a week and every employed woman 3 shillings 6 pence. Younger persons would pay correspondingly less, the contributions in all cases being made through the purchase of stamps.

Four shillings 3 pence for men in the higher-paid occupations would not be an important weekly expenditure, but it would be a considerable item for persons receiving low wages—the lower the wage the higher the proportion represented by the tax. When compared with the rate of contribution in 1942—1 shilling 10 pence a week—the increase becomes over 130%, an increase, moreover, which would take full effect in the second half of 1944.

This would seem to be a heavy burden for the man who lives close to the margin of subsistence. In support of this part of the program, the Report points to the large amount of voluntary insurance carried by wage-earners. The recommendation that the government create a statutory corporation to take over all industrial insurance would relieve many families of the comparatively large weekly payments that this kind of protection has, according to the Report, involved. Reference is made to studies which show that families with incomes of less than 2 pounds a week spend on an average in voluntary insurance 2 shillings 3 pence a week. Including individual expenditures for medical care, which under the proposed national health service would no longer be necessary, the Report estimates that, "for purposes covered in whole or in part" by the Beveridge plan, the wage earning man pays in weekly premiums 5 shillings 10 pence as compared with the suggested contribution of 4 shillings 3 pence.[335n] These figures, however, are averages, and for the person at the lower end of the average the amount of the required contribution would present a problem.

The whole Beveridge program as it relates to insurance is built upon the existing system of flat universal payments and benefits universal within the categories to which they apply. It does not change the principle of everybody paying alike and receiving alike. It merely broadens the coverage of the established system, eliminating the restriction that allowed no non-manual worker receiving more than 420 pounds a year to participate and admitting everybody, rich or poor, to payments and benefits, the same payment and the same benefit within the various categories. Against the fact that the worker with the lowest wages pays in insurance the largest percentage of earnings is the compensating circumstance that when misfortune comes or old age arrives he receives a larger proportion of his previous income and, under any circumstances, an amount calculated to provide him with basic essentials.

It is interesting to contrast this system with Old-Age and Survivors Insurance as established in the United States under the Social Security Act. Here the contributions are based upon a percentage of wages, employer and employee paying the same percentage. As of the close of 1942 this was 1 per cent. The benefits are likewise related to wages but are weighted in favor of the man with the lowest pay, an actual record of the wages of every insured person being maintained. Properly developed, this plan would seem to involve less financial sacrifice for the lowest-paid groups and would more fairly effect the redistribution of income, which is one of the aims of the Beveridge plan.

Conditioning the success of the whole program, it must again be pointed out, is the essential and critical premise that employment be maintained and mass unemployment be eliminated. This involves putting an end to the kind of unemployment that we had in the 1930's and of "unemployment prolonged year after year for the same individual." Whereas "in the industries now subject to unemployment insurance the finance of the Unemployment Fund has been based . . . upon an average rate of unemployment through good years and bad of about fifteen percent," the new program assumes in these industries an unemployment of 10 per cent and, including the proposed expanded coverage of the system, an over-all unemployment of 8½ per cent. The Beveridge Report, therefore, contemplates a reduction of unemployment to two-thirds of the present actuarially calculated base of the British system of unemployment insurance.

This assumption, to quote the Report,

does not imply complete abolition of unemployment. In industries subject to seasonal influences, irregularities of work are inevitable; in an economic system subject to change and progress, fluctuations in the fortunes of individual employers or of particular industries are inevitable; the possibility of controlling completely the major alternations of good trade and bad trade which are described under the term of the trade cycle has not been established; a country like Britain, which must have exports to pay for its raw materials, cannot be immune from the results of changes of fortune or of economic policy in other countries. . . .

In 1913 and 1914, it was found that less than five percent of all the unemployment experienced in the insured industries occurred after men had been unemployed for as long as 15 weeks. Even if it does not prove possible to get back to that level of employment, it should be possible to make unemployment of any individual for more than 26 weeks continuously a rare thing in normal times.[335i]

This is, indeed, a large assumption; but during both world wars we have seen mass unemployment eliminated, and the conditions existing before the Second World War are certainly conclusive evidence that the conquest of unemployment is as essential to the preservation of our civilization as the defeat of the Axis. In some degree the distribution of income involved in the Beveridge proposals would provide a cushion against industrial depression, but it would not put an end to unemployment. The assumption remains as a question for further study.

The essence of the attack upon want made by the Beveridge Report is contained in the recommendation of the principle of the national minimum with the corollary proposal of the children's allowance. The Interdepartmental Committee on Social Insurance and Allied Services has made many important suggestions for improvements in administration, but its great contribution is the official advocacy of the floor of living below which no citizen of Britain shall be allowed to fall. It is this proposal which gives the Committee a significance (but positive instead of negative) comparable to that of the Commission of 1834, the Royal Commission for Inquiring into the Administration and Practical Operation of the Poor Laws. Just as the principle of less eligibility and no relief for the able-bodied outside the workhouse dominated thought about the problem of want throughout all the following decades of the nineteenth century, so the principle of the national minimum adopted by Sir William Beveridge promises to set the standard for the next stage in British history.

The plan for a universal coverage by a basic insurance marks the highest point which England has reached on her road to social security. When Sir William Beveridge writes out the means test with his statement "management of one's income is an essential element of a citizen's freedom," [335j] he is leading the way toward the goal that has been the aim of the people since their emergence from feudalism six centuries ago.

The realization in statute and administration of the ideals of the Beveridge Report may take time; but there is a quality of inevitability about the project and its auspices. The widespread attention and support which the principal proposals have received demonstrate the extent of the social revolution that has taken place in Great Britain during the twentieth century. The same state which in 1349, with the Statute of Laborers, proclaimed its intention to restrict the liberty of its workers, and which as recently as 1834 offered relief from distress only in an atmosphere of threat and punishment, now in the midst of war gives attention to an official recommendation for a national minimum based upon a system of universal social insurance. The people of England in their long pilgrimage have come at last "to the top of the hill called Clear," whence they can see opening before them the way to freedom with security.

BIBLIOGRAPHY

LAWS AND STATUTES

The laws of Ethelred and Cnut will be found in *Ancient Laws and Institutes of England*, printed by command of King William IV, 2 vols., 1860, pages 343 and 397–98 in Volume I. For the Statutes between Henry III and the end of the reign of Queen Anne, I have consulted the *Statutes of the Realm*, printed by command of George III, in nine volumes, the first of which appeared in 1808, the last in 1822. After George III, I have used Danby Pickering's *Statutes at Large*, the *Statutes of the United Kingdom of Great Britain and Ireland*, and, from 1860, the *Public General Acts in the Law Reports*.

Italic numerals in this section are page references to the text of this book.

1. The Laws of King Ethelred
   17
2. The Laws of King Cnut
   1
3. 23 Edward III, the Statute of Laborers, 1349
   1, 4, 5–6, 8, 28, 166, 246
4. 25 Edward III, Statute the Second [the Second Statute of Laborers], 1350–51
   4, 6, 8
5. 1 Richard II, c. 6, 1377
   7
6. 12 Richard II, c. 3, 1388
   7, 15
7. 12 Richard II, c. 4, 1388
   7
8. 12 Richard II, c. 7, 1388
   7–8
9. 15 Richard II, c. 6, 1391
   18
10. 2 Henry V, Statute 1, 1414
    16
11. 4 Henry VII, c. 19, 1488–89
    9
12. 11 Henry VII, c. 2, 1495
    8
13. 19 Henry VII, c. 12, 1504
    8

34. 3 William & Mary, c. 11, 1691
    42, 81–82, 83–84

35. 7 & 8 William III, Private and Local Acts 32, Bristol, 1696
    53, 86

36. 8 & 9 William III, c. 30, 1697
    87

37. 9 George I, c. 7, 1722
    60, 63, 66–67, 68, 84, 86, 88–89

38. 2 George III, c. 22, 1761
    65

39. 7 George III, c. 39, 1767
    65

40. 22 George III, c. 83, 1782 [Gilbert Act]
    67–68, 85, 86, 155

41. 35 George III, c. 101, 1795
    43–44, 155

42. 36 George III, c. 23, 1795
    73

43. 39 George III, c. 81, 1799 and 40 George III, c. 106, 1800 [The Combination Laws]
    170, 240

44. 42 George III, c. 73, 1802
    168

45. 59 George III, c. 12, 1819
    83

46. 59 George III, c. 66, 1819
    168–69

47. 2 & 3 William IV, c. 45, an Act to Amend the Representation of the People in England and Wales, 1832
    170

48. 3 & 4 William IV, c. 103, 1833
    169

49. 4 & 5 William IV, c. 76, an Act for the Amendment and Better Administration of the Laws Relating to the Poor in England and Wales, 1834
    44, 127, 128, 131, 136, 138, 139, 140, 154, 155, 157, 211, 246

50. 10 & 11 Victoria, c. 29, 1847
    169

51. 10 & 11 Victoria, c. 109, 1847
    138

52. 28 & 29 Victoria, c. 79, the Union Chargeability Act, 1865
    155

73. 7 & 8 George V, c. 64, the Representation of the People Act, 1918
      210

74. 9 & 10 George V, c. 29, the Ministry of Health Act, 1919
      210

75. 9 & 10 George V, c. 102, the Old Age Pensions Act, 1919
      206

76. 10 & 11 George V, Chapter 30, the Unemployment Insurance Act, 1920
      207, 208

77. 15 & 16 George V, c. 70, the Widows', Orphans' and Old Age Contributory Pensions Act, 1925
      207–08, 221

78. 16 & 17 George V, c. 20, the Boards of Guardians (Default) Act, 1926
      213–14

79. 19 George V, c. 17, the Local Government Act, 1929
      214–15

80. 21 & 22 George V, c. 48, the National Economy Act, 1931
      219–20

81. 22 & 23 George V, c. 54, the Transitional Payments (Determination of Need) Act, 1932
      220

82. 24 & 25 George V, c. 29, the Unemployment Act, 1934
      220–22, 225–26

84. 2 & 3 George VI, c. 93, the Unemployment Assistance (Emergency Powers) Act, 1939
      222

85. 3 & 4 George VI, c. 13, the Old Age and Widows Pensions Act, 1940
      222

86. 4 & 5 George VI, c. 11, Determination of Needs Act, 1941
      223–25

87. 4 & 5 George VI, c. 39, the National Health Insurance, Contributory Pensions and Workmen's Compensation Act, 1941
      207, 208

STATUTORY RULES AND ORDERS

The relief orders cited below will be found in *Statutory Rules and Orders,* an official series that has been published annually since 1890. The Out-door Labour Test Order was not issued as a general order but was directed to individual Poor Law unions. It appears in William and Reginald Glen (see list of Authors).

101. The Out-door Relief Prohibitory Order, December 21, 1844

102. The Out-door Labour Test Order, see # 445

103. The Out-door Relief Regulation Order, December 10, 1852
104. The Relief Regulation Order, 1911
105. The Relief Regulation Order, 1930
106. The Supplementary Pensions (Determination of Need and Assessment of Needs), Amendment, Regulations, 1941
107. The Unemployment Assistance (Determination of Need and Assessment of Needs), Amendment, Regulations, 1941

PARLIAMENTARY DEBATES

201. *The Parliamentary Register*, or the *History of the Proceedings and Debates in the House of Commons*, Vol. XLIV, 1796, pp. 25 & 26
202. *Parliamentary Debates, Fourth Session of Twenty-eighth Parliament*, Vol. 4, Col. 488
203. *The Parliamentary Debates*, Series 5, Vol. 5,　Col. 507
204. ....　"　223　"　71
205. ....　"　283　"　1077, 1090, 1092
206. ....　"　357　"　1207–08
207. ....　"　358　"　854–55
209. ....　"　368　"　1557
211. ....　"　368　"　1602
212. ....　"　"　"　1606
213. ....　"　371　"　380
214. ....　"　"　"　372
215. ....　"　378　"　1230
216. ....　"　"　"　1235 & 1236

REPORTS OF ROYAL COMMISSIONS, COMMITTEES OF PARLIAMENT, ANNUAL AND OTHER DEPARTMENTAL REPORTS

301. *Orders and Directions Together with a Commission for the Better Administration of Justice and More Perfect Information of His Majestie; How, and by Whom the Laws and Statutes Tending to the Reliefe of the Poore, the Well Ordering and Training up of Youth in Trades, and the Reformation of Disorders and Disordered Persons, Are Executed throughout the Kingdome, 1630. (N.S. 1631)*
a. pp. 1–33; I–XVI

302. *Report of a Committee Appointed to Inquire into the State of the Parish Poor Infants under the Age of Fourteen within the Bills of Mortality, 1767,* House of Commons Journals, Vol. XXXI, November 11, 1766 to March 10, 1768
    a. p. 248

303. *Report of the Select Committee of the House of Commons on the State of the Poor in Ireland;* Part III, Second Report of Evidence; May 18–June 5, 1830, The Rev. Thomas Chalmers, D.D.
    a. pp. 296 & 297, Question 3455
    b. p. 308, Question 3492
    c. p. 294, Question 3446

304. *Extracts from the Information Received by His Majesty's Commissioners as to the Administration and Operation of the Poor Laws,* Published by Authority, 1833
    a. p. 389

305. *The Report from His Majesty's Commissioners for Inquiring into the Administration and Practical Operation of the Poor Laws,* Published by Authority, 1834
    a. pp. 31–32
    b. p. 55
    c. p. 36
    d. p. 83
    e. p. 72
    f. p. 68
    g. pp. 150 & 151
    h. p. 5
    i. p. 13
    j. pp. 88 & 89
    k. pp. 44 & 45
    l. p. 46
    m. pp. 46 & 47
    n. pp. 247 & 248
    o. p. 271
    p. p. 228
    q. p. 262
    r. p. 297
    s. pp. 297–331
    t. pp. 306 & 307
    u. pp. 264
    v. pp. 362
    w. p. 264
    x. p. 362

305A. *Report from His Majesty's Commissioners for Inquiring into the Administration and Practical Operation of the Poor Laws.* Appendix F. Foreign Communications. Ordered Printed by the House of Commons, 1834

   · a. *Foreign Communications Relative to the Support and Maintenance of the Poor.* p. xxxii.

306. *The Parish and the Union, or, the Poor and the Laws under the Old System and the New; Being an Analysis of the Evidence Contained in the Twenty-two Reports of the Select Committee of the House of Commons, Appointed in the Session of 1837, to Inquire into the Administration of the Relief of the Poor, under the Orders and Regulations Issued by the Commissioners Appointed under the Provisions of the Poor Law Amendment Act,* London, 1837

   a. pp. 72–74

307. *Report of the Poor Law Commissioners to the Most Noble the Marquis of Normanby, Her Majesty's Principal Secretary of State for the Home Department on the Continuance of the Poor Law Commission, and on Some Further Amendments of the Laws Relating to the Relief of the Poor.* 1840

   a. pp. 45–47

   b. p. 47

308. *Report to His Majesty's Principal Secretary of State for the Home Department from the Poor Law Commissioners on an Inquiry into the Sanitary Condition of the Laboring Population of Great Britain, with appendices.* Presented to both Houses of Parliament by Command of Her Majesty, 1842

309. *Letters of the Poor Law Commissioners Relative to the Transactions of the Business of the Commission 1847,* House of Commons, No. 148

   a. pp. 30 & 31

310–11. *Report of George Coode to the Poor Law Board on the Law of Settlement and Removal of the Poor, Being a Further Report in Addition to Those Printed in 1850,* 1851

   a. p. 253

   b. p. 188

312. *Report of the Royal Commission on the Aged Poor,* 1895

   a. p. 705

313. *Local Government Board, Poplar Union,* Transcript of Shorthand Notes Taken at the Public Inquiry by J. S. Davy, C. B., Chief General Inspector of the Local Government Board into the General Condition of the Poplar Union, Its Pauperism, and the Administration of the Guardians and Their Officers, 1906

   a. p. 216

314. *Report of the Select Committee of the House of Commons on the*

Aged Deserving Poor, together with the Proceedings of the Committee, Manuals of Evidence and Appendix, 1899

315. *Report of the Royal Commission on the Poor Laws and Relief of Distress,* 1909, Appendix, Vol. 1, Minutes of Evidence
    a. Question 2230
    b. Question 2781
    c. Question 3219

316. *Report of the Royal Commission on the Poor Laws and Relief of Distress,* 1909, (Cd. 4499) (The Majority Report)
    a. Part IV, c. 1, p. 96
    b. Part VI, c. 1, p. 359
    c. Part IV, c. 5, p. 140
    d. Part VI, c. 3, p. 364
    e. Part IV, c. 6, p. 159
    f. Part IV, c. 6, p. 161
    g. Part IV, c. 5, p. 140
    h. Part V, c. 3, p. 299
    i. Part VI, c. 4, p. 445
    j. Memorandum by Miss Octavia Hill, p. 678
    k. Part VI, c. 4, p. 423
    l. Part VI, c. 4, p. 424
    m. Part VI, c. 4, p. 425

317. *Report of the Royal Commission on the Poor Laws and Relief of Distress,* 1909, (Cd. 4499). Separate Report by the Rev. Prebendary H. Russell Wakefield, Mr. Francis Chandler, Mr. George Lansbury, and Mrs. Sidney Webb
    a. pp. 1078 & 1079
    b. p. 1063
    c. p. 1006
    d. p. 1020
    e. p. 1078
    f. pp. 1031 & 1032
    g. pp. 1028 & 1029
    h. pp. 756 & 757
    i. p. 750
    j. p. 1028

318. Ministry of Labour, *Final Report of the Committee of Inquiry into the Scheme of Out-of-Work Donation,* (Cmd 305), 1919
    a. pp. 3 & 4

319. Ministry of Labour, *Report on National Unemployment Insurance to July 1923 with a Short Account of the Out-of-Work Donation Scheme* (November 1918 to March 1921) *and Appendices,* 1923
    a. pp. 41–51

331. Eleventh Annual Report, 1929–30
    a. p. 164
332. Thirteenth Annual Report, 1931–32
    a. p. 198

Unemployment Assistance Board

333. Report for the year ending 31st December, 1938
    a. pp. 71–72
334. *Unemployment Assistance and Supplementary Pensions*. Report by the Assistance Board on the Administration of the Determination of Needs Act, 1941–42
    a. p. 7
335. *Social Insurance and Allied Services*, Report by Sir William Beveridge, Presented to Parliament by Command of His Majesty, November, 1942. Cmd. 6404, London. The Macmillan Co., New York, 1942
    a. p. 214, table XVIII
    b. p. 7
    c. p. 158
    d. p. 87
    e. p. 49
    f. p. 134
    g. p. 154
    h. p. 112, table XIII
    i. p. 164
    j. p. 12
    l. p. 167
    m. p. 166
    n. p. 114
336. International Labour Office. *Year Book of Labour Statistics*, Sixth Year of Issue, 1941, Montreal, 1942
    a. p. 125
337. International Labour Office. *The Minimum Wage, An International Survey*, Geneva, 1939
    a. p. 123
    b. p. 112–114

BOOKS

401. Anonymous—*Greevous Grones for the Poore*. London, 1621.
    a. Title page
402. Anonymous—*An Account of Several Workhouses for Employing and Maintaining the Poor*. The Second Edition very much enlarged. London, 1732.

a. p. 160
b. pp. 7, 11, 14, 15
c. pp. 17–20
d. p. 6
e. pp. 101, 106, 128–29

403. Sir William James Ashley—*An Introduction to English Economic History and Theory*. Second Edition. 2 vols. Longmans, Green & Co., London & New York, 1892–93.
a. Part II, p. 318
b. Part II, p. 350

404. C. R. Attlee—*The Labour Party in Perspective*, Victor Gollancz, Ltd., London, 1937.
a. p. 28

405. W. H. Beveridge—*Unemployment, A Problem of Industry*, Longmans, Green & Co., London & New York, 1909, New Edition, 1930.
a. p. vii

406. Eric H. Biddle—"Answers to Specific Questions of Federal and Chicago Agencies." (An unpublished document.) Washington, D.C., 1941.
a. p. 101

407. Charles Booth, ed.—*Life and Labour of the People in London*. 9 vols., Macmillan & Co., London & New York, 1892–97.
a. Vol. IX, p. 427

408. Charles Booth—*Pauperism, a Picture; And the Endowment of Old Age, an Argument*, Macmillan & Co., London & New York, 1892.
a. p. 240

409. [Mary Booth]—*Charles Booth—A Memoir*, Macmillan & Co., Ltd., London, 1918.
a. pp. 13–15

410. Helen Bosanquet—*Social Work in London, 1869 to 1912; A History of the Charity Organization Society*, John Murray, London, 1914.
a. p. 53
b. pp. 98–99

411. Sir Thomas Browne—*Religio Medici*. 7th Edition. London, 1672.
a. p. 48

412. John Graham Brooks—*Compulsory Insurance in Germany*. (Fourth Special Report of the Commissioner of Labor.) Washington, D.C., Govt. Printing Office, 1893.
a. p. 45

413. Richard Burn—*The History of the Poor Laws: With Observations*, London, 1764.
a. p. 211
b. pp. 134–35

c. p. 211

d. pp. 210–11

e. pp. 213–15

f. p. 106

414. Eveline M. Burns—*British Unemployment Programs, 1920–1938.* Washington, D.C., Social Science Research Council, Committee on Social Security, 1941.

a. pp. 35–51

415. John Cary—*An Essay toward Regulating the Trade and Employing the Poor of This Kingdom.* Second Edition. London, 1719. The Appendix, "An Account of the Proceedings of the Corporation of Bristol."

a. pp. 150–62

416. Edwin Chadwick—*Report to His Majesty's Principal Secretary of State for the Home Department from the Poor Law Commissioners on an Inquiry into the Sanitary Condition of the Labouring Population of Great Britain, with Appendices,* Presented to Both Houses of Parliament by Command of Her Majesty, London, 1842.

See 308

417. Thomas Chalmers—*The Christian and Civic Economy of Large Towns.* 3 vols. Glasgow, 1821–26.

a. Vol. II, pp. 99, 106

b. Vol. I, p. 3

c. Vol. I, pp. 55, 56, 57

d. Vol. I, pp. 99, 100

e. Vol. I, p. 271

f. Vol. II, pp. 55–59, 65, 66

g. Vol. II, p. 27

h. Vol. II, pp. 151–52

418. Thomas Chalmers—*Directory of Procedure for the Deacons of St. Johns,* in Appendix, "On the Sufficiency of the Parochial System, without a Poor Rate for the Right Management of the Poor," Glasgow, 1841.

a. p. 293

420. Thomas Chalmers—*On the Sufficiency of the Parochial System Without a Poor Rate for the Right Management of the Poor,* Glasgow, 1841.

a. pp. 11, 14

b. pp. 73, 74

421. Thomas Chalmers—"Reflections of 1839, on the Now Protracted Experience of Pauperism in Glasgow—An Experience of More Than Twenty Years, Which Began in 1815, and Terminated in 1837," in *Select Works of Thomas Chalmers,* Vol. X. London, 1856.

a. p. 723
b. p. 721

422. Thomas Chalmers—*Statement in Regard to the Pauperism of Glasgow, from the Experience of the Last Eight Years.* (First printed in 1823.) In *Select Works of Thomas Chalmers*, Vol. X. London, 1856.
a. p. 618
b. p. 626

423. Sir William Chance—*The Better Administration of the Poor Law*, London, 1895.
a. pp. 3–4
b. p. 80
c. p. 82

424. Sir Josiah Child—*A New Discourse of Trade*, London, 1696.
a. p. 80
b. p. 98

425. Winston Spencer Churchill—*Liberalism and the Social Problem*, Hodder & Stoughton, London, 1909.
a. pp. 208–10
b. p. 80
c. p. 376

428. G. D. H. Cole—*A Short History of the British Working Class Movement*, G. Allen & Unwin, Ltd., London, 1927.
a. Vol. II, p. 23

429. G. D. H. Cole and Raymond Postgate—*The Common People, 1746–1938*, Methuen & Co., London, 1938.
a. pp. 443, 445–46

430. William Cunningham—*The Growth of English Industry and Commerce*, Cambridge University Press, 1890.
a. p. 304

431. [Daniel Defoe]—*Giving Alms No Charity and Employing the Poor a Grievance to the Nation*, London, 1704.
a. p. 12
b. p. 20

432. Sir Frederic Morton Eden—*The State of the Poor: Or, An History of the Labouring Classes in England, from the Conquest to the Present Period.* 3 vols. London, 1797.
a. Vol. I, pp. 57–59
b. Vol. I, p. 28
c. Vol. I, p. 412
d. Vol. I, pp. 182–83
e. Vol. I, pp. 269–70
f. Vol. I, p. 576

g. Vol. II, p. 384

h. Vol. I, p. 270

433. Edward Denison—*Letters and Other Writings of the Late Edward Denison, M.P. for Newark*, edited by Sir Baldwyn Leighton, bart., London, 1872.

a. pp. 46, 59, 207, 228

434. Benjamin Disraeli, Earl of Beaconsfield—*Sybil: or, The Two Nations*, Hughenden Edition, London, 1881.

a. pp. 76–77

b. p. 340

435. A. Doyle—"The Poor Law System of Elberfeld," in *Poor Laws in Foreign Countries, Reports Communicated to the Local Government Board by Her Majesty's Secretary of State for Foreign Affairs*, London, 1875.

a. pp. 344–65

436. Henry Fawcett—*Pauperism: Its Causes and Remedies*, London, 1871.

a. pp. 56–57

437. Thomas Firmin—*Some Proposals for the Imploying of the Poor, Especially in and about the City of London*, 1678.

a. pp. 3, 4, 6, 13, 14

b. pp. 14–15

c. p. 19

438. T[homas] F[irmin]—*Some Proposals for the Imployment of the Poor, and for the Prevention of Idleness and the Consequences Thereof; Begging, a Practice so Dishonorable to the Nation and to the Christian Religion. In a letter to a Friend, by T. F.* London, 1681.

a. pp. 45–46

439. *Forma subventionis pauperum quae apud Hyperas Flandrorum urbem viget, universae Reipublicae Christianae longe utilissima*, 1531. Translated by William Marshall into English and Published by Him in 1535; in Frank R. Salter, M.A., ed., *Some Early Tracts on Poor Relief*, London, 1926.

a. pp. 73–74

b. pp. 52–71

440. T. W. Fowle—*The Poor Law*, London, 1881.

a. p. 163

441. Thomas Fuller—*The Church History of Britain from the Birth of Jesus Christ until the Year MDCXLVIII*, London, 1655.

a. Book II, p. 126

b. Book II, pp. 289, 299

442. Thomas Fuller—*The Historie of the Holy Warre*, Cambridge, 1639. The Epistle Dedicatorie.

443. Thomas Fuller—*The History of the Worthies of England*, London, 1662.
   a. p. 223

444. Thomas Gilbert—*Plan for the Better Relief and Employment of the Poor*, London, 1781.
   a. p. 7

445. William Cunningham Glen and Reginald Cunningham Glen—*The General Orders of the Poor Law Commissioners, the Poor Law Board, and the Local Government Board Relating to the Poor Law*. Tenth Edition. London, 1887.
   a. pp. 299–306

446. John Richard Green—*Stray Studies*. Second Series. Macmillan & Co., Ltd., London, 1903.
   a. p. 133

447. John Richard Green—*Stray Studies from England and Italy*, Harper and Brothers, New York, 1876.
   a. p. 25

448. R. H. Gretton—*A Modern History of the English People*, Single-volume Edition. Longmans, Green & Co., London, 1930.
   a. p. 689

449. The Rev. S. Humphreys Gurteen—*A Handbook of Charity Organization*, Buffalo, N.Y., 1882.
   a. p. 25

450. R[ichard Haines]—*England's Weal & Prosperity Proposed: Or, Reasons for Erecting Publick Workhouses in Every County, for the Speedy Promoting of Industry an the Woollen Manufactury, Shoewing How the Wealth of the Nation May Be Encreased, Many Hundred Thousand Pounds per Annum. And Also That Many Thousand Persons May Be So Reformed, to Their Own and the Whol Kingdoms Present and Future Wealth and Glory, That There May No More Be a Beggar Bred up in the Nation*. Humbly Offered to the Consideration of the Great Wisdom of the Nation, and Presented to the Honourable House of Commons by R., London, 1681.
   a. Title page

451. Sir Matthew Hale—*A Discourse Touching Provision for the Poor*. (Bound with) *Pleas of the Crown*, London, 1716.
   a. pp. 109, 122–28

452. Mary Agnes Hamilton—*Sidney and Beatrice Webb*, Houghton Mifflin Co., Boston, 1933.
   a. p. 120
   b. p. 39

453. J. L. Hammond and Barbara Hammond—*The Village Labourer*. Fourth Edition. Longmans, Green & Co., London, 1936.

a. p. 17
b. p. 153
c. p. 61

454. The Rev. William Hanna—*Memoirs of the Life and Writings of Thomas Chalmers, D.D., LL.D.* 4 vols. London, 1850–52.
a. Vol. I, p. 406
b. Vol. I, p. 180
c. Vol. II, pp. 149–50
d. Vol. I, p. 382
e. Vol. IV, pp. 114, 115
f. Vol. II, pp. 300–301
g. Vol. II, pp. 511–12

455. Jonas Hanway—*An Earnest Appeal for Mercy to the Children of the Poor.* London, 1766.
a. p. 68
b. pp. 41–43
c. p. 3

456. Jonas Hanway—*Letters to the Guardians of the Infant Poor, Also to the Governors and Overseers of the Parish Poor; Recommending Concord, Frugality, Cleanliness and Industry, with Such a Pious, Humane, Resolute, and Judicious Conduct in the Executing of This Office as May Effectually Answer the Good Purpose for Which They Are Chosen and More Particularly in the Preservation of Infants,* London, 1767.
a. p. 15

457. William Hay—*Remarks on the Laws Relating to the Poor with Proposals for Their Better Relief and Employment by a Member of Parliament.* First published in 1735. London, 1751.
a. Preface, VI

458. Octavia Hill—*Homes of the London Poor.* A New Edition. London, 1883.
a. pp. 55, 56

459. Octavia Hill—*Official and Volunteer Agencies in Administering Relief in Third Annual Report of the Local Government Board,* 1873–74.
See 326a.

460. Octavia Hill—*Our Common Land and Other Short Essays.* London, 1877.
a. pp. 54–56
b. pp. 155–56, 159–60

461. Harry M. Hirsch—*Compilation of Settlement Laws of All States in the United States, September, 1939,* American Public Welfare Association, Chicago, 1939.

462. Helen Fisher Hohman—*The Development of Social Insurance and Minimum Wage Legislation in Great Britain*, Houghton Mifflin Co., Boston, 1933.
   a. pp. 245–50

463. [Charles Kingsley] Parson Lot, Pseud.—"Letters to the Chartists," No. 1 in *Politics for the People*, London, 1848.
   a. p. 29

464. George Lansbury—*My Life*, Constable and Co., Ltd., London, 1928.
   a. pp. 135–36
   b. p. 139
   c. p. 133

465. E. M. Leonard—*The Early History of English Poor Relief*, Cambridge University Press, 1900.
   a. p. 266

466. Sir Charles S. Loch—*Charity and Social Life*, Macmillan & Co., Ltd., London, 1910.
   a. p. 198

467. David Lloyd George—*Slings and Arrows;* Sayings Chosen from the Speeches of the Rt. Hon. David Lloyd George, Cassell and Co., Ltd., London, 1929.
   a. p. 5
   b. p. 8

468. John Locke—*Board of Trade Papers*, 1697, quoted by H. R. Fox Bourne in his *Life of John Locke*. 2 vols. New York, 1876.
   a. Vol. II, p. 378.

469. Sophie Lonsdale—*The English Poor Laws*. Third Edition, Revised and Enlarged. P. S. King & Son, Ltd., London, 1902.
   a. p. 67
   b. p. 68

470. Martin Luther—"Ordinance for a Common Chest," in F. R. Salter, ed., *Some Early Tracts on Poor Relief*, Methuen & Co., London, 1926.
   a. p. 87

471. Martin Luther—[*Liber Vagatorum*], *The Book of Vagabonds and Beggars: With a Vocabulary of Their Language, Edited by Martin Luther in the Year 1528, Now First Translated into English, with Introduction and Notes,* by John Camden Hotten, London, 1860.
   a. pp. 4–5

472. Thomas Mackay—*A History of the English Poor Law*. Vol. III. P. S. King & Son, London, 1899.
   a. p. 540

473. Frederic William Maitland—*Domesday Book and Beyond, Three Essays in the Early History of England*, Cambridge University Press, 1921.
   a. p. 42

b. p. 437

474. Bernard Mandeville—"Essay on Charity, and Charity Schools"; in *Fable of the Bees*, London, 1723.
   a. pp. 286–88.

475. C. Edmund Maurice—*Life of Octavia Hill as Told in Her Letters*, Macmillan & Co., Ltd., London, 1914.
   a. p. 14

476. Frederick Maurice—*The Life of Frederick Denison Maurice, Chiefly Told in His Letters*. Edited by his Son, Frederick Maurice. Macmillan & Co., London, 1884.
   a. Vol. II, p. 305
   b. Vol. II, p. 13

477. John Stuart Mill—*The Letters of John Stuart Mill*. Edited with an Introduction by Hugh S. R. Elliot. Longmans, Green & Co., London, 1910.
   a. Vol. I, pp. 50–51

479. William Flavelle Monypenny—*The Life of Benjamin Disraeli, Earl of Beaconsfield*, The Macmillan Co., New York, 1910.
   a. Vol. I, p. 374

480. Sir Thomas More—*Utopia*, Cambridge University Press, 1922.
   a. p. 33
   a. p. 161

481. Sir George Nicholls—*A History of the English Poor Law*. New Edition. P. S. King & Co., London, 1898.
   a. Vol. II, p. 91
   b. Vol. II, p. 15
   c. Vol. II, p. 438
   d. Vol. II, p. 391
   e. Vol. II, p. 338
   f. Vol. I, p. iv
   g. Vol. I, p. 2
   h. Vol. II, pp. 70–71, 97–98

482. Robert Owen—"A Report of the County of Lanark, May 1, 1820," in *A New View of Society and Other Writings*, E. P. Dutton & Co., New York, 1927.
   a. p. 244

483. Robert Owen—*A New View of Society*, London, 1813.
   a. pp. 9, 23

484. Robert Pashley—*Pauperism and Poor Laws*, London, 1852.
   a. p. 274

485. Edward R. Pease—*The History of the Fabian Society*, E. P. Dutton & Co., New York, 1916.
   a. p. 43
   b. p. 213

486. M. A. Richardson—Extracts from the Municipal Accounts of Newcastle-upon-Tyne in *Reprints of Rare Tracts and Imprints of Ancient Manuscripts, etc., Chiefly Illustrative of the History of the Northern Counties,* and Printed at the Press of M. A. Richardson, Newcastle, 1849.

    a. Vol. III, p. 44

487. James E. Thorold Rogers—*Six Centuries of Work and Wages,* New York, 1884.

    a. p. 117

488. B. Seebohm Rowntree—*Poverty, A Study of Town Life,* Macmillan & Co., Ltd., London, 1903.

    a. p. 117

490. Thomas Ruggles—*History of the Poor; their Rights, Duties, and the Laws Respecting Them, in a Series of Letters.* 2 vols. London, 1793.

    a. Letter 17, Vol. I, pp. 199 & 200

491. Frank Reyner Salter, M.A., ed.—*Some Early Tracts on Poor Relief,* Methuen & Co., Ltd., London, 1926.

    a. p. 2

492. John Scott—*Observations on the Present State of the Parochial and Vagrant Poor,* London, 1773.

    a. p. 55

    b. p. 37

493. Nassau W. Senior—*Historical and Philosophical Essays.* 2 vols. London, 1865.

    a. Vol. II, pp. 56, 57

494. George Bernard Shaw—*The Fabian Society, Its Early History.* Fabian Society Tract No. 41. London, 1892.

    a. pp. 3, 4

497. Margaret M. Sherwood, Translator—*Concerning the Relief of the Poor or Concerning Human Need,* A Letter Addressed to the Senate of Bruges by Juan Luis Vives, New York School of Philanthropy (now New York School of Social Work), New York, 1917.

    a. pp. 11–12, 14–17, 22–23, 30

498. Adam Smith—*An Inquiry into the Nature and Courses of the Wealth of Nations.* 2 vols. London, 1776.

    a. Vol. I, pp. 170, 171

    b. Vol. I, pp. 173, 174

    c. Vol. I, p. 176

499. Carl R. Steinbicker, S.T.L.—*Poor-Relief in the Sixteenth Century,* Catholic University of America, Washington, D.C., 1937.

    a. pp. 124–25

500. Benjamin [Thompson], Count of Rumford—*Essays, Political, Economical, Philosophical,* London, 1796.

a. Vol. I, p. 34

b. Vol. I, p. 5

c. Vol. I, pp. 14–16, 37–38, 42, 87–88, 93, 100

501. [Joseph Townsend]—*A Dissertation on the Poor Laws by a Well-Wisher to Mankind*, London, 1786. Republished 1817.

a. p. 80

b. pp. 39–51, 57, 96, 97

502. Juan Luis Vives—*Concerning the Relief of the Poor or Concerning Human Need*, A Letter Addressed to the Senate of Bruges. Translated by Margaret M. Sherwood, New York School of Philanthropy (now New York School of Social Work), New York, 1917.

a. pp. 11, 12, 14, 15, 16, 17, 22, 23, 30

503. Baron [Kaspar] von Voght—*Account of the Management of the Poor in Hamburgh between the Years 1777 and 1794, in a Letter to Some Friends of the Poor in Great Britain.* Published in 1796, now Republished by Permission of the Author and Dedicated to the Rt. Hon. George Rose, M.P., London, 1817.

a. pp. 9–20

504. Beatrice Webb—*My Apprenticeship*, Longmans, Green & Co., London, 1926.

a. p. 173–74

b. p. 389

c. pp. 167–68

505. Sidney Webb—Article in *St. Martin's Review*, February, 1929, quoted in Mary Agnes Hamilton, *Sidney and Beatrice Webb*, Houghton Mifflin Co., Boston, 1933.

a. p. 31

506. Sidney and Beatrice Webb—*English Poor Law History: Part I. The Old Poor Law*, Longmans, Green & Co., London, 1927.

a. pp. 424–25

507. Sidney and Beatrice Webb—*English Poor Law History: Part. II. The Last Hundred Years.* 2 vols. Longmans, Green & Co., London, 1929.

a. Vol. I, pp. 206–07

b. Vol. I, pp. 1042–43

c. Vol. II, pp. 896–99

508. Andrew Yarranton—*England's Improvement by Sea and Land to Out-do the Dutch without Fighting, to Pay Debts without Moneys, to Set at Work All the Poor of England with the Growth of Our Own Lands*, London, 1677.

a. pp. 46 & 47

509. [Arthur Young]—*The Farmer's Tour through the East of England, by the Author of the Farmer's Letters.* 4 vols. London, 1771.

a. Vol. IV, p. 351

INDEX

(For index to laws and statutes, see Bibliography)